THE
CULTURE CLASH

Jean Donaldson

The Academy for Dog Trainers
www.academyfordogtrainers.com

The Culture Clash
Jean Donaldson

Published by The Academy for Dog Trainers
www.academyfordogtrainers.com

Distributed by:
Dogwise Publishing
403 South Mission Street
Wenatchee, Washington 98801
509-663-9115, 1-800-776-2665
www.dogwisepublishing.com / info@dogwisepublishing.com

© 1996, 2005, 2013 Jean Donaldson

ISBN 978-1-61781-112-8
Printed in the U.S.A.

More titles by Jean Donaldson

Oh Behave! Dogs From Pavlov to Premack to Pinker. Dogwise Publishing, 2008

Train Your Dog Like a Pro (With DVD.) Howell Books, 2010

Dogs Are From Neptune, 2nd Edition. Dogwise Publishing, 2009

Canine Fear, Aggression and Play DVD. Tawzer Dog, 2008

Perfect Paws in 5 Days. Featuring Jean Donaldson's Modern Dog Training Methods DVD. Perfect Paws Productions, 2007

Fighting Dominance in a Dog Whispering World DVD. dogTEC, 2007

Predation in Family Dogs. Predation, Predatory Drift and Preparedness Seminar DVD. Distrubuted by Dogwise Publishing, 2006

Fight! A Practical Guide to the Treatment of Dog-Dog Aggression. Distrubuted by Dogwise Publishing, 2004

Mine! A Practical Guide to Resource Guarding in Dogs. Distrubuted by Dogwise Publishing, 2002

Train at the Next Level DVD Set. Tawzer Dog, 2012

The Culture Clash

Contents

For Lassie

Chapter One
Getting the Dog's Perspective

Walt Disney vs. B.F. Skinner

A book published in the early 1990s refers to the "moral code" of dogs. It became a bestseller. It seems that most people still buy into the Walt Disney dog: he is very intelligent, has morals, is capable of planning and executing revenge, solves complex problems, and understands the value of the artifacts in Walt's home. Nobody wants B.F. Skinner's dog: the input-output black box who is so obviously not the furry member of our family. It's been marketed all wrong, I think. Skinner was right but has gotten bad press. The truth must be presented in a way that people will start to buy into. They have to, because not getting it has led to the death of countless dogs. Here is an example to illustrate the difference.

A dog has been reprimanded every time he was caught chewing furniture. Now the dog refrains from chewing furniture when the owner is home but becomes destructive when left alone. When the owner comes home and discovers the damage, the dog slinks around, ears back and head down.

Walt's view: The dog learns from the reprimand that chewing furniture is wrong, and that the owner hates it. The dog resents being left alone and, to get back at the owner, chews the furniture when the owner leaves. He deliberately, in other words, engages in an act he knows to be wrong. When the owner comes home the dog feels guilty about what he has done.

BF's view: The dog learns that chewing furniture is dangerous when the owner is present but safe when the owner is gone. The dog is slightly anxious when left alone and feels better when he chews. It also helps pass the time. Later, when the owner comes home, the dog behaves appeasingly in an attempt to avoid or turn off the harsh treatment he has learned often happens at this time. The owner's arrival home and/or pre-punishment demeanor have become a predictor: the dog knows he's about to be punished. He doesn't know why.

There is no question whatsoever that the second view is the accurate one. The question is not which interpretation is the truth but rather why anyone still argues the point. The medical equivalent would be a significant percentage of the American public thinking disease was caused by imbalance in humors, rather than microorganisms.

The accurate information has been around for decades, yet most people who own dogs haven't learned it yet. One reason for our astonishingly poor understanding of dogs is extremely slow trickle down from experts: those in applied behavior educating one owner or one class at a time rather than something on the scale of public service announcements or spots on Oprah. Not only is this missing, fantastically inaccurate information about dog behavior is actively disseminated on reality TV.

But I think there's a second reason for the slow acceptance of realistic interpretations of dog behavior: simple reluctance to let go of anthropomorphism. Behaviorism, made famous by Skinner, has suffered some serious backlash since its assault on the world of psychology in the mid-twentieth century, largely because it could be successfully argued that hardcore behaviorism comes up short for understanding humans in all their mega-brain complexity. When it comes to animal training and behavior modification, however, the fit is incredibly good. But so far no amount of evidence makes the behaviorist model palatable to the average dog owner. The implications of this are really important.

2

The impressive staying power of Walt's warmhearted but distorted view of dogs is a perverse measure of how much we like them. We want them to be smart, morally "good." Many cynics see dogs as superior to people in their loyalty and trustworthiness. By contrast, the behaviorist model hasn't caught on in the mainstream because it seems to reduce dogs to input-output machines. Our fear is that if we accept this viewpoint, we strip dogs of their status as honorary humans, with the logical extension of negative ramifications for their welfare.

In other words, humans are tribal. Our compassion and consideration for other beings is strongly aligned with our perception of how similar they are to us, and a strong measure of that similarity is intelligence. IQ is still an acceptable prejudice. Heated ethical discussions ensued when the question of language acquisition in great apes was raised. Without a possible capacity for language, it had somehow seemed more okay to accept a utilitarian attitude towards them. No one much questioned the premise of intelligence as criterion for being considered for compassionate treatment.

Our species has a long history of incredible violence and horror perpetrated, essentially, because the victims were too far outside our perceived tribe. Our current tribal boundaries have a lot to do with species, IQ and moral integrity. Our bond with dogs is obviously strong. But they are the wrong species. To explain the bond, we compensate by exaggerating how much they resemble us in the areas of intelligence and morality. This is a typical example of a bias or attitude coming first and then edifices of explanatory facts or fictions being built in support of it.

But things do change. I think we're more ready than we ever have been to accept the real species. We are now living in a culture that is much more aware of the concepts of tolerance and validation. Dogs are not like us, not nearly as much as we thought, but that's okay. We can still bond with them, share our lives with them and use them as surrogate children without apology. We don't have to

3

build myths surrounding their nature to legitimize how we feel about them. They are valuable and fascinating as they really are. They don't need to be promoted in intelligence or morality to merit fair treatment or places in our families. Empathy and compassion for beings that are clearly unlike ourselves is a phase of ethical progress.

Facing up to reality is important not just because anthropomorphism has outlived its usefulness. It has always had a very real down-side for dogs. Plenty of perfectly good dogs are insufficiently Lassielike to their owners and subjected to still-legal sadistic training practices. The greatest gains for the welfare of dogs are now to be found in abandoning the Disney dog notion and replacing it with information from two sources: dog behavior and the science of animal learning. Indeed, it is our *responsibility* to be informed about the basic needs of the species we are trying to live with as well as the vast and well-developed behavior modification technology available to us. If we achieve this, we can help them fit into our society without totally subjugating their nature.

Lemon-Brains but We Can Still Like Them

The two areas in which there is the greatest amount of myth and knowledge void are:

1) dog behavior, i.e. the genetic endowment and constraints or "hard-wiring" the dog comes with, and
2) animal learning, i.e. the nuts & bolts about how experience affects the behavior of dogs and other animals, including us.

Humans also learn through operant and classical conditioning[1]. In this respect, we are like dogs. However we, unlike dogs, are also masterful at learning through observation and insight. We have language to mediate our thoughts, we can move mentally from past

---

[1] "Classical" and "Pavlovian" conditioning are the same thing

4

to present to future and think abstractly. We internalize values taught to us, most of us developing qualities like compassion and a conscience, a sense of right and wrong. Behaving congruently with our values gives us self-esteem, a feeling of integrity. All of which swishes dogs completely.

Dogs are completely and innocently selfish. They learn almost exclusively through operant and classical conditioning. Although some of their behaviors are socially facilitated, there is no good evidence that they have the all-purpose Swiss Army Knife imitation tool that humans have. Here is the important point: this doesn't make them stupid or any less valuable than they would be if they could think more like us.

In fact, dogs are great learners. They can discriminate extremely fine differences in their environment. They have incredible olfactory powers. They can deal with complex social environments. They may have a rich emotional life. But they do not think abstractly. They are amoral. They cannot move mentally forward and backward through time. And although they can learn to discriminate the relevance of certain words, they do not understand language.

Let's examine our penchant for inflating the importance of intelligence and language in determining the worth of living beings. Psychologist Steven Pinker has noted that little money has been thrown at and no films made on the search for extraterrestrial marsupialism, or, for that matter any other adaptation organisms have evolved or might evolve to make a living. We're looking for *intelligence*. Nobody stops to think that this is evidence of a bias.

So while intelligence is but one strategy to gain evolutionary foothold, it is the only one we feel is worth searching outer space for. The jury is even out on whether our strategy will help us go the distance, long-term survival-wise.

Pinker says:

"Though language is a magnificent ability unique to Homo sapiens among living species, it does not call for sequestering the study of humans from the domain of biology, for a magnificent ability unique to a particular living species is far from unique in the animal kingdom. Some kinds of bats home in on flying insects using Doppler sonar. Some kinds of migratory birds navigate thousands of miles by calibrating the position of the constellations against the time of day and year. In nature's talent show we are simply a species of primate with our own act, a knack for communicating information about who did what to whom by modulating the sounds we make when we exhale." (*The Language Instinct*, 1994)

We all, publicly at least, denounce discrimination based on race, sex, age or body-size but the tyranny of brain-power remains and is ever so subtle. There are few more egregious insults than to call someone stupid. Ponder for a minute how you would feel about using rats in experiments to test drugs if it were discovered that rats are sophisticated, pacifist, psychic beings with IQs greater than the average human. If we still somehow had the might to perpetrate anything we wanted on them, it would raise insurmountable moral questions because our internal justification for using them has less to do with our might than the fact that, well, they're not very smart, are they.

Dogs (like rats) are multitalented but they are also not very smart the way humans are. A recent book, devoted to the intelligence of dogs, is 250+ pages long (Stanley Coren, *The Intelligence of Dogs: A Guide to the Thoughts, Emotions, and Inner Lives of Our Canine Companions*, 1994). Interestingly, despite careful qualifications by Coren regarding definitions, the ranking of breeds by intelligence literally made newspaper headlines. We are obviously fascinated by the notion that dogs - or at least certain breeds of dog - might, just might, be really, really smart. It all makes as much sense as evaluating humans on our ability to sniff for bombs or echo-locate.

6

We crave anecdotes about genius dogs and these abound. Everyone knows a story that illustrates how smart dogs are. But a fundamental question has never been answered by proponents of reasoning in dogs: if dogs are capable of these feats of brain power at all, why are they not performing them *all the time*? Why never in controlled conditions? What is most tedious about these claims is the lack of rigor in evaluating them. It reminds me of people who leap to unlikely conclusions about things like circles in English wheat fields. Before theorizing that the circles were made by extra-terrestrials, more likely explanations have to be ruled out, such as sophisticated pranksters. The latter turned out to be the case, but not before a huge amount of interest (not to mention a film) was generated by extra-terrestrial theories. It would seem parsimony when evaluating possible interpretations is not mankind's natural inclination. Likewise, before jumping to the conclusion that the dog thinks abstractly and moralizes, first rule out an explanation based on operant and classical conditioning. I actually find it disturbing that my dogs' value is based on myth and exaggeration, as though their reality wasn't good enough. Their value comes from their real beings, their dogginess. They don't need mental upgrading. They are worthy and wonderful as they are.

So what is the fallout for dogs of the Lassie myth? As soon as you bestow intelligence and morality, you bestow the responsibility that goes along with them. In other words, if the dog knows it's wrong to destroy furniture yet deliberately and maliciously does it, remembers the wrong he did and feels guilt, it feels like he merits a punishment[2], doesn't it? That's just what dogs have been getting - a lot of punishment. We set them up for all kinds of punishment by overestimating their ability to think. Interestingly, it's the "cold" behaviorist model that ends up giving dogs a much better crack at meeting the demands we make of them. The myth gives problems

---

[2] The word "punishment" here is used in its everyday sense – those already familiar with operant conditioning jargon will recognize from the context that what I'm referring to is positive punishment

to dogs they cannot solve and then punishes them for failing. And the saddest thing is that the main association most dogs have with that punishment is the presence of their owner. This puts a pretty twisted spin on loooving dogs 'cause they're so smart, doesn't it?

Learning theory, i.e. behaviorism, is the best means we have to understand and modify the behavior of our dogs. It is best both in terms of effectiveness and therefore, by extension, in terms of minimizing wear and tear on the dog and on the dog-human relationship. The large-scale unwillingness to accept and develop our expertise in applying the principles of animal learning is defended on grounds that don't hold up when scrutinized. The basis in science leaves people cold yet the warm model, as we've seen, lays the foundation for endless punishments of these brilliant, moral, yet law-breaking beings. My argument is that dogs aren't demeaned or reduced to the status of laboratory rats by applying what has been learned by behavioral science. I'm incensed, in fact, by the incredible irony that zillions of rats AND dogs lived pretty awful lives in laboratories and were subjected to zillions of rotten experiments in order to come up with basic principles of how animals learn. One of the most obvious applications of the knowledge so gained would be dog training, no? Kind of a double whammy for your species to be used in the experiments and then have the mass public ignore the results and continue to punish you because you're so smart. Of all the windows in existence to communicate with dogs, operant conditioning is the window that is open the widest. We should start using it.

The Eager to Please Fallacy

The anthropomorphic spin on dog behavior is not limited to exaggerations of their intelligence. We also misinterpret their regard for us. When are we going to put to bed once and for all the concept that dogs have a "desire to please?" What a vacuous, dangerous idea. I'm still waiting to meet this dog who wants to please his owner. Indeed, where is this dog who is interested at all in the internal state of his owner except with regard to how manifestations of this state impact events of relevance to the dog? Actually, let's start by tracking down a dog who can form representations of another being's internal states at all. Although praise works as a reinforcer for some individuals in the total absence of any competing motivation, this effect is limited, and casts some pretty extreme doubt on a "desire to please" module.

Closer scrutiny makes the case even weaker. Rule out, for starters, that the praise functions as a safety cue - a predictor of extremely low likelihood of aversives. This is evident in traditional obedience classes. The primary motivation is said to be praise. The primary motivation is actually avoidance of aversives, called "leash corrections." If the trainer is any good, the dog learns that if a response is praised, a correction has been avoided, and so the praise acquires meaning and relevance. But does this mean the dog is employing this sound as evidence of some internal state of the maker of the sound? This is unlikely.

Praise can also acquire some "charge" as a secondary reinforcer in the day-to-day life of a dog. People tend to praise dogs more before doling out cookies, attention, walkies and games. This all is more evidence of what we already knew and should be exploiting with a tad more sophistication: *dogs learn by the immediate results of their actions, and by tip-offs to important events in their lives.*

And yet the use of food in training meets moralistic resistance among a staggering number of owners. I once spoke to a traditional trainer who poured scorn on the use of food as a motivator. The line he trotted out, and which still makes me retch even to this day, was: "If you use food to train, the dog is doing it for the food and not for you." This man's dog, trained by avoidance with a strangle collar, was supposedly doing it for him because the only *positive* reinforcer was praise. Trainers who make claims about dogs working "to please" or strictly for praise seem oblivious to the main motivator they employ: pain.

The first task in training any animal is finding out what motivates it. No motivation, no training. All animals are motivated by food, water, sex, and avoiding aversives. If they are not motivated by these at all, they die. A lot of animals can be motivated by play, attention, and the opportunity to socialize with or investigate other dogs and interesting smells. All animals can be motivated by signals that represent one of these primary reinforcers, provided the relationship between the signal and the primary is kept adequately strong. This is mostly where praise comes in, as a sort of imprecise marker that tells the animal the probability of a primary has improved. If you opt not to use positive reinforcement, you end up, like they all do, using aversives and announcing that your dog is doing it for you. How pathetic.

None of this is to say praise isn't good or important. I personally praise my dogs an embarrassing amount because I like them and I like doing it. They like it when I'm in a good mood because Good Things Happen for Dogs when She's in a Good Mood. I personally love it when someone like my Kung Fu instructor, who has power over me, is in a good mood, but not because I'm genetically wired with a desire to please him. My interest in my teacher's mood is pretty selfish, and *I'm* supposed to be a morally advanced human. Any interest your dog has in your mood is based on what he has learned it means for him. And that's okay.

Praise does work as a primary reinforcer for some dogs. They like it enough to work for it, especially when it's the only game in town. But this is weak grounds on which to marginalize those dogs for whom praise does not work as a primary. It is also weak grounds to support the hypothesis of an underlying mechanism of desire to please. A lot of dogs seem to kind of like praise but won't reliably work for it. This is fine. There's a difference between expressing affection to the dog, for what it's definitely worth to the human and for whatever it may be worth to the dog, and relying on praise as a principal means of motivating an animal in training or behavior modification. In other words, don't confuse bonding activities with training and behavior mod. For the latter, heavier artillery is usually needed.

Some people feel disappointed to discover the necessity of using heavier artillery like food and access to fun and games and other primaries in order to condition their animal. They feel like their particular dog is a lemon because he "listens when he wants to," "only does it when I have a cookie," and has in short little or no desire to please. *Generations of dogs have been labeled lemons for requiring actual motivation when all along they were normal.* In fact, many people are actually put off by the intensity with which dogs will work for strong primary reinforcers such as food. It assaults any belief they might have in the desire to please myth, and makes them feel less important to the dog ("wow, is *this* what motivation looks like?"). I'm still waiting to meet a real dog with desire to please. If he shows up, I'll send him for therapy.

The desire to please thing has been fed, largely, by the misreading of certain dog behaviors. Dogs get excited when we come home, solicit attention and patting from us, and lick us. They are very compulsive about their greeting rituals. They often shadow us around when we're available and become gloomier or even anxious when we leave. They are highly social and genetically unprepared for the degree of absence from family members they experience in a human environment. They also bounce back amazingly well, to a point, from the immense amount of punishment we mete out at them. They monitor our every movement. I can see how this could be interpreted as worship, but it's important not to get a big ego about it: they are monitoring our every movement for signs that something might happen *for dogs*.

My dogs' brains are continuously and expertly checking out the behavior of humans, working out to eight decimal places the probability at any given second of cookies, walks, attention, Frisbee and endless hours of deliriously orgasmic games with the latex hedgehog. They appear devoted to me because I throw a mean Frisbee and have opposable thumbs that open cans. Not to

11

say we don't have a bond. We are both bonding species. But they don't worship me. I'm not sure they have a concept of worship. Their love is also not grounds for doing whatever I say. It is, in fact, irrelevant to training. To control their behavior, I must constantly manipulate the consequences of their actions and the order and intensity of important stimuli. Interestingly, some of the most sophisticated training jobs are done where no love and little bond is present. This is not to say that training is not one of the best ways around to *foster* a bond. It is. But it's not a prerequisite of training.

The Dominance Panacea

The other model that has been put forth as a quasi-justification for the use of aversives in training is pack theory. Ever since the linear hierarchy was postulated in wolves, dog people have gone cuckoo in their efforts to explain every conceivable dog behavior and human-dog interaction in terms of "dominance." We really latched onto that one. It is a great example of a successful meme. Dogs misbehave or are disobedient because they haven't been shown who's boss. You must be the "alpha" in your "pack." Aside from amounting to yet another justification for aversives-oriented training methods - the dog is supposedly staying up nights thinking up ways to stage a coup so you'd better keep him in his place with plenty of coercion - dominance has provided a panacea-like explanation for dog behaviors.

For the owner, this simple explanation makes unnecessary the work of boning up on a myriad of other topics, like how animals learn. Notions like dogs rushing through doors ahead of their owners or pulling on leash to exert dominance over their owners are too stupid for words. Some poor people have it so backwards that they view appeasement behaviors such as jumping up to lick or pawing as dominance displays and thus fair game for aversive training. The dominance panacea is, once again, a case of leaping to a conclusion before ruling out more obvious explanations. Dogs chew furniture because what else could furniture possibly be for?

12

They are disobedient because they have no idea what is being asked of them, are undermotivated to comply, or something else has won the behavioral gambit at that moment in time, like a fleeing squirrel. Rank is not likely on their minds.

So, a separation has to be made between a dog behaving appeasingly and a dog being under aversive control. If you apply continuous shock to an animal after giving the recall cue, turn it off when the dog makes contact with you, and the dog learns he can escape and later avoid the shock by coming as soon as you give the cue, you have aversive control. You can do the same thing more clumsily, and many do, by using strangle collars or rolled up newspapers. This is not necessarily a dominance maneuver, however. How it impacts rank, if that exists, is up for grabs.

Likewise, if a dog knows that he has a one in five chance for a reward if he comes and that the great likelihood is he will be able to return to what he is doing if he comes immediately, and will in fact *lose* a few minutes' freedom if he fails to comply, he's also going to exhibit a strong recall. This is control without aversives. What's important here is not what brand of motivation you use, avoidance or positive reinforcement, but the near total absence of bearing this has on the whole question of dominance. When most people say they have a dominance problem, usually they mean one of two things: they have a *compliance* problem, or else the dog is biting or threatening them. It may very well be in both cases that the dog's self-perception is that he is dominant over the owner. It could also be the case that the dog's self-perception is he is second-to-last in rank of all organic matter on the planet yet is still undermotivated to comply and/or bites people. You could have a dog whose self-perception is that he is very dominant yet is a world-class obedience dog and never bites or wants to bite anyone.

If the problem is compliance, the dog can be successfully trained to comply using operant conditioning. This is the direct-access means to modifying behavior. Using concepts like dominance to explain that a dog doesn't want to come when he has not been conditioned

13

to do so and had the behavior proofed against competing motivation is needlessly muddying the water. You can flip him on his back all you want and he will still fail to come if he's untrained and unproofed. And, you can flip him on his back and hold him down all night (and precede him through doorways) and he's still going to bite you if you set up conditions that push him past his bite threshold. There is a staggering lack of rigor and parsimony in the dog world, and the popularity of dominance as explanation is a prime example.

Top Ten Behaviors People Attribute to "Dominance"

1) **Biting/aggression, especially towards family members**

2) **Pulling on leash**

3) **House-soiling, especially when accidents occur on beds, shoes etc.**

4) **Chewing valuable owner possessions**

5) **Jumping up to greet and pawing**

6) **Failing to come when called**

7) **Begging at table/pestering for handouts**

8) **Going through doorways first**

9) **Sleeping on forbidden furniture**

10) **Food/laundry stealing**

My favorite myth is going through doorways first. What silly person came up with the notion that a dog would understand, let alone exert dominance, by preceding his owner out the front door? When dogs are rushing through doors, mustn't we first rule out that

14

they are trying to close distance between themselves and whatever is out there, as quickly as possible, because they are excited, because they are dogs, and because they have never been presented with a reason not to?

Whenever there's this desperate grasp for "whywhywhy" a dog does something, rather than being taken by a red herring like "pack theory," first rule out:

1) because it's being reinforced somewhere in the environment

2) because no one ever made a case to do otherwise (i.e., why not?)

The dominance panacea is so out of proportion that entire schools of training are based on the premise that if you can just exert adequate dominance over the dog, everything else will fall into place. Not only does it mean that incredible amounts of abuse are going to be perpetrated against any given dog, probably exacerbating problems like unreliable recalls and biting, but the real issues, like well-executed conditioning and the provision of an adequate environment, are going to go unaddressed, resulting in a still-untrained dog, perpetuating the pointless dominance program.

None of this is to say that dogs aren't one of those species whose social life appears to lend itself to beloved hierarchy constructs. But, they also see well at night, and no one is proposing retinal surgery to address their non-compliance or biting behavior. Pack theory is simply not the most elegant model for explaining or, especially, for treating problems like disobedience, misbchavior or aggression. People who use aversives to train with a dominance model in mind would get a better result with less wear and tear on the dog by using aversives with a more thorough understanding of learning theory, or, better yet, forgoing aversives altogether and going with the other tools in the learning theory tool box. The dominance concept is simply unnecessary. So, what do we know about real dogs?

Top Ten Things We Know About Real Dogs

1) It's all chew toys to them (no concept of artifacts)

2) Amoral (no right vs. wrong, only safe vs. dangerous)

3) Self-interested (like all living organisms)

4) Lemon-brains (i.e., small and less convoluted brains)

5) Predator ancestry (search, chase, bite, dissect and/or chew software in most individuals)

6) Highly social (bond strongly and don't cope well with isolation)

7) Finite socialization period (fight or flight when not socialized to some social stimulus category)

8) Opportunistic scavengers (if it's edible and within reach, eat it, NOW)

9) Resolve conflicts through ritualized aggression (never write letters to editor, never sue)

10) Well-developed olfactory system

Chapter Two
Hard-Wiring:
What the Dog Comes With

If you had to boil the preceding top ten list down to two things that really captured the essence of dogs, it would be numbers 5 and 6: they are social predators. A lot of dog behavior can be traced to their evolutionary legacy as predators and as beings that lived constantly around others. It is true that dogs are not exclusively carnivorous; they can eat and digest a lot of vegetable matter and are keen scavengers. But there's a reason gerbils and ponies don't reflexively chase moving objects whereas puppies and kittens do.

Behaviors pertaining to food acquisition are, understandably, pretty deeply imbedded. Even hundreds of generations of selective breeding that ignored, stylized or even actively sought to eliminate predatory behavior in various dog breeds have failed, in the vast majority of individuals, to stop dogs visually tracking, chasing and biting moving objects. Those same hundreds of generations of selective breeding also preserved the strong tendency to form social bonds and the rich array of affiliative behavior.

Predatory Behavior and Its Offshoots in Dogs

The hunting behaviors that crop up in so many dogs derive from wolf biologist David Mech's wolf predatory sequence:

- Search (find prey, mainly using nose)
- Stalk (stealthy approach to prey)
- Rush (move rapidly towards prey)
- Chase (if prey flees)
- Bite/hold/shake/kill (the prey)
- Dissect and eat (the prey)

There are two other behaviors that I would lump under the food acquisition constellation though they are not found in fixed sequence: chewing and food-guarding. Both were sufficiently adaptive to ensure their presence in the repertoire of the ancestors of our pets and both seem alive and well in a good many individuals today. Chewing keeps the crucial equipment, jaws, in good working order through isometric exercise. Dogs also can successfully consume bone as part of their diet. Food guarding was selected for in social carnivores because of the relative scarcity of food.

By contrast to dogs, consider a herbivore who must consume vegetation twelve or more hours a day in order to extract enough nutrition. There's grass as far as the eye can see. It would be an ineffective strategy to expend energy guarding your daily acres from your confrere. Predators, on the other hand, invest an immense amount of energy in finding, catching and hauling down a dense source of protein, and may not eat again for days. If you're a predator, you're going to make sure you don't lose your hard-won chunk of carcass, hence the strong propensity in dogs to food guard.

It's compulsive rather than logical behavior: no matter how plentiful resources are made to appear - continuous kibble in the bowl for instance - the dog's genetic program fires in a particular context so the dog guards. Not to say it's not modifiable: it is. It is a common fallacy that behavior with a strong genetic basis is immutable. Modification, however, requires active intervention in the form of conditioning exercises, rather than simply resolving the actual scarcity by feeding to the point of obesity.

The other reason dogs, and many other animals, can *afford* to engage in behavior like food-guarding is that they have evolved highly ritualized forms of aggression. They are capable of aggressing without fatal or maiming force. They have, in fact, a huge spectrum of threat levels and means of resolving disputes that, although spectacularly scary looking to humans, result in minimal

18

damage to the victim. This is also likely why some dogs' possessiveness extends to other things besides food: squeaky toys, sleeping locations, Kleenexes or socks stolen from the laundry basket can all trigger guarding. There has been insufficient breeding pressure against ritualized level misfiring. If, however, a dog guarded Kleenexes with maim force bites, he (hopefully) wouldn't be bred.

Predatory Sequence Behaviors

A great way to develop outlets for your dog is to come up with stylized games involving behaviors in the search, stalk, chase, grab and hold sequence. Doing so is not just being an enlightened owner who Meets Their Dog's Needs. Providing this kind of stimulation on a regular basis is the first line of defense against behavior problems. What follows are suggested games owners can play with their pets to burn off that predatory energy. The choice of games would depend on the individual dog and the owner's preferences. Simply experiment and come up with a selection that best suits.

Hide & Seek

Put the dog in a sit-stay out of visual contact with the room where you will hide the object (for details on teaching sit-stay, see chapter 6). Alternatively, you can simply shut the dog in another room to prevent him from peeking. Hide the object and then initiate the search by releasing him from the room (or the sit-stay) and asking him excitedly "where's your toy?!" Then prompt and coach him to search. The object can be a cookie, a stuffed chew toy, a ball or a tug of war toy. There must be some motivation for the find. If the dog is a maniacal retriever, a ball or other retrieve toy is perfect: when the dog makes a find, you may celebrate with a few intense retrieves before setting up another search. Likewise, if the dog is a tug of war addict, give him a ten or fifteen second round of tug as reinforcement[3] for a find. If he's more food-motivated, use a Kong stuffed with something delicious.

Start off with easy finds and big celebrations to get the dog hooked on the game. It only takes a few rounds for the dog to learn that he is looking for something of great interest to him. As he gets into it, go for tougher hiding places. As soon as possible, stop helping him to make finds so that he gains confidence in his own ability. If you constantly bail the dog out, he will learn that giving up is the most effective strategy, rather than persevering. Most dogs will naturally begin to use their noses to make the find. This is magical to watch. At this point, they can find objects buried deeply into sofa cushions or anywhere else you might try to stump them. The main benefits of this game are:

1) predatory energy burner: both by making the dog use his nose to find and by working in some retrieve and/or tug of war ("Find it!" is the ultimate Rainy Day Game. Fifteen to thirty minutes of it results in happily panting doggies who otherwise would have their disappointed noses pressed to windows)

2) teaches the dog to actively search for his chew toys (!)

3) multiple rehearsals of sit-stay with excited dog

4) fun, the very best thing to have

Another variation of this game involves the owner hiding himself somewhere in the house. The disadvantage of this version is that it is more limiting as far as hiding places, whereas there are virtually limitless places you can hide a squeaky toy or other small item.

---

[3] Reinforcement is a more precise word than "reward" because it refers to a "reward" that by definition served to increase responding, as opposed to reflecting solely the *intention* of the rewarder

You can also use this finding skill to help the dog kill time when you're away. Before leaving, plant cookies, stuffed chew toys, stuffed chew toys wrapped in dissectible rags with multiple knots, and stuffed chew toys wrapped in rags enclosed in old margarine containers all over the place. Even the dog's meal in installments can be hidden around the house, while the dog waits behind a closed door. Good sniffer dogs will crack virtually any hiding place you cook up. This provides constructive activity for the dog when he's alone and is a blow-softener for him and guilt-reducer for you, given that you're about to leave him alone. Please note that if your dog has an existing destructiveness problem, refer to the section on chew-training as well. And, if your dog has bona fide separation anxiety, you must get at the root of that.

Retrieving

It has been long held that there are dogs who like retrieving and dogs who have no natural inclination. More likely dogs who are strong natural retrievers have a stronger (indeed, sometimes compulsive) inclination whereas other dogs have it in them but it's not as strong and/or is buried deeper, requiring some awakening. Their apparent reluctance could be due to any combination of things: they are laid back individuals in general, they have early histories of being punished or reprimanded for chasing and/or putting anything in their mouths, they have histories of lots of coercive training and are globally inhibited, they have a history of understimulation and have a hard time relaxing and focusing when anything interesting starts happening, or something in the immediate environment while training is stressing or distracting them.

In formal training, many methods would advise force to teach these dogs to retrieve. In fact, some methods advocate force-training the natural retrievers too. My point is not only that reluctant dogs can be trained with positive reinforcement to retrieve, but many will at some point as though triggered, start to get into it. It will become inherently enjoyable to them. I've seen this time and time again. In

21

fact, I've never seen it not happen, given enough time and an adequate approach.

With a dog who is not interested in retrieving, it's important to obtain that first little spark of interest and nurse it along until it develops into a flame. The first spark of interest is likely to be visual tracking - following the movement with the eyes, rather than actual pursuit. This is fine: get excited when the dog watches the movement, tease him with the object, make it retreat rapidly from him, play peek-a-boo. The sudden disappearance may trigger some movement from the dog. Again, this is to be encouraged. If you get any actual pouncing or attempts to bite the object, praise enthusiastically and try to get the dog to follow it as it moves, like a kitten follows a piece of string. Do as many repetitions as the dog is up for. The limiting factors are your own patience, how long the dog is in the room and interested in the game itself and the reinforcers you are offering for nice responses.

It's a big risk for dogs who are inhibited about chasing or picking up objects to actually try doing this, so it is extremely important that you give unambiguous and enthusiastic approval when you see the first tentative experiment. In fact, the first time the dog tries *anything* is always a critical juncture.

A dog's early attempts at retrieve-like behaviors may have been squashed: the dog picked up something the owner would rather he didn't touch and was told off. It is only much later, after innumerable punishments for chasing bikes and feet, and for picking up shoes, Kleenexes and garbage that the owner tries to teach retrieving. A lot of chasing and object holding have been drummed out of the dog by then. A much better policy with young puppies, who will quite naturally chase anything that moves and bite all matter, is to direct this behavior towards predatory outlets from the start.

If your dog has some punishment baggage, it may take time for him to loosen up enough to risk chasing and biting, so persevere. Once the dog starts blossoming, you can start shaping the desired chain of behaviors. An informal retrieve consists of a chase, pick up, carry and presentation (putting it in your hand or dropping it nearby). In reluctant retrievers, each of these behaviors needs to be added separately, like pieces of a puzzle. One crafty and efficient short cut is to develop an ultra-strong presentation using food rewards and then shape the other steps in reverse order, always leading up to the final step with its huge reinforcement history. Other trainers forward shape retrieves and get nice results too.

Shaping is a technique that involves reinforcing the dog's best efforts and then gradually raising the standard until the behavior is as you wish. Most people's downfall when shaping is that they arbitrarily set too high a standard for reinforcement, and ignore behaviors that are on the right track. For chasing, this might mean initially reinforcing even visual tracking. The foundation of shaping lies in the fact that behavior is always variable. If you decide, for instance, to reinforce the dog half the time, you will reinforce the better half of what he's already doing, however far that might seem from your ultimate goal. Over time, this differential reinforcement will push the average up along with the cluster above and below the average, allowing you to differentially reinforce responses that are closer to the final product. Here is an example.

Kurt

Kurt, a golden retriever, is totally disinterested in retrieving. In his first training session, out of thirty trials consisting of the trainer teasing him and making an object move and disappear etc., eighteen of his responses consist of watching with mild to little interest and not moving. Twelve responses are different. Of those twelve, seven consist of him not even looking at the object, sometimes even scratching, yawning or walking away. These are the worst duds. But five of his responses are little nuggets of brilliance. One time he watched with greater interest, his ears going up, his head cocking. Four times he actually moved. Three times he moved tentatively in the direction of the object, and once he actually moved a bit quicker and tried to paw it. These responses are all reinforceable. The selection of responses is made using a clicker: a cricket-noise making device that informs the dog if the precise instant (and behavior) he has won a treat. More on clicker training in a bit.

In the next training session of thirty trials, two consist of him not looking, six consist of him looking with mild to little interest, thirteen times he follows, five times he follows and paws, twice he follows, paws *and* mouths, and twice he pounces with some vigor. Kurt is starting to follow. An astute trainer may reinforce this several times and then see there are bigger fish to fry. The new standard becomes pawing and/or mouthing. A couple of sessions later, this dog is, with border collie intensity, exploding after every throw with a fast chase, grab and pick up plus a carry about two thirds of the way back. The reinforceable response is now a perfect retrieve, all the way into the trainer's hands.

What's amazing is not that this dog learned to retrieve and to love it, but that most people would have given up on him after that first session or else failed to reinforce the mild interest and achieved a training stalemate. The behavior would have remained clustered around that initial average and may have even deteriorated through extinction. In any session there are always going to be variations in the responses the dog gives. The trainer's job is to identify those that are reinforceable among those the dog is already offering: not those that meet some arbitrary standard the trainer has in mind (perfect retrieving), but those above average for that dog on that day. Individual judgment calls about whether to reinforce a given response at any moment are part of the art of training. Trial to trial judgment calls will get better with experience because more rapid progress after better calls will be a reinforcing event for the trainer!

All training with positive reinforcement is greatly facilitated by using some signal that tells the dog exactly when he has won a primary (tangible) reinforcer. Most sophisticated dog trainers use

24

clickers, cricket toys, which have been previously associated with food reinforcement. Timing is absolutely everything in training: if the dog does a reinforceable pick-up and carry, it's critical this behavior be marked for reinforcement instantly and not seconds later when he may be doing some other behavior. Delivering food reinforcers to dogs is not feasible in those kinds of time envelopes, so the click tells the dog that he just won and may now come to collect a reinforcer. The same system is used in marine mammal shows: the animals have been shaped to perform tricks, and the trainer's whistle tells them precisely when they have scored a mackerel.

Improving Presentation

Many dogs will chase with gusto and either fail to pick up, pick up and drop/lose interest, or else pick up and hoard rather than bring the object to the trainer. Improving presentation in retrieval stymies many people but the principles are the same. In any series of carries (or putter outs), there will be variation. Sometimes the dog will chase and not pick up at all. Sometimes the dog will pick up and run the other way. Sometimes the dog will pick up, turn and drop. Occasionally, the dog will pick up, turn and take any number of steps in your direction. The devil is in the details. Whatever is above average[4] is reinforceable and will, if reinforced enough, become the new average, enabling you to set a higher standard. There is no limit to how tightly you can crank the standard provided you do it gradually and follow the rules. These rules have been well laid out in Karen Pryor's outstanding book "Don't Shoot the Dog." This book is worth reading and rereading to grasp the finer points.

With a dog who is a natural chaser but who actively wants to play keep-away/chase-me, it's doubly valuable to cultivate a nice retrieve and presentation. Things are stacked slightly more against

---

[4] The "best half" rate of reinforcement is a rule of thumb - some green dogs may need more, and savvy dogs can often tolerate lower rates

you in this case than when there is simple disinterest because the dog actively tries to avoid you when he gets control of the object. This could be the dog choosing another game (keep-away) or it could be more serious object guarding, or a bit of both. With these dogs, never show any interest in the object. In fact, you're not interested in the object. You are controlling both the food reinforcement and the ability to make the object come to life again with your throw. So relax, watch and shape. You've got him. Your failure to notice his attempts to get you to chase him may give that behavior a bit of a jostle and give you a few more reinforceable approachlets. As you won't get nearly as many trials in during a session, try multiple objects. Regardless of whether any are returned to you, you should deliver at least half as many reinforcers as there are objects.

When you teach a dog to bring something to you rather than guard it or play keep-away, it is an example of DRI (differential reinforcement of an incompatible behavior): teaching a behavior which is mutually exclusive to the one you're trying to get rid of in a given context. Any behavior that's occurring with such annoying regularity as the one you're trying to eliminate has a payoff already from somewhere in the dog's environment, very often from you, the owner. The payoff with keep-away types is the chase. The dog is ignored for lying quietly, picking up or chewing his own toys but becomes a human chase magnet as soon as he picks up a piece of laundry or runs off with the ball in a retrieve-training session. This is a very potent reinforcer and usually happens on the first trial, which is particularly potent. So, in the context of objects and dogs, retrieving is the Ferrari DRI exercise against grabbing and running, and object guarding.

Savvy owners will do a number of things:

1)   provide reinforcement in the form of attention to the dog for playing with his own toys
2)   actively teach some predatory outlets to channel the energy

3) ignore the dog's initial experiments at picking up forbidden objects, or keep forbidden objects out of reach until #'s 1 and 2 have been well installed
4) do object guarding prevention (or treatment) exercises
5) make the dog a maniac retriever to combat keep-away
6) put keep-away on cue

Putting keep-away on cue is one more line of defense against spontaneous keep-away as well as another fun game to play with the dog. Putting a behavior on cue simply means that you take charge of the time and place the dog may engage in the behavior: the dog learns that he gets regular enough doses of the activity he likes but that the game only "works" when you give the cue. In the case of keep-away, teach him that when you give a certain cue, it predicts that you will actively and gleefully start chasing him ("I'm gonna GET you!!!") and he must pick up the nearest dog toy and run. Try heading him off, tackling, any variation you like. When you've had enough, sit down wherever you are and watch what happens. The dog, having had a thrilling time, will try to solicit more chasing from you. You must refuse to bite unless he actually brings you the toy and drops it. If he does, flip it to him and start another round by saying "oooooooh, I'm gonna GET you!!" The one predictor of your chasing him is the cue "I'm gonna get you" and your wiggling outstretched fingers. The only way he can influence your decision is by relinquishing the object. I would advise simply waiting (or shaping) rather than trying to prompt the relinquishment behavior in this case.

Practice initiating and ending the game over and over. Use an end cue such as "time for a break" to signal that the game is over. The dog learns that when you give this cue, you stop playing and the toy drop stops working, so he may as well wait for the next time you say those magic words. I also love alternating keep-away rounds with retrieve or tug of war rounds. This way the dog is reinforced for running away but only on cue, and has multiple, varied reinforcers for presenting on cue. There is an important maxim in training: control the games, control the dog.

For the duration of the training period, keep laundry and other grab-ables out of reach. This is an example of another important maxim: you must manage during training. This means physically preventing the old problem, and studiously avoiding rehearsal of the old pattern while you train something new. This way you avoid putting yourself in the position of feeling "forced" to reinforce behavior you are trying to extinguish ("I HAD to chase him, he had a $300 shoe" etc.). When the "I'm gonna GET you" toy game is well rehearsed, you may start leaving the (selected) illegal objects around again. The first time he tries to get you to engage by grabbing, ignore him completely. Not even a blip. Even if you have to sacrifice that item (hence the selection), don't even cast a glance his way. Later that same day, play the game with a toy, giving the cue first. What we're after now is discrimination learning. Think of discrimination learning as the dog saying to himself: "Oh, it only works when she says 'I'm gonna get you' first, and only when it's the squeaky hedgehog or rubber ring...I get it now." This renders laundry stealing a useless waste of energy.

My dog, Lassie, had quite possibly the worst genetic predisposition on the planet for search and destroy and for object guarding, all kept at bay by regular bouts of "I'm gonna get you," object exchange exercises (discussed later) and regular predatory fixes. If, out of the blue, I'd say "I'm gonna get you" she would immediately pick up the nearest object and start maneuvering briskly around just out of reach tail until I stopped chasing. There is nothing cuter.

Today It's Not Sitting
Can a Coup D'état be Far Behind?

You can recognize traditional obedience training by the following signs: 1) some sort of special collar is usually put on the dog, 2) praise is considered adequate reinforcement, and 3) the pack theory mumbo jumbo gets thrown around a lot. This style of training has, in spite of an evolution in its trappings and rhetoric, remained essentially unchanged since the 1950s. Its latest incarnation is usually couched in rhetoric such as "eclectic" or "balanced," meaning that aversives are used as well as praise and possibly food.

"He knows, he's just stubborn" or "He knows, he's trying to be dominant" are extremely common attitudes. There is a true epidemic of people who witness one, two or several correct responses by their dog, presume learning is accomplished and then hunt around for reasons to explain subsequent wrong responses. It's no wonder people are clinging to stuff like pack theory. There's a serious knowledge void. In actual fact, a correct response, provided it has been reinforced, is merely like one more grain of sand on a scale: it increases the probability of the same response occurring in the same context in the future. A steady history of reinforcement is necessary to tip the scale in favor of that behavior occurring. It will become highly probable given sufficient volume of training.

Most people do not have a good understanding of how animals learn (or of probability), and dog owners are no exception. Many would also dearly love to avoid having to spend a lot of time installing responses through "a sufficient volume" of training. Many are also near their rope's end, emotionally, in their own hectic lives. Coping with the normal behavior of another species is breaking the camel's back. This all makes for fertile soil for explanations like dominance and stubbornness and training methods that employ aversives.

Where a behaviorist or marine mammal trainer might see a simple shaping of some behavior as the task, anyone schooled in traditional dog training typically sees either an ethology brain-buster or a battle of wills. What traditional trainers always fail to rule out when a dog does not "obey a command" are: 1) WHAT: does he know what that cue means and is it generalized to the context in which it's currently being given, 2) WHY: has the trainer supplied motivation, i.e., is there a strong history of reinforced responses to that cue, and 3) OTHER OPTIONS: is the behavior proofed against competing motivation. If all these have not been well covered, the dog is not sufficiently trained. Period. No hidden agenda, no rebellion, no spite, no mule-headed stubbornness or attitude in need of adjustment, simply an undertrained response. If you're taking tango lessons and make a mistake or your kid gets 60% on the math quiz, there's usually no BIG reason. You got it wrong because you need more practice. Your kid needs more study. The dog needs more training. It's sad, the astounding reasons that obedience hobbyists and pet owners come up with to explain poorly trained responses.

Top Ten Non-Compliance Excuses for Undertrained and Undermotivated Dogs

1) **Dominance play by dog (or its watered down version – dog in need of more "leadership")**

2) **Dog spiteful because of some recent event**

3) **Dog stubborn (i.e. disobedience "on principle")**

4) **Dog too excited or distracted**

5) **Dog tired, bored or in wrong mood**

6) **Dog over-trained (!) and so bored with responding**

7) **Particular breed-related difficulty**

8) **Dog under-exercised**

9) **Dog recently boarded/other disruption in routine**

10) **Life-phase-related disobedience (too young or too old)**

My personal absurdity gold medalist on this list is "over-trained." Behavioral scientists often measure conditioning histories for simple behaviors by animals in the thousands of reinforced trials so it staggers the mind to see a dog owner announce that his dog "knows" something after having witnessed a few correct responses (sometimes not all of which have even been reinforced). As soon as the assumption of learning is made ("he knows but he's...": choose your favorite from the list), people quite naturally need an explanation for subsequent incorrect responses, hence the top-ten list. Presuming learning on the basis of a few right responses is dangerous, especially given the variety of conditions under which dogs are expected to respond to cues. I have yet to meet the mythical "over-trained" dog. Over-*aversives*-trained is, of course, a different story. The lethargy and paralysis that characterize some competitive obedience dogs is the result of the installation of behavior with the use of pain and startle. This is almost always accomplished by means of some sort of collar. Entire methods of training are founded on specific types of collars. It must seem like bad science-fiction to dogs that their owners' choice of training methods was, until quite recently, a choice of pain-infliction hardware around their necks.

Ear Pinching

Another application of the use of aversives in dog obedience is the routine use of ear-pinching to force retrieving. Done correctly, it's an example of negative reinforcement: the dog learns first to turn off the ongoing pinch and later to avoid it altogether by taking (and later retrieving) a dumbbell quickly enough. The nuts and bolts of perfecting this technique are laid out by trainers whose main focus is competitive obedience. Some of these trainers have great hands-on skills (training "chops") and most are disciplined and diligent. What is frightening is the matter of fact way they use avoidance training to obtain and perfect stylized behaviors like heeling and retrieving. They have done it for so long on so many dogs, associate only with people who do likewise, and are so often reinforced for it with wins in obedience that they have lost all perspective. If this weren't disturbing enough, the technique inevitably trickles down to less skilled trainers, people with no chops. In the hands of someone who has poor timing and little

31

understanding of negative reinforcement, ear-pinching is basically animal abuse.

If there were any justification for the use of aversive methods in dog training, the dogs' own well-being might qualify. Might we use any means necessary to install behaviors that could realistically be expected to one day save his life or improve his quality of life? It's an arguable point. If so, we'd use such aversives only under the following conditions:

1) non-aversive means, well and thoroughly executed, have been exhausted
2) you know what you're doing and have sufficient chops that wear and tear on the dog is minimized (one would think it might cool the jets of even the keenest aversives apologist to know that most trainers have a fuzzy understanding of operant quadrants, let alone their astute application)

Forcing recalls after sufficient positive reinforcement groundwork has been laid is a case in point. I personally wouldn't elect to do this (good enough results can be obtained without force), but it's a plausible theoretical argument. But a formal *retrieve*? A formal retrieve is of use only in an obedience routine or field trial, to receive a qualifying score and maybe win a trophy. This is good for the handler and, if avoidance trained, very crummy for the dog. Dogs regularly screech when ear pinches are done to them. It amazes me to this day that anyone can attend a seminar, watch an "expert" make dogs scream in the name of winning a competition, and not dial the local humane society. How important are these little ribbons and plaques?

A strong avoidance response might improve the probability of the cue working. You've increased motivation. The Spanish Inquisition got innocent people to admit they were supernatural demons by using torture. They increased motivation. Aversives-oriented trainers argue that a dog who is not avoidance trained might - horror of horrors - refuse a retrieve in the ring. They make this sound like the dog could be squashed by a car. I would furthermore argue that if a dog is skillfully shaped, using positive reinforcement, to do the retrieve exercises in obedience, the reliability will be excellent. But it might be less reliable than if you added avoidance. So what. You lose an occasional ribbon and keep your soul.

I once heard a competitive trainer characterize the use of force as a justifiable means to reduce the dog's perception of choice. But this doesn't even work in theory: the dog always has a choice, even if it's between two pretty scary options, one of them cooked up by the trainer. Training is merely the setting up of context-driven contingencies: "If you do this, this happens, if you do that, this other thing happens." The animal can always opt for the aversive. The choice for the trainer is a simple one: train with positive reinforcement or aversive techniques or some of both. I know trainers who have never avoidance trained a retrieve on any breed and are, to date, refusal free in the ring. By contrast, I have seen avoidance-trained dogs crack up in trials and fail to retrieve, so even the increased reliability argument is not unassailable. No one will ever convince me that it's okay to coerce behaviors like retrieves. It's morally bankrupt.

Tug of War

Dog owners have been admonished for decades by trainers, breeders and veterinarians to never play tug of war with their dogs because it risks increasing aggression and/or dominance in the dog. I think they've muddled predatory behavior, which tug actually is, with agonistic (conflict resolution) behavior, which tug is not. Played with rules, tug of war is a tremendous predatory energy burner and good exercise for both dog and owner. Like structured roughhousing, it serves as a good barometer of the kind of control you have over the dog, most importantly over his jaws. The game doesn't make the dog a predator: he already is one. The game is an outlet.

Tug, or any vigorous activity for that matter, played without rules or functioning human brain cells is potentially dangerous. But the baby has been thrown out with the bath water in this case: why deprive dogs and owners of one of the best energy burners and outlets there is? It's good because it is intense, increases dog focus and confidence, and plugs into something very deep inside dogs. The owner becomes the source of a potent reinforcing activity, and there is a payoff in terms of lowered incidence of behavior problems due to understimulation. It's also extremely efficient for the owner in terms of space and time requirements, and it can be used as a convenient reinforcement option in obedience.

The "tug might make him more dominant" argument is extremely lame. The implication is that dogs or wolves ascertain rank by grabbing the ends of an object and tugging to see who "wins." If anything, the best description of tug is that it is cooperative behavior. It's not you vs. the dog, it's you and the dog vs. the tug of war toy. When you're playing tug of war with a dog and he "wins," i.e. you let go, a tug-addicted dog will try to get you to re-engage in the game rather than leaving and hoarding. You have control of the supreme, ultimate reinforcer here: the ability to make the toy appear to resist, to feel like living prey. The dog learns this.

When dogs do leave and hoard, it's often because the owner has made simple tactical errors. With a dog who tends to run the other way after getting control of the tug object, playing hard to get is an infinitely smarter owner strategy than chasing the dog. Avoid battles with dogs involving speed and agility - you cannot win. Psych-outs are much better. Pretend you couldn't care less and usually the object will be brought back much more quickly. Once the dog learns that playing with the toy *with* you makes it come to life, you gain this extra leverage.

The only study ever performed on owners who play tug with their dogs vs. those that do not (Borchelt and Goodloe) yielded zero correlation between regular tug of war games and increased aggression. I will definitely come to full alert if anyone comes up

34

with some hard, well-controlled data to the contrary, but so far all there has been is the attitude that, well, it must be bad because the dog gets so revved up. People have such a hard time witnessing real dog behavior.

Tug of war intensity is similar to the gusto seen in dogs engaging in Flyball, lure coursing, herding, field and den trials, all activities that plug into the predator in the dog. But remember, when dogs are playing tug of war, they are not playing against you, they are cooperating with you to make a kill. Watch footage of wolves or African Wild Dogs killing large prey animals. A few pack members will have hold of the animal at the same time, maybe one on the tail, one on a hamstring and one with a nose hold. They are all pulling like mad (rank unlikely on their minds). This portion of the hunting sequence in social carnivores is indistinguishable from a dog pulling on a tug toy with his owner or another dog. I would even go so far as to say that this cooperative "killing" is a bonding experience for pack members. It's an intense, pleasurable experience the dog will intimately associate with you. That said, it is absolutely critical that tug games with pet dogs incorporate the following rules.

Tug Rules

1) Dog "Outs" on Cue

This rule means the dog must let go immediately when cued. Here's how to teach it:

Decide on a release cue such as "out," "give" or "let go." Before revving the dog up to pull on the object for the first time, practice some low-key exchanges with him. The sequence is 1) your cue to out, 2) the dog releases, 3) a food reinforcer from your pocket and 4) your cue to retake. If the dog doesn't take the object in his mouth in the first place, practice the exchanges anyway, simply by giving the object to the dog (put it down right in front of him) and then taking it back, giving the reinforcer and then replacing it.

35

Rehearse dozens of exchanges for good treats. We want the "give" part strongly primed before anything else happens.

If the dog takes the object and runs away, practice exchanges without completely releasing the object, so that the dog experiences having something taken away, getting a treat, and then having it returned to him. Possessive types stand to benefit enormously from the exchange practice (much like object exchanges for object guarders, which will be addressed in chapter three) and from learning that it's more fun to play *interactively* with an object than to have it to themselves. Object guarders must be loosened up with a solid history of exchanges before proceeding with the actual game.

If the dog hangs on and will not out when encouraged, prompt an out by putting the treat he could win near his nose. Once the dog has done a few this way, hide the food so that the dog is doing his part of the bargain first, on faith. The maxim about prompts, such as visible food reinforcement, is to get rid of them as quickly as possible. If the dog is a reluctant outer, you will food-reinforce every exchange until he 1) outs without hesitation on the first cue every time and 2) knows and enjoys the tug game. The retake will eventually become reinforcement for outing on cue, but provide the food fringe-benefit in pre- training and in early rounds of tug.

If the dog still hangs on despite freeze-dried liver in his nostrils, try the following: abruptly let go of the object, whirl around and walk away. Do a two minute time out and then try again. You can also try making the toy go "dead" close to your body – cease all provocative movement and wait him out. This is ultimately about building up the dog's confidence that outing won't end the world, but *will* get him a food reinforcer and another retake on a livelier object. To teach him this, you must manufacture the first few outs to get the ball rolling. Exploit your ability to make the object simulate living prey, or be dead and more boring.

When the out is rehearsed and you are engaged in a game of tug with the dog, any failure to out should immediately end the game. This policy is carved in stone: his breaking of a (sacred) rule wrecked the game for himself. When the dog knows, loves and is hooked on the game, ending it abruptly is by far the most effective way to get your point across that failure to out is a boo-boo.

2) Dog May Not Take or Retake Until Invited to Do So

This rule prevents the dog from being grabby or initiating the game off cue. The easiest way to get this rule installed is to practice while playing. Present the designated tug toy to the dog and then a unique take/retake cue like "GET THAT ROPE" or "MAKE A KILL". Having two ingredients to the "take" (the verbal cue and the designated object presentation) is insurance against the dog ever misfiring in day-to-day life: you don't want someone innocently picking up the tug toy and being enthusiastically jumped by your dog, and you don't want to have your dog grab some other object you're holding because he thought he heard the cue. The likelihood of someone presenting the right object *and* mistakenly saying "make a kill" are more remote. So, have one and only one official tug toy, reserved especially for that use. It can double up as a retrieve object or hide & seek target too, but have no other things with which you play tug of war. Limit this activity to one target.

Play as usual when the dog takes on invitation. If, during an obedience break (see below), the dog goes for a retake before you've invited him to do so (perhaps he felt a particular response was especially deserving), immediately cue a time out and then reinstitute the game with a long obedience break. Then invite him to take. This rule infraction is extremely common in tug of war, so don't sweep it under the rug. If he goes for another retake before being invited, i.e., makes the same mistake twice in a row, end the game for that day. There must be clear consequences to clear criteria regarding rule breaking, otherwise your rules are valueless.

3) Frequent Obedience Breaks

Tug of war is one of the great recyclable reinforcers for obedience training. Alternate back and forth between tug games and obedience to spot check out and retake control during the game and to obtain snappy obedience from the dog when he's in Excitement Mode. Every initiation of the tug game is a potent reinforcer that you can use to select the most stunning obedience response he gives you during the break. The dog will try fanatically hard to improve his obedience to get you to restart the game. Through their repeated association over time, the two activities will blur in the dog's mind, eventually making the dog love obedience training.

4) Zero Tolerance of Accidents

When taking the object or readjusting their take, dogs will sometimes make contact with your hand or other part of you by mistake. Don't let this go unnoticed. Screech "OUCH!" even if it didn't hurt and abruptly end the game. Dogs are capable of controlling their jaws with great precision if you give them a reason to do so. The obvious fringe benefits to this rule are that you remind the dog of the sensitivity of human skin and the great necessity to keep their jaws off people at all times, *and* you've installed this while the dog is in Excitement Mode, which is most often where sloppy jaws are a problem.

During tug, if the dog is not breaking any of the rules, allow him to get as excited as he wants. This includes head-shakes, strong tugging and growling. Once these rules are established, they need to be maintained by constant practice and testing. When things go wrong, it's inevitably because the human slacked off on enforcing the rules.

Reluctant Tuggers

At the other end of the spectrum from overzealous dogs who need scores of priming to teach them to "out" reliably and constant rule checks, are dogs who are hard to engage in the game at all. These reluctant dogs, very much like reluctant retrievers, may be inhibited, worried types who are apologetic by nature or have histories of punishment for touching or picking up objects. These guys must be built up. They are reluctant to take, hold and hang on. Go for each of these in turn, praising enthusiastically any move in the right direction. The praise, in these cases, functions mostly  as a safety cue. You are giving the dog permission to loosen up and act like a dog without fear of reprisal. Reluctant tuggers can be turned around. My dog Meggie was quite a dismal tug of war prospect initially, but grew to adore tug, hanging grimly on like it was the Last Bison on Earth.

I'm not convinced food reinforcement is the best strategy to build tugging, as the out-prompting aspect of food can slow down all but the most crafty trainers. So, once the out is past initial installation, forego the food with these dogs.

Dissections and Chewing

There was a time when chewing in domestic dogs was viewed as either a stage that "teething" puppies went through or else a sign of a neurotic, screwed up dog. Now we know better. Chewing is a normal canine pastime that is both enjoyable for the dog and keeps the jaws and teeth in good shape. Dogs get into chew toys the way humans get into spy novels or an absorbing movie. The problem is simply one of choice of chew object: we would like the dog to discriminate between dog chew toys and all the other items in the house, indeed the universe. This is an easy discrimination for us but not at all obvious to the dog. Remember, dogs have no concept of things in your house being "worth" anything apart from their obvious suitability as chew objects. They also have no concept of right and wrong, only safe and dangerous. They also don't particularly care what your opinion is of their actions unless there is some impact on them.

With all this in mind, the urgency of installing a chew toy habit becomes clear. Under no circumstances should a dog of any age or breed be given access to anything but his chew toys unless he is actively, and I mean actively, supervised. This prevents experimentation which might result in the dog finding out he likes leather loafers or carpets. Once he finds out these things are mighty fine chew toys, subsequent punishments will likely teach him to wait until you are gone to employ them. This goes for regressions too. If the dog has been perfect for three months or three years but then conducts an experiment on the suitability of antique tables as chew toys, restrict his access until you've renewed his focus on his own toys and done a few interrupt and redirect set-ups to rule out the heirlooms.

People are often incapable of taking these obvious steps because they endlessly muddy the water with a refrain of "whywhywhy…" trying to get into the depths of the dog's psyche to discover what Big Agenda is making a dog chew a piece of wood. They paralyze themselves against effective action. As so often is the case in dog training, "the reason why" is an interesting chat over coffee but the solution is the same, regardless of the latte discussion. Take immediate action to: 1) stock up on suitable chew toys and get the dog hooked on them, 2) prevent the dog acquiring an addiction to any wrong objects by careful dog-proofing or confinement, especially when he's not supervised, and 3) after these measures have been in place for some weeks, start giving the dog full access (i.e. out of confinement) under close supervision and redirect him to a chew toy whenever he guesses wrong. This is accomplished through sting operations: you repeatedly set the dog up to make the mistake when you are Good and Ready (i.e. spying) to catch the *initiation* of the boo-boo and immediately redirect him to his own chewies. It's dangerously late to re-direct him after a minute or two of mouthing on a furniture corner.

Order of Events in Chew Training

The preceding order of events is very important. The third step, when you do actually interrupt the dog for touching the chair or shoe, would have yielded the "fine, I'll wait till you're gone" syndrome if implemented alone. The dog has to chew something. You must establish legal and attractive chew objects before interrupting and redirecting his chewing.

An excellent model to conceptualize this is called the hydraulic model. Think of the dog's total behavioral output as being fuel in a tank. The tank has X amount of fuel in it every day. The fuel will be drained every day into several reservoirs (fuel burners), which represent the dog's various behavioral outlets. One outlet is likely labeled "chewing" (others might include "chase and grab," "bark like crazy" etc.). If you plug the hole (by interrupting) leading to one of the reservoirs, there will be a backlog of fuel that will still have to drain. Thus, you might get more barking or chasing but the likelihood is that you'll get the drainage into the chewing reservoir at times when the plug (you) are not there to block the behavior. Only if you have already opened up another reservoir ("chewing chew toys") does your interruption have a chance of plugging "furniture chewing" more permanently. Dogs must have outlets for their natural behavior. If you can't or don't want to provide for the basic behavioral needs of a dog, do not own one. Subjugating natural dog behavior through punishment and morbid obesity is no longer acceptable.

Another way to view the whole chewing issue is to consider the sheer number of things you consider wrong for the dog to chew. Remember? Virtually all matter in the universe is prohibited except for the half dozen items you have decided are dog chew toys. The chances of the dog guessing right every time are astronomical. It is neither feasible nor advisable to try and rule out

41

each and every wrong item. And, if you elect to use punishment, each punishment makes you the bad guy and increases the likelihood that the dog will delay his entire day's chewing for when you are gone so he can behave normally in peace. Direct the bulk of your efforts at getting the dog chewing chew toys in your presence *and* absence by: 1) making the chew toys really attractive and interesting, 2) giving the dog no other choices and 3) playing interactive games incorporating the toys.

The Art of Chew Toy Stuffing

Individual dogs will demonstrate individual preferences for what they like in a chew toy and some dogs don't chew much, if at all. The crème de la crème of chew objects are hollow bones, Kong toys, bully sticks and Greenies. Hollow bones are made of actual cow bone and are available in various incarnations like smoked, sterilized and pre-stuffed with marrow. The great thing about them is that they are safe, relatively indestructible and hollow (knuckle bones are great too, though not stuffable). Every day you can fill the hollow inside with a new taste sensation for the dog. If you stuff the inside artfully enough, the dog will extract the stuffing near the ends with great ease but have to work harder to get out the goodies in the middle. Every minute he spends on this project is draining the chewing reservoir for that day. Yippee!

Some people can put the same old stuff (e.g. canned dog food and raw carrots) in the bone every day and the dog is thrilled. Other people, by choice or necessity, vary the contents. Most dogs love some novelty in their diet. Anything that is reasonably nutritious is okay with the exception of chocolate, onions, raisins and grapes, all of which are potentially harmful to dogs. The stand-bys are cheese cubes, cream cheese, Cheese-wiz, canned dog or cat food, peanut-butter, leftovers and commercial dog treats. Into Kong Toys can go the above along with variable sized pieces of dog cookie. The small pieces will tumble out easily, the medium sized pieces will come out with some effort and the large pieces will require you to squash the hole to get them in, and require some considerable labor by the dog to extract. Another variation is to put the dog's dinner or part of his dinner into a few Kongs, each with something more attractive, a piece of freeze-dried liver for instance, at the back. The dog works through the kibble to get to dessert.

Some dogs love doing dissections, i.e. tearing things apart rather than simply gnawing on them. Others hang onto the same stuffed animals for years. For the dissecting types, it can become expensive to keep the dog supplied so it's worth developing collections of used old socks and clean rags that can be nested inside each other. If you want him to find treasure, nest a cookie or piece of liver in the very center. If he's a really industrial dissector, tie many knots as tightly as you can to make it tougher. Present it to the dog and behold a predator in action. Witness the first few dissections to be sure your dog doesn't ingest the non-edible parts, as the occasional dog might. If he's an ingester, he can't do dissections.

A case can definitely be made for making the dog work for much of, if not all his food ration by putting it into Kongs, bones and dissectibles and even hiding these around the house so the dog has to first play hide & seek to get the toy before unpacking it. It is very unlikely you will ever over-challenge your dog. The vast majority of dogs are severely under-challenged in their day to day life. Free food in a bowl plays against the genetic legacy of dogs. The search, chase, bite and hold, and dissect urge is perhaps best met around mealtime. So, even if you choose to continue giving food in a bowl, why not precede each meal with a couple of minutes of predatory sequence games?

Many zoos and research institutions have been criticized, and rightly so, for providing unstimulating environments for their animal captives. Behavioral enrichment, usually taking the form of housing in social groups and making the animals work to acquire their food in order to better simulate their natural environment has improved the quality of life for many animals. These institutions wouldn't get away with the impoverished, unchallenging environment many pet dogs are given.

Organized Dog Sports

In the seventies and eighties, if you wanted to participate in an organized, structured activity with your dog, you were pretty much limited to competitive obedience, tracking and Schutzhund. Competitive obedience is a more stylized, rule-intensive version of behaviors like heel, stay, come, find my lost glove etc. Most cities and towns where there are dogs will have one or more obedience clubs. Schutzhund is a stylized simulation of police dog training, incorporating obedience, tracking and protection/suspect disarming. It is usually organized by clubs but, unlike obedience where any dog can join, is somewhat limited to the larger breeds of dog. Schutzhund is a great predatory energy burner as a lot of tug toy style motivation is employed by the more progressive organizations and the tracking and protection portions are terrific, predatory fun for the dog. In both obedience and Schutzhund, there's a real lottery regarding how the training is accomplished from club to club. Be wary of traditional "you must come with a choke collar" style mentality. All leading edge training methods make virtually exclusive use of positive reinforcement these days, so there is no reason to hammer obedience into the dog using aversives anymore. Be a choosy consumer.

Tracking can be done independently of Schutzhund training. The dog is taught to follow the path of the track-layer. In tracking, the goal is not to teach the dog to scent - he already knows how to do that - but to motivate him to want to keep tracking the layer's scent, indicate articles the layer has dropped, and discriminate between the layer and other people who cross the layer's track. The scenting ability of dogs is truly amazing. Experienced tracking dogs can retrace your path, footstep for footstep, six or more hours after you

44

have walked through an area, make multiple turns, cross a road, go through changes of vegetation, indicate personal articles you drop along the way, and ignore other fresher tracks which cross yours. It's a time-intensive sport but truly satisfying if you like witnessing dogs employing their natural gifts. Motivation tends to be positive in tracking: the vast majority of tracking courses now food-train rather than force-track, though I don't doubt that there are remaining pockets of force enthusiasts around.

I have had the good fortune to make the acquaintance of many search and rescue (SAR) people. This is no sport, as the dogs are called out to find lost kids, people missing after disasters and often cadavers. The dogs employ predominantly air-scenting to accomplish their work, rather than re-tracing paths taken, as tracking dogs do. If you have a well socialized dog with some strong desire to work, and you would like to be of service, this is an activity worth pursuing.

Flyball is a relay race between teams of four dogs who must, in turn, jump over four hurdles, trigger a mechanism called a Flyball Box with their paws, catch the tennis ball that flies out and then come back to their handler over the four hurdles with the tennis ball. The first team to complete successful runs with their four dogs wins the race. This is an extremely predatory, addictive activity for dog and an exciting spectator sport. Flyball is overseen by the North American Flyball Association, which makes the rules and sanctions official tournaments. Unlike obedience and tracking, which are limited to registered purebred dogs, sanctioned Flyball is open to all dogs, including mixed breeds. Many Flyball participants play just for fun and exercise and never enter a tournament.

Agility is an obstacle course for dogs, consisting of things like jumps, tunnels, climbing frames, teeter-totters and weave-poles which the dog must negotiate in the order specified by his or her handler. It's great fun for the dogs and good for developing timing for the trainer and dog-trainer rapport. It is sanctioned by various groups, including the AKC and the United States Dog Agility Association, the latter of which will grant titles to both mixed breeds as well as purebreds, like Flyball. The elitism (purebreds only at the official level) in dog sports like AKC agility, obedience and tracking is a sad relic of the vested interest kennel clubs have, through collection of registration fees and income from dog shows, in promoting purebred dogs. This doesn't mean anyone can't participate, they just can't compete in American or Canadian Kennel Club sanctioned obedience or tracking trials.

Lure coursing is a flat-out chase in a large open field of an artificial prey object ("bunny") that is moved ahead of the dog by a mechanical pulley. The course is planned in advance; the dogs each take a turn and are judged on their speed, agility, keenness and style. At the official level, it is usually restricted to sight hounds but is open to all dogs at places such as dog camps. Watching a dog with no prior experience click into coursing mode can take your breath away. The focus and intensity of the dog makes a believer out of any owner who doubted their dog was a predator. People who attend dog camps regularly rate lure coursing as their favorite activity, above the many others offered.

Dog Social Behavior and Its Implications

One of the reasons we have such a longstanding and strong relationship with dogs is that they form strong social bonds, just as we do. Separation from other group members typically is followed by behaviors which help reunite: increased agitation and exploratory activity, distress vocalizations and, if physical barriers are present, scratching, digging and chewing to escape. Although they are not very well genetically prepared to be alone (let alone all day as is the norm in our society), the dog can be readily taught to tolerate periods of isolation. Because it is against the genetic grain and is unlikely to come naturally, deliberate steps must be taken to make the dog alone-proof.

46

Alone Training

To improve alone training in puppies and in newly adopted dogs without severe separation anxiety problems (or even in an established companion), here are the things you can do. First, if it's a new dog or puppy in your house, set the precedent right away. The tendency with a newcomer is to be constantly with him because he's novel and fascinating and you want to make him feel at home and secure. However, if you are constantly available and heaping attention on the dog, you are setting him up for a terrific letdown when normal life resumes. He will have to face The Void of aloneness. So, right off the bat, leave baby dog or newly adopted dog alone for brief durations, over and over. With dozens of trials, he will learn that: 1) people are not always going to be available and 2) when people leave, they always come back again. Leave him in a dog-proofed area or comfy dog-crate with stuffed chew toys so that he won't guess wrong about what to chew. And, be sure he is getting nice predatory fixes on a daily basis. Fetch, tug, and hide & seek are the first lines of defense in all cases.

Come and go continually, all without hellos and good-byes so the puppy or dog becomes somewhat less attentive to all these departures and arrivals. It is absolutely normal for puppies to distress vocalize when you leave them alone, even for these brief practice periods. It's in the programming, remember. Luckily, it is modifiable. It can be made stronger through reinforcement or weakened and killed through the withholding of reinforcement. The latter is known as extinction. The reinforcement in question is your return. If noise making is ever, even by chance, reinforced by the arrival of a human, it will become a stronger response, possibly even in the absence of any underlying anxiety.

The rule, therefore, with distress-vocalizing puppies is: wait for a lull before going to them. Resist thoughts like "what if he needs to go out" or some other vital communication from dog to human and worry about the potent behavior modifying influence of your arrival chez dog. Always ask yourself what behavior you want to reinforce. If you like the noise, respond to it. If you don't, wait however long it takes for a lull before going to the dog. It is not that you're not going to meet your dog's needs: it's just that you're not going to train in noise-making in the process.

Keep all your departures and arrivals low-key. The gushing hellos and long-winded good-byes with tons of cuddling and begging ("pleeeeeeeze be good while I'm gone") are not only useless but serve only to increase the contrast between when you're home (Bliss) and when you're gone (The Abyss). Employ every conceivable strategy to *reduce* this contrast. Save the very nummiest chew toys for when he's alone. Incorporate lots of fetch and tug toys into your interactions with your dog, even into greeting ceremonies (celebratory fetch or tug rather than just gushing). Get the dog out into the outside world so he has novel sights, sounds and experiences to process every day. This increases mental fatigue.

If you must leave the dog alone all day, consider hiring a dog walker at lunchtime to break up the time. Eight or ten hours is a very long stretch, especially if you have limited time in the morning getting ready to go to work (dog walked, fast fetch and tug game, fed then ignored). I am aware that many dogs can hang onto bladder and bowels that long, just as many humans can hang on longer than they'd ideally like to on occasion. However, I do wonder about what it must be like for the dog those last couple of hours. Just because he *can* hold on is not justification that we *should make* him.

It used to be thought that dogs needed mainly space, that it was the ideal life to be "on a farm" with "plenty of room to run." Now we know better. **Dogs are not space-intensive, they are time-intensive.** Given a choice between your time and a yard, virtually every dog on this earth will opt for more time hanging out with living beings.

48

Preventing mistakes through dog-proofing is not a frill to alone training. A puppy or an untrained dog must be enclosed in an absolutely dog-proofed room, crate or pen with nothing but chew toys whenever you're not supervising. If housetraining is an issue, the dog should be crated when not watched. Management failure derails or delays many a training project.

Think of establishing a new behavior or outlet as cutting a new path through dense jungle with a machete: the more times you go up and down that path, clearing as you go, the easier it is to walk. Think of the undesired behavior or outlet you're trying to get rid of as an established trail you'd like to abandon so that it overgrows: any journeys along that path will keep it clear and usable that little bit longer. Every time the dog gets a crack at the undesired behavior, he's keeping that old path alive. Therefore nipping embryonic problems is a good idea, before they become worn paths. If your "trained" dog suddenly chews furniture one day, don't let there be a second day: refresh chew training rather than waiting for a history of misbehavior to develop. I'm always astounded at how people wait for weeks or months to address their dogs' chewing problem because "well, he doesn't do it every day" or some other excuse.

Separation Anxiety

Most dogs that are destructive when alone are engaging in recreational chewing. Many dogs have small but discernible levels of depression – disappointment is a good word - at being left alone. Some dogs, however, develop a bona fide anxiety disorder, separation anxiety. While a bored dog might chew and play while alone, a dog having a flat-out panic attack might injure his paws and break teeth while digging and chewing at points of exit such as doorframes. Other cardinal signs that can be used to distinguish separation anxiety from more garden-variety owner-absent behavior problems are: signs of anxiety prior to departure (panting, pacing, salivating, trembling, lethargy and hiding), and anorexia while alone and often shortly before departure. The onset of separation anxiety often occurs after some triggering event such as

49

being re-homed or major routine change especially if it involves a sudden contrast between having the owner around a great deal and suddenly having to endure long absences. Shadowing is often raised as a sep-anx flag, but I'm not sure it's particularly diagnostic. Following owners all over the house, including, if allowed, into the bathroom is par for the course for most dogs.

Fortunately, separation anxiety, once identified, can be treated with a combination of gradual desensitization and anti-anxiety medications. Under no circumstances should you attempt to punish any chewing or noise-making already committed while alone, hours or even minutes earlier. If well-timed punishment is a slippery technique, late punishment is abuse, and late punishment to a dog who is already anxious blenderizes the dog's remaining brain. The overall anxiety level of the dog is exacerbated by the punishment that is predicted by the owner's arrival home. Now the dog has two reasons to be upset. He's alone (genetic programming he can't control) and he will be attacked when his owner returns home (human idiopathic aggression he can't control). If you've ascertained that your dog is severely anxious about being left on his own, the treatment of choice is systematic desensitization.

Systematic Desensitization

Systematic desensitization is the same technique used on people who are excessively afraid of spiders or flying in airplanes. The subject is first taught to relax and then introduced to the fear-evoking stimulus at whatever level he or she can tolerate without anxiety while practicing the relaxation exercise. Then the stimulus is gradually intensified at whatever rate the subject can handle, always building on success. A spider phobic might only be able to tolerate pictures of spiders at thirty feet in initial training but, if a hierarchy of difficulty is made gradual enough, can be made to eventually tolerate the proverbial tarantula on the arm. The same can be done with dogs who are phobic or who experience separation anxiety. The best results are usually obtained if the dog can be kept safe from panic-inducing levels of aloneness for the duration of treatment. This often means that, early on, the dog can't be left alone at all. This sounds absurd to some owners, but to others it's a small temporary price (and one they already may be paying) for resolving the disorder.

One potential way around the inter-session exposure problem is to use a safety cue, like the radio, during training sessions. The radio becomes a signal to the dog that only short, non-anxiety producing absences are in store. It is important to understand that it is not the radio, per se, that relaxes the dog but it's *reliable pairing* with tolerable levels of aloneness that *establish* it as relaxing. This effect can be quickly decimated by putting the radio on and leaving for longer than the dog can handle. Radios are frequently used without any desensitization procedure, usually to no avail. This is because when owners put the radio on to mimic the ambiance when people are present or to "keep the dog company" it immediately loses any power it had by coming to predict anxiety-producing lengths of absence. This is a classic example of mistaking the building of a tool with its use. So, whenever you're doing exercises, have the radio on. When you're leaving for real and therefore distressing the dog, leave the radio off.

Early training revolves around desensitizing the dog to your pre-departure ritual. Only when the dog is no longer exhibiting the panting, pacing etc. would you even open the door and step out for a second or two. These programs are best attempted under the guidance of a competent professional. See the Resources section to track down good behavior counseling.

Adjuncts to Alone Training

There are basic mental hygiene measures you can take to help the alone training cause. Practice semi-absences by closing the dog in various rooms of the house for different lengths of time when you're at home so he can't always shadow you around. Increase regular, vigorous exercise, predatory stimulation and walks so the

51

dog has some novel sights, sounds and experiences to process every day.

One excellent trend I see emerging is double dog households. Be advised: having two dogs doubles your food, medical and accessories expenses. It also doubles the amount of hair in the house and on your clothing, and time and money spent grooming and training, not to mention double the likelihood of a dog regurgitating grass and bile onto the wall-to-wall carpet and double the number of eyes following you into the bathroom. Double dogs also frequently bond more strongly to each other than to anyone else, especially if the two dogs are littermates. You will need to spend quality time with them individually if you wish to reduce this. It is also advisable to have them practice time away from each other so that it's not too traumatic an event when one is hospitalized or otherwise not available. It's a serious decision.

In terms of quality of life for the dogs, though, given that both dogs are socialized to their own species and the like each other, things are much better. They are almost never alone. They have a target for a lot of their doggie behavior, a built-in playmate. They have the opportunity to develop a richer percentage of their doggie communication and interaction patterns. Their day to day life is more complex: even the inevitable conflicts and disappointments which come with being one of two rather than an Only Dog help in the never-ending war against understimulation. I am in no way suggesting that getting a second dog is a quick fix for existing behavior problems (most notably, acquiring another dog almost never ameliorates separation anxiety in the existing dog). Life is never that simple. Indeed, it may have no impact at all. It merely shifts the odds more in your favor and improves the quality of life of a dog whose owner must leave him alone a great deal. Interview people who own two dogs. Most will tell you that their dogs hang out together all the time and play with each other vigorously "every day." I often wonder where all this energy is going in single dogs.

Chapter Three
Socialization, Fear and Aggression

Aggressive behavior in domestic dogs is an issue that has long needed to come out of the closet. There is incredible stigma attached to dogs that bite, as though they have character flaws and are qualitatively different from dogs who have never bitten. They are not. There are not two kinds of dogs: nice dogs who would never bite and less nice dogs who do. *Biting is natural, normal dog behavior*. This is why it is so prevalent.

Biting and threat displays (which are simply the indication of intention to bite) are how dogs settle both minor and major disputes and defend themselves from any perceived threat when they cannot or opt not to flee. In dog culture there are no letters to the editor, slanderous gossip and backstabbing, guilty feelings, democratic institutions, or lawyers. There are growls, snarls, snaps and bites. Aggressive behavior does not fracture relationships in dog society. It's all taken very much in stride. The problem is that aggression often changes things a great deal in dog-human relationships. We routinely execute dogs who bite. That's quite the culture clash.

There is an important distinction to be made: between dogs who inflict egregious damage when they bite – breaking bones, mutilating flesh, putting people in hospital or killing them – and garden-variety biters who inflict no damage or damage equivalent to a minor kitchen injury. In the wake of dramatic incidents of maulings and human fatalities that get massive media play, there is some understandable terror among the general population. It is terribly, terribly important to understand the rarity of these kinds of attacks. There are, and have been for as far back as records have been kept, in the neighborhood of twenty-five dog-related fatalities per year in the US. Considering the degree of exposure – the

53

number of dogs and people in close contact for extended durations every single day – this is a vanishingly tiny incidence.

Headline-grabbing dog attacks put the idea non-representatively into human minds. Usually no effort is made to distinguish dogs involved in fatal and near fatal maulings from kitchen injury level biters. In human terms, this is exactly akin to lumping sharp words with felony assault and murder.

If we can get over this preliminary hurdle in understanding, what do we make of normal dogs, the vast majority? The domestication of dogs has made it easier to socialize them but it has not provided any guarantee against anti-social behavior. Selective breeding practices dance with the devil all the time by stating, in breed standards, temperament characteristics such as "aloof," "wary of strangers," "one family dog" etc. etc. The behavior these stated ideals flirt with (and too often consummate) is fear and aggression toward strangers. The mythical dog is one who can tell the good guys from the bad guys. Gentle with toddlers and accepting of family friends, the mythical dog instantly springs into action, attacking would-be robbers and muggers. For every anecdotal report of an otherwise (allegedly) perfectly friendly dog who nailed the burglar there are scores, hundreds, perhaps thousands of dogs that, for *identical reasons*, nailed the neighbor, the delivery guy or a child in the park.

The mundane, unglamorous reason in the vast majority of cases of dogs biting people is the falling short of breeding and rearing practices of what is an absurd ideal in the first place (no bites, ever). Breeding practices range from bitches' choice "accidental" (from the humans' perspective) matings to a prodigious cranking out of dogs by well-meaning owners and hobbyists. They include backyard breeders lacking knowledge or even consideration of the genetics of behavior to fanciers who breed to a conformation standard or who may even deliberately breed for low ease of socialization ("one family dog" euphemism breeding). It's hard to know what to do with this last group, the fanciers. On one hand,

54

many fine dogs are produced and many interesting breeds are maintained. On the other hand, animal shelters on this continent are forced to slaughter millions of dogs per year, most of which are healthy and friendly. All other kinds of breeding have been indicted for their role in this insanity with the exception of the dog fancy.

As far as the deliberate breeding of harder to socialize dogs, society may decide it's perfectly acceptable to deliberately breed dogs who are less easily made friendly to strangers. Indeed, that seems to be the current standard, if by default and not careful consideration. Alternatively, society may decide it wants multiple lines of defense against dog bites, and breeding practices will come under greater scrutiny. The attitude among breeders of hard to socialize dogs seems to be one of side-stepping any culpability by implicating owners' failure to implement adequate compensatory socialization. I'm for strong socialization as much as anyone can be but, when it comes to dog bites, redundant lines of defense would be better.

As laws currently stand, I could spend twenty or thirty generations combining genes to produce the most aggressive dog possible and sell that dog to pretty much anyone I want. A buyer of one of my dogs may then do all the right things vis a vis socialization and training. Should that dog ever bite someone, however, the owner (or, depending on which State one is in, whoever is holding the leash at the time) is liable but I, the breeder, am not. This is like being allowed to build a bomb in my basement, deliberately making it as dangerous a bomb as possible, and then selling it, with no legal ramifications. I think it is partly because we live in a nurture-biased society, where we seem determined to deny any genetic influence on behavior. This is lucidly discussed in Steven Pinker's *The Blank Slate*.

Gene Team Passes the Baton

As Ian Dunbar has said, once the gene team has had its turn, rearing practices are what's left to manipulate. In other words, there's no crying over spilled milk: the dog very well may have unhelpful genetics, but there's nothing that can be done about it with current technology. The focus, once sperm meets egg, must be on environment. Two additional considerations worth noting at this juncture are prenatal environment and maternal behavior. There is some research that suggests that stress during pregnancy, at least in rodents, can potentiate stress over-responsiveness in adult offspring. There is also some suggestion that maternal behavior alone in dogs can influence the development of fear in puppies. Although neither of these are under control of dog owners, pressure could be brought to bear on breeders via consumer education of prospective purchasers of their puppies.

Once the baton is passed to the dog's owner, the socialization effort is often retarded by the extreme head-in-the-sand attitude regarding the potential for garden-variety aggression. Most owners have never actually done any active aggression prevention training. Most would agree with the statement "my dog would bite only with extreme provocation." What's insidious is that almost all owners of dogs who bite seemingly "without provocation" believed their own dog to be safe the day before or the minute before the dog bit for the first time. Because of the normalcy of the behavior and the spotty track record by the gene team to breed Superfriendly dogs, *all* dogs must be acknowledged as potential biters.

Dogs are unaware that they've been adopted into a culture where biting is considered a betrayal of trust and a capital offense. Incredibly little is actively, consciously done to reduce the probability of biting. Flight-bite is the dog's hardwired program for increasing their distance from anything that spooks them. Dogs, like most animals, are extremely aware of and constantly manipulating social distance. There are only two ways to do this: move yourself away or get the other guy to move away, plan A or plan B. Getting the other guy to move away is the function of aggression.

56

Which plan an individual dog chooses first (threaten or run) is a function of his genetic predisposition and learning history. Dogs will do what tends to have been successful in the past. They will also, if plan A is not working, switch without hesitation to plan B. Cornered dogs switch to threat display. Dogs spooked by your presence into behaving aggressively will turn and run if aggression doesn't work. It is a matter of great urgency when the "increase distance" alarm goes off in a dog's head. Genetic predisposition simply makes one plan or the other more likely and influences how likely the dog is to spook in the first place, all other things, such as how well socialized he is, being equal. An important piece of the puzzle that is missing in mass education is information about the seemingly innocuous events and contexts that elicit spooking in domestic dogs.

To accept aggression as normal behavior would require a fundamental shift in our view of domestic dogs. The potential payoff is that we could, starting today, reduce the number and severity of dog bites by facing up to the problem: dogs are animals and animals bite. It would simply take a large scale initiation of **routine preventive intervention** to minimize risk. There are things whose safety we take for granted: books, pillows, hats, flowers. We don't have safety programs for these things. There are also things we see as potentially dangerous - safe only if knowledge and care go into their management or use: kitchen knives, electrical outlets, swimming pools, chainsaws, matches, bleach. We put normal dogs in the safe category when they belong in the potentially hazardous category. Dogs are seen by many as being dangerous only if really pushed, like a pillow is dangerous only if you really go out of your way to cook up a smothering scene. Dogs are animals and animals bite. They are still *really* great animals.

The Real Epidemic

Whenever there is a headline-making dog attack, where someone is seriously injured, public officials are pressured to do something about "the epidemic." The reason these incidents make the news, as opposed to, say, a kid getting a comparable injury in a car accident or falling out of a tree, is that it is an incredibly rare event. As I mentioned earlier, there *is* no epidemic of extremely serious dog bites. There is, however, an epidemic of people being growled at, snarled at and bitten to the tune of spit only, or a small puncture wound or two.

When a dog bites at the level of kitchen injury, he is stigmatized, and often killed. The mythology of dogs in general goes relatively unhurt because the individual biter is blamed and labeled deviant, often lumped in as a potential killer, even by some (less rational) dog professionals. From a normal dog's perspective, however, allowing a decrease in social distance between himself and anyone to whom he's not habituated or *socialized* would more likely qualify as deviant behavior. So why aren't dog bites a daily occurrence? For one thing, kitchen injury bites are. Statistics in western countries where the number of bites is recorded are invariably mind-boggling. And these are the *reported* bites. A much larger number go unreported. Many other dogs simply never meet up with the particular combination of elements that would cause them to bite, but this is a stroke of luck. There is no qualitative difference, or even necessarily a quantitative difference, between their temperament and that of the repeat biter next door.

Just as it's inherently clear to dogs that a good proportion of matter is chew toys, it's equally obvious that you should threaten to bite or bite anyone who is spooky and comes too close, or who tries to obtain important resources in your possession. The mental hurdle people seem to have is accepting that *the dog decides what is spooky or threatening.* This is a dangerous place to be anthropomorphic. We humans had better start to pay attention to what these things are or we will be left with the tired refrain of "I don't understand it, suddenly and without warning and with no provocation blah blah blah."

So, a major element of the culture clash between dogs and humans is differing perceptions of what constitutes a threat. The most commonly uttered phrase following a bite is that the dog bit "unprovoked" or "suddenly, for no reason." This is because the number one bite provocation in domestic dogs is some variation on a behavior we humans consider unprovocative, or even friendly: *approach or reaching out with a hand.* We are mired in the belief that the friendly intention behind this gesture is read and understood by all dogs. We've been reinforced in this belief by the dogs who tolerate patting and handling. For sure, some dogs actively enjoy and solicit patting from people. Many dogs, however, just tolerate it or actively dislike it. And, for a dog who is not socialized to, say, men, the mere presence of a man is provocative. What's important to understand is that bites are rarely cases of something going awry, such as abuse or trauma, but failures of omission: not enough was done to get the dog prepared for life in a human environment. Desensitizing dogs to approach and handling must be actively installed to proof them against spooking. Dogs who bite people or are afraid of people are usually behaving like normal animals. To understand why dogs bite for reasons indiscernible to most owners, it is first necessary to understand socialization.

Socialization: What is it Anyway?

Socialization means habituation, or getting used to environmental elements through exposure to them. In a natural setting, it is highly adaptive to increase distance between yourself and anything unusual and then to proceed with extreme caution when approaching. This is because unusual things are potentially very bad news. (They certainly aren't *necessary* for survival because you've made it this far without them.) Animals adhere to rules governing social distance. So do we, if you think about it. We tolerate someone standing right against us in a crowded elevator but would be instantly spooked by the same person standing that close if we were the only two in the elevator. Someone can walk up and stand right behind you if you're in a line-up at the grocery

59

store, but someone doing exactly the same thing when you're in the driveway washing your car is a whole other story. We can also, like other animals, be very weird about being touched.

In animals, curiosity is antagonistic to fear, and usually less pronounced. While it is potentially adaptive to explore novel things in case they yield some advantage (especially in the case of predators), excessive curiosity would eventually result in exposure to danger and hence reproductive disadvantage. In other words, the cost of a false positive (spooking away from something that is in fact harmless or beneficial) is greatly outweighed by the cost of a false negative (failing to spook away from something that is dangerous). You can't pass on those curious genes if you're dead or injured. Consider, for instance, what you'd think about any wild animal in the forest that didn't flee from you or didn't put on an aggressive display if you cornered it. Would you think he was a "nice" animal or would you think he was, say, sick? Avoidance of novelty is the default setting for animals. All these truths about animals are pretty self-evident. And, lest we forget, dogs are animals.

Because it would not be adaptive for animals to be continuously spooking at rocks and trees and bird song, a mechanism is wired in to ensure the animal habituates to normal environmental features. This is the socialization period, a finite time when young animals are much less fearful and are much more likely to approach and investigate novel things. They readily form social bonds.

Adult animals can habituate to novel things too; it simply takes much longer. The socialization window cannot remain open forever. If it did, then you *could* have animals trotting up to you in the forest. Every species of animal has acquired, through natural selection, an average time to assimilate and accept things in their environment. After this period, they will behave to increase distance, through the mechanisms of flight or aggression, from anything to which they have not been socialized. There is also a "use it or lose it" clause: some animals will become increasingly fearful of things they may have encountered in the critical period but see too seldom thereafter.

Notice that the pressure is always in the direction of increasing fearfulness and avoidance, never the other way. Artificial pressure needs to be constantly exerted to get animals to behave tolerantly. It must be installed in the socialization period and maintained thereafter. As soon as there is any weakness in this system, the animal starts leaning towards fight/flight. By definition, the socialization period, be it one day or several months, is what works well for that species in the environment in which it evolved. In the case of domestic dogs, the socialization window closes somewhere between three and five months of age, depending on the breed and individual make-up, with easy habituation drying up by around four and a half months of age in the majority of cases. These thresholds are a matter of consensus, by the way, not strong empirical research. Many of us would really, really like to know what's going on regarding critical socialization periods in dogs, and any relevant details regarding breed differences. The trend among hard-core dog people is toward earlier and earlier formal socialization, i.e. puppy classes for puppies in the seven to eleven week old range. There is increasing willingness to balance the socialization imperative with the need for pathogen avoidance in young puppies with inadequate immunity.

The importance of a critical period for socialization is hard to overestimate. If, for instance, a puppy doesn't get sufficient exposure to men with beards before the socialization clock runs out, the risk for fear responses and aggression directed at men with beards runs higher for that dog as an adult. It's particularly wrinkly because dogs are expert discriminators: adequate socialization to women or eight year-old kids, for example, does not guarantee a generalization to men or two year-old kids. Therefore, it's advisable to go way overboard covering all the bases before the socialization window closes, especially for spookier breeds or individuals. This means exposing the puppy to as wide a social sphere as possible in terms of human age groups, sexes, sizes, shapes, colors and gaits. The experiences should be positive (play, treats, nothing scary) and include a wide variety of patting, handling and movement by the humans. It also means getting the puppy used to anything it may have to encounter in later life, such as car rides, veterinary exams (make the first one or two fun rather than scary), cats, traffic, soccer games, elevators and pointy sticks.

Pumped Up Socialization

I think there are dual benefits to heavy socialization. One is obvious: the more you socialize the puppy, the fewer things you'll miss. The second advantage is a more global effect: the more the puppy encounters novel situations in which it initially is reluctant or spooky and then gets over it and habituates (as puppies do so well), the more the underlying trait of stability or "bounce-back" is developed. The puppy's overall confidence grows. The more puppyhood experiences a dog has to draw on, the more resilient the character. The mild stresses of regular novelty in early life are like inoculations. So, provided the puppy had really thorough socialization and developed good bounce-back, individual elements that were missed during socialization will be handled more easily by the adult animal. The passive approach ("get the puppy out to a few shopping malls and dog shows") is inadequate for some individuals. Aim for a systematic, continual, assault style program. Not only do you end up with a dog who is at reduced risk for fearfulness and biting, but one who also is under much less chronic stress as an adult.

The puppy that has had positive experiences is less likely as an adult to spook in a challenging situation than the dog who had only neutral experiences. So, why not improve your odds of getting a relaxed, confident, solid adult temperament by *actively* increasing the number of strongly positive experiences? This is like putting money in the bank. (Also note, if the puppy has a negative experience on the first trial of exposure to something, a full-blown phobia can be acquired.) Why go for a dog who's more or less habituated to screaming toddlers or teenagers on roller blades when you can end up with one who actively likes them?

In socialization to any category of people, the single best way to obtain this cushion is through hand feeding. Rather than simply getting the puppy around young children, have young children hand feed the puppy small tasty treats. Each treat builds up a little more money in the bank for young children. Another method, suitable for predatory types who are addicted to games with toys or balls, is to have people in the category you're trying to cover engage in favorite games with the puppy.

Socialization Hitlist

CATEGORY	NEUTRAL	POSITIVE
ADULT WOMEN	Meets in corridor	Hand fed by
ADULT MEN	Visits house	Hand fed by
TEENAGERS	Sees on street	Hand fed by
8-12 YEAR-OLDS	Patted by in park	Hand fed by
4-7 YEAR-OLDS	Sees in schoolyard	Hand fed by
TODDLERS	Visits house	Hand fed by (assisted)
BABIES	Sees one on street	Fed when near
BEARDS	Sees on TV	Hand fed near
HATS/SUNGLASSES	Sees on pedestrians	Wear while playing
ODD GAITS/DANCING	Might see by chance	Snacks at Salsa class
ALL RACES	Sees occasionally	Hand fed by
CROWDS	Outdoor event	Snacks at
UNIFORMS	Puppy meets mailman	Hand fed near
WHEELCHAIRS	Sniffs one	Hand fed near
CRUTCHES	Sees at train station	Hand fed near

64

BIKES	Sees on street	Hand fed near
IN-LINE SKATES	Sees on street	Hand fed near
TRAFFIC	Walks near	Walks to fun places
CAR-RIDES	Around block	To fun places
CATS/LIVESTOCK	Sees and sniffs	Treats near
DOGS	Meets & greets	Off-leash play

This list is not exhaustive. **You cannot overdo socialization**. The payoff is enormous. I have often thought that owners who are inclined to leave their dogs' socialization to everyday life (i.e., chance) should meet families of garden-variety biters or dogs with world-class phobias of innocuous environmental elements. They would hear a lot of "if only": many of these dogs appeared fine as puppies. They reacted well to what they were exposed to, but it wasn't enough, either in volume or range. Experiences were neutral, rarely positive. They saw people but not up close. They saw women but rarely men. They saw plenty of people but were never manhandled. There was an omission. Doing remedial socialization on an adult dog is a slow, labor-intensive undertaking, if it is do-able at all. It is infinitely easier to work on puppies because of that open window of the socialization period.

IF YOU HAVE A PUPPY, BITE THE BULLET AND SOCIALIZE IT NOW

It's criminal to not put massive effort into a dog like a kuvasz who we already *know* is hard-wired to be spookier. Remember, smokescreens like, "reserved with strangers" or "takes a while to warm up to people" or "great with the family" or "protective" mean one thing and one thing only: uncomfortable around strangers. Period. There is no longer any excuse for dogs to reach adulthood

65

emotionally crippled and at risk for execution after they bite someone because of insufficient socialization. The information has been out there for years. Dog bites continue to be common, despite all the information on how to prevent them. Perhaps there's a late feedback effect: the punishing results of failing to adequately socialize a dog appear too late to modify owners' behavior. Heavy socialization is the single smartest investment you can make in a dog.

Socialization Case History

The Campbell family consists of Mom, Dad and three kids, aged seventeen, fifteen and eleven. They recently put to sleep their ten year-old German shepherd due to illness. Their other shepherd, aged seven, has always lived with another dog, so the Campbells bought a new shepherd puppy a few months after the death of their older dog. The puppy, Bruce, was bright and naturally very compliant, got along well with the other dog and fitted into the family easily. It was much easier raising this puppy than previous puppies because the family was better off financially than years earlier, had a house in the suburbs with a fenced yard for the dogs to play in and the kids were older and able to take more responsibility for feeding, training and clean-up. The family was shocked and appalled when Bruce, at age eight months, bit a visiting four year-old girl when she tried to pat the dog.

This story is so common it makes me want to scream. The owners are experienced German shepherd owners. Their first two dogs never bit anyone, never threatened anyone. One was reserved around strangers, simply retreated when they approached, and never in his life felt cornered enough to switch to plan B: biting. The Campbells bought from the same breeder and are at a loss to explain Bruce's biting because they raised him the same way. What they don't realize is that they got away with no active socialization with the first two dogs for a number of reasons. They were raised in a household with young children, who had friends over constantly, which covered that base. At the time, the family lived in an apartment so the dogs had regular walks, which exposed them to sights and sounds in a busy city. And their shepherd who avoided strangers was simply a time bomb that never went off.

Time Bomb Dogs

Bruce experienced the same passive socialization but with a couple of differences. The kids were older when he was a puppy so the occasional kids he saw felt to him like aliens from Mars. The yard offered exercise and elimination which was more convenient than taking him out on leash, so he missed out on regular walks. No walks = no meeting people. The other difference is that his response when spooked was a threat display rather than flight like their previous shepherd, even though his motives were the same as the other dog: to increase distance between himself and the child who tried to touch him.

It's important to understand that this is not a case of the Campbells doing a good job on the first two dogs and then failing on the third dog, or of the breeder producing a lemon. They never actively socialized *any* of their dogs but got away with it with the first two. Their timid shepherd would likely have resorted to threat if flight had been unavailable when encountering strangers (plan B). It just never happened. These owners never considered what they were doing to be insufficient until, inevitably, one of their time bombs went off. Many people raise time bomb dogs who, because of some combination of passive socialization, absence of sufficient challenge and that individual dog's reaction style (flight being plan A), don't explode and bite during their lifetimes. So generations of dog owners continue to gamble unknowingly. Heavy socialization, although it does not provide a guarantee against biting, vastly improves your odds.

Socialization can be upgraded from neutral to positive experiences and from passive to active. It's far better to actively seek out those categories of people and things than to hope that enough bases will be covered by whatever experiences happen to come up in the pup's

67

day-to-day life. This is especially important for puppies who are at greater risk. These are: puppies of certain breeds, any puppy observed to already be reserved, timid, reactive or sensitive, puppies from litters not whelped and raised in a human-infested home (i.e. litters whelped in kennels, barns etc.), puppies belonging to owners who live in rural or quiet suburban areas, puppies whose owners have yards, puppies of small breeds with overprotective owners, puppies raised in multi-dog households (including dog exhibitors) and puppies of large or scary-looking breeds which strangers may avoid.

The breeds at risk are an interesting mix. Herding dogs are, I think rightly, often put forward as dogs that need package warnings, for their high drive and higher risk of shyness with strangers. I would speculate here about the absence of selection pressure for gregariousness in dogs whose work and lives are, by definition, in a rural environment, and the high pressure on working ability and style in the early foundation stock. Where herding dogs come by their shyness by happenstance, the Us vs. Them breeds come by it more by design. One collection of Us vs. Them breeds is the flock-guardian dogs, notoriously hard to socialize, which is understandable when one considers their original task: living with a flock of sheep and noticing and driving off predators. The other lot is the guard dogs that guard people and other sorts of property besides livestock. They are not only less comfortable around strangers, but more sensitive to environmental changes such as people with odd gaits, people appearing suddenly, moving unexpectedly and presenting other odd pictures. There's a case to be made, for example, for mandating rehearsal of strangers doing odd, sudden stuff around great Dane and giant schnauzer puppies, among others.

Puppy Classes

A marvelous innovation has been the introduction of quality puppy kindergarten classes. Although puppy classes have been offered in the past, these were barely distinguishable from traditional jerk 'n'

68

praise obedience classes and often did more harm than good, especially in the case of puppies. This may be part of the reason behind the old admonition by veterinarians and other dog resource people to not begin formal training until a dog is at least six months old. The puppies couldn't withstand the "training." Pioneering puppy trainers like Dr. Ian Dunbar turned it all around with gentle, amazingly effective puppy-friendly methods that teach compliance while performing aggression prophylaxis and improving sociability all at the same time. There's little limit to what young puppies are capable of learning if the method is right. It's a tragic lost opportunity to delay taking a dog to class till he's an adolescent. Puppy classes are the way of the future.

Another benefit of puppy classes is the instant provision of age-mates for the developing pup. The problem of basic dog-dog socialization is very often obliterated simply by showing up to class. This assumes that the class in question is a true puppy class, limited to vaccinated puppies under the age of eighteen weeks rather than a beginner level obedience course masquerading as a puppy class. All training in a good puppy class should use positive reinforcement as motivation rather than some form or other of "training collar." There should also be frequent puppy play sessions. Aside from the dog-dog social repertoire development, play is one forum for the acquisition of bite-inhibition.

Bite Inhibition

Dogs are animals equipped to kill, tear apart carcasses and crack bone with their jaws. They are also highly social and, as animal species go, argumentative. If they are to live among others with this kind of weaponry as standard issue, they need some means of preventing serious injury to each other during altercations. That is the function of ritualization. Ritualization is a series of conventions that evolve in an animal species to allow the resolution of conflict with reduced risk to all participants. This is because, in a natural environment, flat-out aggression is expensive behavior. Injury risk to winner as well as loser, energy expenditure, time

69

away from other pursuits and, if you're a prey species, reduced vigilance and increased conspicuousness to predators are the costs. To mitigate these costs, animals often ritualize agonistic (conflict-resolution) encounters. In the case of normal dogs, postures, stares, growls, snarls, snaps and reduced-force bites all stand in for flat-out attacking.

The cornerstone of ritualized aggression is bite inhibition. Dogs are not born with soft mouths, but they are wired up to easily acquire the ability to bite softly if conditions are right. The right conditions means: plenty of feedback about bite strength during the first few months of life. To ensure that puppies get plenty of feedback about bite strength, nature has made puppies into veritable biting machines with needle-like teeth. Normal puppies can and should play-bite continually in social interactions. Of high concern is the fact that puppies are removed from their litters early in life and often placed in a relative social vacuum. This is greatly compounded if the puppy is forbidden from play-biting his owners. Suppressing puppy biting too early means the puppy doesn't get the repeated doses of feedback on his jaw strength; the puppy grows up with a hard mouth. Ironically, this is a serious squandering of a critical line of defense against dog-bites.

Smart puppy owners allow some puppy biting in order to give the puppy information on his own strength. Puppy biting is such a valuable thing, in fact, that puppies who do not play bite should be actively encouraged to do so in order to rehearse soft mouth. Start off by targeting harder bites. Let the puppy chomp away on your hands and monitor the level of pressure. Although puppy teeth are sharp, puppy jaws are undeveloped so this will not be unbearable. As soon as the puppy bears down a little harder, screech "OUCH!" as though it hurt much more than it did, look at the puppy like he's a little ax-murderer and leave the room for a minute or two. This time out is a clear refusal-to-play consequence with the "OUCH!" as the conditioned punisher. Many puppies also have an innate understanding of the screech, making the system work even better. After the minute or two has passed, return and resume play. He

70

may be more prudent temporarily and he may not. Be prepared to repeat this procedure over and over so the trend emerges. Puppy learns that if puppy bites too hard, puppy plays by himself.

It's beneficial from a generalization standpoint if more than one person implements these same rules. The exception is young children. Young kids and puppies are an extremely dangerous combination. Kids do all the wrong things around dogs: they scream, flap, move a lot, fall down and react in a fun (for the puppy) way when the puppy bites them. They expertly simulate wounded animals and bring out the predatory rehearsal repertoire in the dog all too well. They are not good candidates to install soft mouth in excitable puppies. Young kids should be around puppies, and well-socialized adult dogs for that matter, only when actively supervised by an adult. All their interactions should be carefully refereed. When the puppy starts to rev up, the kids must exit so the adults may do the soft mouth exercises or redirect the puppy's energy. Kids should never, ever, ever be allowed to go up to strange dogs. The "kids and dogs" as wonderful playmates is an overblown and highly dangerous myth. Two lines of defense is the way to go: 1) socialize puppies to kids and 2) supervise all interactions between dogs and kids.

When the puppy has consistently demonstrated some greater self-control, you may start targeting even low pressure bites. The reason for doing it in stages is to get in plenty of *soft* biting practice. Plus, the puppy would be unable to comply if you set too high an initial criteria. He's got to be able to manage the task you set for him. Little biting-maniac puppies can and do learn to hold back on the hard bites but they are simply unable to hold back on most bites too early on (unless you obliterate the puppy with harsh punishments). You're teaching him self-control in manageable chunks. When he is mouthing you with very little pressure you may then teach him "don't touch" and redirect him to appropriate bitable objects like his toys. He now knows that he may not bite humans at all and you've got the critically important fringe benefit

71

of acquired bite inhibition. Good puppy classes do a splendid job on these "don't touch" exercises.

I very much like the idea of maintaining bite inhibition in grown-up dogs. The best way to do this is to hand feed the dog, do mouth exams and teeth-brushing, and engage in structured roughhousing. You'll be doing a lot of hand feeding anyway if you use food reinforcement in training. Rather than letting the dog eat out of your flat hand, hold food morsels in your fingers. If you feel incisors on your fingers, screech "OUCH!" and withhold the food. Only relinquish food, regardless of the brilliance of the behavior you are reinforcing, if the dog is demonstrably prudent with his jaws and you feel no pressure on your fingers. Dogs need these constant reminders so they don't get rusty. Another good way to get your hands into the dog's mouth is to regularly brush his teeth. This is a good idea anyway and super palatable dog toothpastes exist now. Regular dental maintenance like this gives you opportunities to remind the dog to be gentle with his mouth as well as giving the dog nice breath and tartar-free teeth. Yet another opportunity to fine-tune bite inhibition is during tug and fetch games. Without exception, screech in pain and end the game if the dog makes a grabbing error and nicks or bites you instead of the toy.

Play and Roughhousing – With Dogs and With People

Young dogs that are socialized will usually spar and jaw-wrestle with other dogs endlessly if given the chance. One function of play is thought to be rehearsal of the "four F's": fighting, fleeing, feeding and courtship. In the case of play-biting, the fighting and feeding (i.e. hunting) skills are getting a workout. This behavior is normal, healthy and adaptive, with the important benefits of soft mouth practice, keeping the social skills well-oiled and constantly re-associating the close proximity of other dogs with fun.

Owners of dogs usually identify dog play as a problem for one of three reasons:

1) normal play is extremely rough and intense and therefore frightening for some owners to witness, so they want to curb it in case the dog "becomes aggressive"

2) the owner can't compete with the attractiveness of other dogs as playmates and has obedience problems in the presence of other dogs

3) the play is directed at humans

The logic behind number 1 is back-to-front. Dogs who do *not* regularly play with other dogs usually have the poorest social skills. They have a difficult time both delivering and reading dog body language. These naive animals come in two varieties. One kind is tense, asocial and proximity sensitive. They may present as shy and snappy if dogs come too close. This can evolve into pre-emptive lunging and aggression as they learn that displays work to keep other dogs away, and then cut to the chase when a dog approaches. The other variety is hyper-motivated and keen, but still with extremely coarse skills. They are often described by their owners as "too excited." When they meet dogs, they engage in annoying, gross play solicitations and rude investigations, all of which evoke defensiveness in other dogs.

Regular play builds confidence, improves the dog's repertoire of intraspecific communications and maintains the dog's soft-mouth. The more dogs he interacts with, the more slick his social skills grow to be, culminating in a dog who is a veritable doggy-diplomat, able to coax even worried or asocial dogs into play, appease tough guys and defuse potential fights with mind-bogglingly subtle body language.

At the other end of the spectrum is the two-sided coin of fear and aggression - dogs who are basically unsocialized to their own species. This is pretty much a travesty, considering the genetic predisposition dogs have to become socialized to and form bonds with any living thing they have sufficient contact with before 4 months of age. Owners of socially inept animals often say things like "he's dominant with other dogs" and "I can't bring him around other dogs, he gets too excited..." What they don't realize is that they will never make the dog blasé by restricting his access.

There is no question that most well-socialized dogs will be extremely attracted to and enjoy playing with other dogs. As a result, obedience that is near-perfect when there is no competing motivation may fall apart in the presence of other dogs. It's important not to go overboard in labeling failure to comply as insubordination when obedience behaviors conflict with enjoyable things like dog-play. **The dog is always perfectly obedient to the contingencies in the environment.**

If the dog is not coming or otherwise being obedient when there are other dogs around, it is because:

1) coming has never been necessary to obtain the dog-access

2) coming has proven to be mutually exclusive to dog-access (it actually *ends* the fun, so has been punished while other strategies have been differentially reinforced)

3) other reinforcers employed by the owner are below dog-access on the reinforcer hierarchy

4) the owner has sufficient leverage but the behavior is not well enough generalized (dog doesn't read "come" in that context; strange but true that dogs are susceptible to this)

This is the most useful way of looking at the problem of competing motivation. I'll get into more detail about training in the presence of competing motivation in the final chapter. The point is that limiting dog play or failing to socialize a dog in order to avoid this distraction is shooting yourself in the foot. You still don't know how to train against competing motivation and now you have an undersocialized, underexercised, understimulated dog. You're in the flames.

The third dog-play problem is an example of the culture clash. Normal dog play directed at humans is both annoying and potentially dangerous. It is essential that the dog be quickly brought up to speed regarding the social norms in a human environment. The rules the dog must assimilate regarding his play behavior vis a vis humans are:

1) keep your extremely soft mouth off human flesh and clothing at all times (exception: when invited to roughhouse)

2) when people walk, run and ride bikes don't chase them

3) paws off at all times

Understand that our having these jaws-paws rules essentially means that the dog must never engage in his pre-programmed play behaviors with people. If you look at dog-to-dog play, there is virtually none of it that we humans would like directed at us in day-to-day life. It's important to inform the dog about this and to provide alternative outlets in the form of regular access to other dogs and/or interactive games with humans that we *can* live with, often involving toys as an intermediary.

Some people opt to roughhouse with their dogs – I am an example. The game is always human-initiated and the dogs are taught to stop on cue. Overly rough mouthing or failure to stop on cue results in abrupt cessation of the game.

Roughhousing with dogs generates ire among many traditional dog trainers, who make a Pandora's Box argument that, in my opinion, just doesn't fly. A common trigger of aggression is intolerance of body handling, so wrestling and roughhousing with the dog is beneficial. It increases the dog's familiarity and comfort with hands and a wide variety of touch on a wide variety of body parts.

The other two benefits of roughhousing are rehearsal of bite inhibition and a terrific outlet for dog energy.

To maintain bite inhibition, monitor the pressure of mouthing during roughhousing and "OUCH!" then abruptly cease the game if the dog is anything less than perfectly gentle with his jaws. Game misconduct penalties can also be used to control the starting and stopping of the game – if the dog starts before being invited or fails to stop when asked. Note the similarity between these rules and those for tug.

Timid Puppies

What we most like to see is a puppy who is outgoing: who readily and confidently, with a wagging tail, approaches any person and who play bites feverishly. This is a puppy who actively seeks to *close* distance with novel humans and is diametrically opposed to flight-or-bite puppies who work to increase social distance. Note that the continuum of temperament is not one with fear and aggression at opposite ends of the spectrum and normal in the middle. Rather, at one extreme there is relaxed, confident, highly affiliative behavior and at the other end the two-headed coin of fear and aggression. Fear and aggression are considered flip sides of the lack of confidence coin because they are really just strategies to accomplish the same end: to keep the scary stimulus far enough away. Dogs readily switch strategy if their usual style doesn't work.

So, the opposite of a fearful dog is a relaxed, confident dog, and the opposite of an aggressive dog is, you guessed it, a relaxed, confident dog. This is why lack of confidence in a puppy is such a major emergency. If we don't see outgoingness in a puppy, the race begins to see how much we can install before the socialization period comes to an end. Timid puppies often come around at an astounding rate with intense socialization, becoming "different dogs" in a matter of days. To achieve a comparable change in an adult dog usually takes weeks or months of formal desensitization and counterconditioning. In fact, if a timid puppy does not make dramatic gains, it is a sign that formal effort, likely extending well into adulthood, will be necessary. One of the debates in the fear literature is whether severe deficits can be reversed with diligent effort. You'll hear biases in applied dog behavior circles ranging from recommendations to write off fearful puppies without fast curves to convictions that all or most can be improved with time and care. This area could use some good research.

Regardless of your personal bias, puppies who present with shyness around strangers *urgently need intervention*. Whatever the puppy seems afraid of or growls at should be the target of a massive effort to get the puppy comfortable and confident. The goal is a puppy who willingly chooses to approach and make contact. The best results I've seen have been obtained with long duration passive socialization in conjunction with counterconditioning where the puppy can set his own pace. This means the handler must find whatever medication or Zen-like mood is necessary to make him abstain from ever forcing the puppy to socialize, as is many people's inclination. Dog trainers, ironically, can be micromanagers, and however well this serves them in their other training endeavors it must be suspended for work with fearful dogs or puppies.

It's critically important when working with timid puppies (or dogs) that it be puppy's choice whether to approach and at what speed. If the puppy wants to keep his distance for a few minutes or half an hour, that must be respected. Rushing the puppy or forcing him to make contact with people or things that frighten him can exacerbate the existing fear. The puppy thought someone was a bit dangerous. Now you've proven him right by associating the strong fear response brought about by coerced contact and the person or thing you're trying to make seem benign. Not a good move. Much better to keep the scary person or thing stationary and let the puppy approach at his own pace. Step out of the "but it's just a ..." posture. It's the puppy's call whether he's afraid, not yours about whether he "should" be or not. This is why a passive approach works so well. Arrange a therapeutic situation and then give it time to unfold.

Imagine yourself strapped to a chair and someone coming at you with a blowtorch. If they said, "there, there, it's okay, it's oooookaaay" would it feel okay? The only thing that would make it okay would be for you to have freedom of movement to access the blowtorch in your own way at your own pace. And, if someone kept putting cash right near it, you might, with great prudence, sneak in and collect the cash and gradually get more comfortable. You might even end up doing some welding.

Desensitizing timid puppies is no different. "Puppy's choice" must be respected. Every time the puppy, of his own accord, takes the risk to approach something scary and lives through it or, better still, has a positive experience, the puppy's confidence gets a boost. Adding tasty bait to the process is enormously helpful. For instance, a strange man remains motionless but has sliced hot dogs sprinkled all over him while he reads a magazine. Each time the puppy finally feels confident enough to approach, the approach is reinforced with a hot dog slice. The probability of future approaches starts to go up. You're off and running. Escalations to moving people, approaching people, people who pat and demographic variations can gradually be added, with "puppy's choice" always respected. The approach is called "passive training" because, once you've set up the scary person or object and the sprinkled bait, your presence or intervention is no longer necessary. Go about your business while the puppy self-trains. Passive training is extremely valuable for socializing timid animals because the time-frames involved in more active training fall out of the limits of most people's patience. This is a slow process. Do not give up or switch to something counterproductive (such as pressuring the puppy) when working with shrinking violets. This is doubly important when working with adult dogs.

Puppy Temperament Testing

An extremely popular topic in the doggie crowd is puppy testing. Numerous formal tests purport to objectively measure fixed traits such as dominance, predatory drive, fearfulness and sociability. Unfortunately, some serious doubt has been cast upon both the reliability and predictive validity of puppy temperament tests. One fly in the ointment is that the presumed immutability of "temperament" has proven iffy if not false. The temperament of dogs, right down to such seemingly basic traits as level of "dominance" and, more importantly, how outgoing the puppy is, is surprisingly plastic. There is no compelling data yet correlating results from existing puppy temperament tests with measurable adult behavior. Temperament test results on any given puppy also vary wildly from one day to the next and from one tester to the next. Contact latency tests ("how long till the puppy goes right up to a person when he enters the room") are one such example: puppies who are slow or non-approachers can be turned into keen approachers in a couple of reinforced trials so how real is the underlying trait which the test allegedly measures?

Most of these tests fail to get at the underlying traits they are supposed to. For instance, a litter of six puppies will be individually tested on their reaction to a novel stimulus like an umbrella suddenly opening. Let's say puppies one and two are not spooked in the slightest; they wag and investigate the umbrella. Puppies three and four spook first and then investigate. Puppies five and six spook but don't come around to investigating by the end of the testing period.

What have we learned about the temperaments of these puppies? The standard test interpretation would read that puppies one and two are very stable, puppies three and four are a bit spooky and puppies five and six are definitely spooky. The reality is that we haven't learned anything about puppies one and two, puppies three and four have demonstrated reactivity but excellent bounce-back and puppies five and six have demonstrated reactivity and some lack of bounce-back. Puppies one and two haven't been tested yet. Remember, the test is to determine the reaction of a dog to something that frightens it, not the puppy's attitude about wet weather gear. Before it's possible to see how well numbers one and two respond to a fearful stimulus, you first have to supply one. All that can be concluded from the test is that pups one and two aren't afraid of umbrellas. We still don't know how they will react when they encounter something that scares them. They may react as did three and four or they may be like five and six or worse. The jury is still out.

Even more interesting is that both the reactivity and bounce-back of *all* of these puppies could likely be modified through early experience. Take numbers five and six, do some exercises and then retest them. Owners of dogs like one and two are conceivably also at risk because their puppies seem solid as rocks because they tend to be non-reactive. Non-reactive puppies or puppies who are very selectively reactive don't get as much of an opportunity to develop bounce-back and do not have as much attention paid to their socialization because they don't seem to need it. This is a big mistake. Remember the dual benefit of socialization: it's not just to reduce the number of items in the universe at which the puppy might spook but to repeatedly provide the *experience of first feeling fearful and then getting over it.* Bounce-back is one of the most valuable traits you can instill in a dog. Flaky or brittle temperaments are those that are unforgiving or acquire phobias more easily. The chances of a dog turning out this way are reduced if bounce-back is developed early, regardless of whether the dog in question was highly reactive (spooks fairly easily) or non-reactive (spooks less often).

Dog-Dog Socialization

Dog to dog socialization is, if you think about it, an odd problem. How far would dogs have gotten as a species if they routinely mutilated each other? An awful lot is wired into dogs to prevent this if we only provide an adequate crucible for the intraspecific

80

social repertoire to develop. This is a big "if only" because many owners make such a mess of it. I have devoted an entire manual to dog-dog aggression problems so will deliver only an overview only here.

Dogs seem pretty compulsive about making contact with one another so that they can engage in the important ritual of mutual rear-sniffing. They really want to know who the other dog is (familiar or unfamiliar, sex, reproductive status etc.), greet, investigate in some detail and posture or initiate play. None of this can be established at a distance.

Many owners find the urgency with which dogs pull on leash towards other dogs or otherwise "act up" (i.e., are motivated and animated) worrisome or irritating. They punish the behavior or prohibit contact with other dogs. This leaves the dog with a corked up backlog of social craving, which ends up actually contributing to unpolished social behavior when contact ever *is* made with another dog. The socially starved and inexperienced dog comes on too strong and the owner's prophecy is fulfilled, so future contact with dogs is avoided, perpetuating the cycle. Bottom line: social skills develop with repeated exposure and deteriorate with isolation.

Things get even worse when the *other* dog is similarly handled, so that now *two* juiced up, socially naive animals are involved. Also, the owners often exacerbate dog-dog tension by choking up on leashes to hold the already frustrated dogs just out of reach. Dogs in general behave much more aggressively on leash than off. This is due to a couple of effects. The first is barrier frustration. Barrier-frustration also contributes to the aggression and displaying observed in kenneled dogs, dogs who are tied out, and dogs who fence-fight. Dogs in these circumstances repeatedly see things they are highly motivated to approach and investigate but are prevented from doing so. If this happens repeatedly the dog develops a Pavlovian response of frustration at the sight of dogs. And, if the

81

dog has had traditional obedience training, other dogs may also become associated with increased probability of leash corrections.

Many have also suggested that tie-outs and fences provide too well-defined a territory and this effect is responsible for the huge increase in aggression in these dogs. I don't personally buy this as a primary cause. Dogs who are timid or aggressive with people or dogs usually need remedial socialization, not fuzzier territorial lines. A well-socialized dog will watchdog bark and then go through all the normal motions: he will excitedly sniff and greet the newcomer, hopefully offering appeasement behaviors. An undersocialized dog will watch-dog bark and then stay back, growling, make tracks to somewhere else in the house and hide, or oscillate between approaching and avoiding, probably barking the whole time.

We do know that fence-fighters are best treated by introducing them, off-leash, without barriers, provided the dogs in question have acquired bite inhibition. Owners typically expect a blood bath given the long history of blustering at each other through the fence, but these dogs almost always fizzle out after some minor, ritualized jostling or scuffling. Many become playmates. Needless to say, the ideal is for the dog to experience as little barrier frustration as possible in the first place. This can be accomplished by not tying dogs out or leaving them interminably in yards. In addition, you should allow regular contact and play between dogs who live on the opposite sides of a fence.

Another flavor of on-leash dog-dog problem occurs when dogs who would choose to *in*crease distance - or approach indirectly - are prevented from doing so by the leash. If the dog is motivated to flee and is thwarted, Plan B, aggressive display may pop out and then be reinforced by withdrawal of the other dog, often as a function of the other owner, sensibly, backing off. Or, if the dog would have made a more nuanced, indirect approach and this is thwarted, he may be made anxious by being forced to approach directly. This in turn could bring out the worst in the other dog, kicking off a vicious cycle. An accumulation of these experiences results in a dog who learns that on-leash dog meeting situations predict stress. The owner contributes by being generally edgy and possibly punitive. The discriminative stimulus is the sight of another dog on the street. All this stress and punishment because a dog has caught sight of another member of his species.

What these proximity sensitive dogs need is well-executed desensitization and counterconditioning (D&C) to other dogs, to build up their confidence and remove the motivation for aggression. My favorite modus operandus is to start with a classical approach (straight D&C) and then develop a competing response. It goes like this. First, teach the dog that other dogs predict a gooey, jolly, treat-raining handler – regardless of response. Then, once the lunge rate falls (my rule of thumb is down to 50%), switch to training a behavior that is mutually exclusive to lunging, such as sit and watch (i.e. no longer "regardless of response" – now the treat depends on the sit and watch compliance). By the time the lunge rate is down to 50%, many dogs will already have a fledgling, if superstitious, sit and watch. This makes for a seamless transition from the classical to operant conditioning.

The other type of naïve dog, the unrefined super motivated ones, do well with off-leash experience in small groups of well-socialized adult dogs, i.e., dogs who have regular contact with a variety of other dogs. They will not tolerate much crude behavior but they will also do no harm when dissuading the puppy or enthusiastic, undersocialized adolescent. The tragedy is that naive dogs are usually kept away from other dogs by their owners who find their gross behavior and resulting scuffles too scary. Valuable social lessons are thus never learned and the dog never improves. This is the vicious cycle described above. The solution is to bite the bullet and let the goofy teenager take his lumps from established well-socialized adults. It's fascinating to watch experienced dogs interact: blasé, subtle, cool, virtually phoning in their greetings, posturing, play solicitations and appeasement.

The limiting factors for such remedial socialization are the dog's bite inhibition and the availability of "therapist dogs" that can be recruited. The goal is for these dogs to make their first doggie friend. Therapist dogs are "bullet-proof," which mean extremely well-socialized, slick, friendly adults who have good bounce back. They are dog park types with scores of novel social contacts under their belts. They will be able to withstand the idiotic behavior of the fighter and stand a good chance of slowly seducing him into a playmate, if given adequate opportunity.

Get the dogs together, off-leash, in a barren, boring environment and watch from the sidelines. You can praise or reinforce neutral to positive interactions or stay passive, depending on what seems to be helping the most. If the dog has a history of damaging other dogs, his bite inhibition is poor and remedial socialization is only an option if the dog is muzzled. With these kids, I'd put most energy into the development of better on-leash handleability so that the dog can be walked.

One interesting innovation is the advent of "growly dog classes," which are designed to help rehab dog-aggressive dogs. The sophistication of these classes has increased astronomically since I first attempted them in the late 1980s.

In the case of inter-male aggression, neutering is often extremely helpful, not so much to turn off the dog's hormonal brain-bath but to make him smell less threatening to other males, thus helping to short-circuit the positive feedback loop two males often get into.

Food Bowl Exercises

Aside from socialization, there are other high-priority exercises for puppies. These are: food bowl exercises, object exchanges, placement cues, and body handling exercises. Left to themselves, a significant proportion of dogs will become resource (food, objects, locations and/or owner) guarders and/or be difficult to manipulate, even routinely. This is because they are normal animals, not

84

because some particular individual is stubborn, touchy or vicious. Prophylactic exercises are therefore important for all puppies.

When you feed your puppy, hang around while he eats. Sit on the floor beside him, patting him and dangling your hands in the bowl. He needs to find out, through repeated experience, that your presence around his food and dish is not a threat. Feed him some meals in small installments to pound in the repeated association between your hand approaching the dish and good news: another helping. Practice taking the bowl away in mid-meal and sprucing it up by adding something tastier. This can be a spoonful of canned food, cottage cheese, a piece of freeze-dried liver or anything tasty you're comfortable giving. Also practice walking up to the dog while he's eating and dropping some nice morsel in. The goal is that your approach or removal of the bowl reliably predicts something good for the dog. This is to counteract his natural inclination to guard his food. In a natural environment, zealous guarding of scarce resources like food would be highly adaptive and thus selected for. It crops up all too frequently in domestic dogs in spite of hundreds of generations of artificial selection and an abundant kibble supply.

When opportunity presents itself, have other people add a bonus to the puppy's dish to better generalize the conditioning. Ian Dunbar conceptualized resource guarding many years ago as a lack of confidence. I think it is most usefully viewed from this angle as it points to prevention and treatment interventions that actually work. Think of the dog as insecure and paranoid, operating under an assumption that someone approaching his soggy raw-hide or bowlful of kibble is a major life-or-death deal. Your goal is to teach him that it's no big deal at all – in fact, it's good news!

If you are working with a dog who has an existing problem rather than doing prevention on a puppy or non-guarding adult, you must proceed more slowly and carefully. A prerequisite to working on a known guarder is that the dog have a soft mouth. To my knowledge, no one has had success installing a soft mouth in a hard-mouthed adult dog for duress situations. If the dog takes treats roughly or mouths too hard, this can be softened up, but a bite delivered in an agonistic (conflict resolution) or defensive context will be at an intensity that seems to be established in young puppyhood. Depending on how damaging the bites of a harder-mouthed dog are, alternative strategies are necessary: muzzling and/or tethering during early treatment, lifetime management or, in the worst cases, putting the dog to sleep. To avoid bleak prognoses, the single most important intervention is to help dogs develop good acquired bite inhibition while they are puppies.

Here is a standard, basic hierarchy for a food-guarding dog. For exhaustively splitty training plans, see *MINE! A Guide to Resource Guarding in Dogs*.

1) approach empty bowl and dog, put a small handful of food in, retreat, wait until dog finishes and then approach with next handful – feed meals this way until dog clearly happy to have you approaching

2) approach empty bowl and dog, remove bowl, put handful of food in, put bowl back down, retreat, wait until dog finishes and then approach with next handful – feed meals this way until dog clearly happy to have you approach and remove bowl

3) repeat exercises 1 and 2 but now with overlap – approach and add next handful before dog has finished previous installment

4) sit next to dog and bowl with one hand on bowl, stroking and talking to dog while dog eats normal ration, occasionally adding a tasty bonus to bowl with other hand

5) sit next to bowl while dog eating kibble, remove hand from bowl to get a tasty bonus and then add it to bowl

6) approach dog and bowl while dog eating, add bonus to bowl, retreat and repeat two or three times

7) approach dog and bowl while dog eating, remove bowl, add bonus, replace bowl, retreat and repeat two or three times

8) add bonus once per meal at random time

9) repeat steps with all family members

If, at a given step, the dog demonstrates any guarding (including growling, stiffness, freezing up), back off to an easier exercise and proceed more gradually to the problem exercise. If the dog, for instance, is fine on exercises 1 - 5, but growls if you approach while he is eating his normal meal (#6), insert the following steps:

5A) approach to a certain distance, say three feet, while the dog is eating and lob the bonus at the dish, retreat and repeat, gradually closing the distance until you are able to touch the bowl

5B) wait until he's only just finished and is licking the bowl before approaching with "dessert" – each meal approach a second or two sooner until you are adding the bonus during the meal

The dog may also fall apart during overlap or at number 5, where you take your hand off the bowl during a meal. From the dog's perspective, this is very different from the previous exercise, where you kept one hand on the bowl at all times. That was sharing. By taking your hand off, you are relinquishing possession. You may need to gradually fade your hand off the bowl if the dog starts guarding when you try exercise number 5. Do whatever it takes to get successful trials so you can prove to the dog that you are not a threat and that he can relax. If you really get stumped at any point, lack confidence with this sort of thing, or if your dog is an explosive guarder or dangerous biter, get yourself into the hands of a qualified trainer or behaviorist.

Object Exchanges

Object guarders typically guard bones, valued chew toys and forbidden objects such as bones, plastic wrap, Kleenexes, stolen laundry items and garbage on the ground. With some of these dogs, there is a compulsive, reflexive quality to their guarding. Others seem triggered not just by the fact that they think the hamburger wrapper is so valuable but by the fact that *you* are treating it as though it is an extremely valuable artifact by demonstrating such heated interest in taking it away. This, I realize, is a catch-22 for the owner. Either ignore the dog and allow him to pick up and even ingest all manner of junk he finds on the ground or else increase the value of the item by showing great interest in taking it away from him. The best solution for all object guarders lies in priming and rehearsing the problem scenarios *in advance.* The dog needs to have done exchange exercises in preparation for the Big Day when he gets something truly dangerous which you have to remove from his mouth pronto. If he's relaxed and confident, he'll relinquish. If he's tense and insecure, he won't. You are one step ahead of the game if you start practicing on your puppy. And, just like socialization, the younger you start the better.

The basic object exchange exercise goes like this:

1) give the dog an object (in early training this will be an object he is unlikely to guard, later you will progress to "hot" objects)

2) say "give" or "thank you"

3) take the object away

4) give a nice treat from your pocket (don't preview it)

5) give the object back and repeat

Do five or so, varying the time between repetitions, and then walk away. Try to do a few "sets" of five repetitions a day, varying the object each time so the trend emerges: when humans take things away, it is a Very Good Thing for Dogs (VGTD). When some history of successful exchanges is in place (several days worth of a few sets per day), you may also start to practice taking away chew toys the dog has spontaneously taken possession of. Do a set of five and then let him carry on chewing. Always be aware of the value of the item you are taking away. For "hot" (highly valued by the dog) objects, increase accordingly the value of the surprise treat he gets in exchange. You may reserve special treats, like a morsel of leftover turkey or chunk of old cheddar cheese, for exchanges with the trickiest objects. These rare reinforcers really make an impression.

Here's a typical hierarchy:

1) set up exchanges with objects of no interest (several sets of five a day for two days)

2) set up exchanges with slightly more coveted objects (several sets of five a day for two days)

3) set up exchanges with hot objects, using extra special treats (several sets of five a day for two to three days)

4) exchanges with low to mid-value objects the dog has spontaneously taken possession of (do several in a row, then leave dog with it unless it is a forbidden object: then, give an extra special reinforcer on the last trial and replace object with a chew toy)

5) exchanges with hot objects the dog spontaneously has taken possession of (do several in a row for extra-special reinforcers, then return object to dog or replace with interesting chew toy)

6) maintenance: occasional "cold trials" when dog has an object (one reinforced rep, then give toy back or replace forbidden object with chew toy)

It's okay to do the exchanges or removals without being armed with a treat in later training and maintenance. Head to the fridge or cupboard for the treat after the success (the dog can now tolerate the lag).

Proceed to the next exercise in the hierarchy only when the dog is good at the exercise you are currently working on, meaning he is demonstrating happy anticipation *before* you have supplied the treat. For the duration of working this hierarchy, it is helpful if the dog is not given access to objects that are above the level you are training. This sets you both up for a guaranteed failure. For example, if the dog is on step 4, keep "hot" objects out of reach until you are ready to start step 5. You can't run until you can walk. For exercise 5, you may have to deliberately leave around a hot object so the dog will "spontaneously" take possession. It is much better to have rehearsed in advance the tissue or plastic wrap guarding drama than to have it sprung on you when you aren't ready.

Sufficient repetition of object exchange exercises results in a dog who is actually eager for you to take stuff away from him. Aside from the behavior being reinforced by the food, the dog is getting a key bit of information: when humans take things away, they very often give them back. It is therefore No Big Deal. This is pretty unheard of in dog culture. When the dog is relaxed about exchanges, be sure to test the system with the occasional cold trial. Walk up to the dog while he's chewing, take his toy away, pop him a surprise reinforcer and then let him carry on. Like any behavior, relaxed relinquishing may drift if it's not maintained. Make spot check cold trials a regular game.

In dogs with existing guarding problems, proceed more slowly or hire a professional trainer who can plan and help you implement a hierarchy that's designed for your dog. Under no circumstances should children be given primary responsibility for this.

If there are kids in the house, they will need to practice with the dog but if and only if:

1) the dog likes the kids

2) the dog has a known soft mouth

3) all adult members of the household have successfully completed the entire hierarchy already

4) the exercises done by the kids are supervised by an adult every second.

This holds for all desensitization exercises (food bowl, location guarding and handleability), not just object guarding. Be aware that, if your dog is an object guarder and you modify it with these exercises but don't have kids at home, your dog is still at some risk to guard against kids. Dogs don't generalize very well. In fact, even if your dog has never guarded against you, there's a chance he will guard against strangers, especially kids, particularly if he is not beautifully socialized to kids.

An extremely cunning move in the object guarding war is to teach your dog to retrieve. Aside from being an efficient exercise and predatory energy burner, using guarded objects as retrieve toys is a potent counterconditioning monkey wrench you can throw into the object guarding machinery. Simply playing with the dog with hot items can be an enormous tension reducer for both dog and handler. Proceed carefully the first few times you try this. The dog should already have an enthusiastic, well-conditioned retrieve of non-guarded items. The first time you try using guarded objects in retrieve games, whatever you do, stay glued to your chair so you don't slip into the rut of chasing the dog and demonstrating hot interest in the item itself. Play it very casual and hard to get, just as you would for the dog's usual retrieval toy. Use safe items so you can relax and train. Encourage the dog to come up with reinforceable retrieves. Set criteria extremely low at first. Be prepared, for instance, to click and reinforce evidence of turning towards you, breaks from chewing or any steps back in your direction once he's got hold of the object. Celebrate each step with enthusiastic cheering and extra nice food reinforcers. Then gradually crank up the standard as he gets better. It is perfectly reasonable to expect, with sufficient practice, your previously rabid object guarder to happily fetch and drop in your lap items that used to be hot. That's confidence.

Placement Cues

The classic location guarder is a dog who jumps on the bed and then won't let you in. Or, the dog who stakes out the sofa and growls or snaps when you order him off or ask him to move over. The antidote is to teach what are called placement cues. You condition the dog, with positive reinforcement, to move his body to or from wherever you indicate. A certain percentage of dogs will, one day, actively location guard, so start practicing before there's a problem. It's also handy to be able to easily move the dog around without a lot of pushing and pulling. Typical placement cues include: "into the crate," "off the bed," "into the car," "off the sofa," "out of the kitchen," "onto the (grooming) table" etc. You simply make it another clicker-training exercise, a game. First, give the cue and then prompt the behavior. Any kind of coaching goes, including food lures if you bog down. When the dog performs smoothly, you fade the prompt as you would for any obedience exercise.

For example, practice "off the sofa" as follows. First, ask the dog onto the sofa. You need some fluency at getting him on so that you can have plenty of opportunities to practice getting him off. After you say, "onto the sofa," pat the cushion and make encouraging sounds ("c'mon, c'mon" + enticing kissy sounds is a nice prompt). When the dog jumps on, praise him and mess up his hair a bit ("clevvvvver boy!!" + pat-pat-pat-ruffle). Reserve the heavier artillery of food reinforcement for getting him off. Now cue him off and start prompting him down ("off the sofa," pat the floor, snap fingers, clap hands, make kissy noises to move him off). If he moves off, give him a click and a treat and order him back up for an encore. You also may want to order him on and tell him to lie down to better simulate the eventual real-life scenario. If he doesn't move off, crank up the prompt a bit: try backing away from the sofa, making the best lovey-dovey sounds you can. As a last resort you will manufacture the reinforceable response with a food lure. If you had to go to a food lure to get him off, do this a couple more times and then put the food into your pocket during the prompting step for the remainder of the session. Always supply one for correct responses but fade it as a lure ASAP.

Do a couple of sessions and then practice cold trials. Cold trials are once-only repetitions of an exercise, preferably sprung on the dog when he is not expecting it, to test response to cues in real life. You will get the best mileage out of cold trials if you vary the reinforcer. This is quite a natural thing to do because a lot of the most potent reinforcers are not easily reusable within formal training sessions. A good example of this is walks. Unlike food reinforcement and tug-retrieve games, which can be repeated again and again within a training session, the potent, reinforcing event is the initiation of the "taking the dog for a walk" ritual. Because this happens, at most, a few times scattered throughout the day, try to exploit its value as a reinforcer by preceding it with an "off the couch" placement. It is the perfect cold-trial reinforcer. Wait until the dog is dug in on the couch before doing your cold trial. The sequence is: 1) "off the couch" cue, 2) dog complies, 3) click and "want to go for a walk?" and 4) initiate walk.

Do your utmost to not bribe him off by using the promised walk as a prompt. Say "wanna go for a walk?" *after* he vacates the couch (and then take the walk). This is worlds away from offering the walk while he is still dug in, having not complied with the placement cue. The offering of the walk is a conditioned

93

reinforcer, bridging to the walk, the primary reinforcer for his complying with the "off the couch" cue. So, to re-iterate: once the dog is primed up in initial training sessions with cue-prompt-response-reinforcement trials and then cue-response-reinforcement trials with the recyclable reinforcers (i.e. food), don't use lures of any kind. He must keep his part of the bargain on faith before you keep yours.

Your eventual goal may be a variable schedule of reinforcement. He won't always be getting a walk after his compliance. He may have to gamble that on this occasion he only gets his hair messed up.

If the dog guards locations (such as the sofa or bed) against one specific person, that person must do some of the placement cue work. If it is a child or someone who lacks confidence around the dog, make sure the dog has a soft mouth, and supervise the sessions. If the problem is really severe, especially if there are kids in the picture, engage a competent behaviorist or trainer. I would also stress again the enormous value of doing placement-cue exercises with puppies, before a problem develops. Teach on and off the bed sequences, in and out of the car and in and out of the crate. Dogs who are raised to be happily compliant are at reduced risk for aggression directed at family members.

Body Handling

Dogs have to be handled for a multitude of reasons including veterinary exams, being groomed, held down or otherwise physically restrained, and being hugged, grabbed and patted by a wide variety of people. Good relaxed tolerance of handling does not come naturally for most dogs. One of the best favors you can do your dog is to teach him, while he's still a malleable little puppy, to happily accept all the handling he will have to put up with during his lifetime. You, your friends, family and puppy classmates can all simulate the main handling situations and pair them with food and play reinforcements.

94

Start with grooming and basic physical exams. A good first exercise is to lay out all the grooming tools (brush, comb, tooth brush, toothpaste, nail clippers, scissors and any other equipment), let the dog come over and investigate these items and, as he does, click the clicker and give him an above average reinforcer to make a good first impression. Then, practice holding the dog still and, with your hands, examining all his body parts, giving a small treat after each part. Look in one ear, treat. Look in the other ear, treat. Run fingers over gums, treat. Practice gently opening his mouth and putting a treat on his tongue. Then put a finger followed by a treat. If he tolerates this, depress the tongue a little more firmly each time before the treat. If he struggles, back off and do something less intrusive. Keep the treats coming furiously so that his participation is voluntary. When he does not comply, simply say "too bad!" and withhold reinforcement. Feel his windpipe, treat. Go down each leg, between the toes and apply pressure to each nail. Treat after each nail. Many dogs dislike having their feet handled, often the result of having nail-clipping forced on them rather than being allowed to gradually tolerate and enjoy grooming by early association with goodies. Palpate the dog's belly and feel all the way down the tail. Each time you do a doctor session, do a little more examining for each treat. The final routine consists of an entire once-over for one treat or play reinforcement. Dogs can learn to love being handled and restrained.

Play doctor with the dog often and also practice grooming. Early on in your dog's grooming career, the ratio of reinforcers to procedures will be high. One brush stroke, one treat. Then two brush strokes, one treat. Then four. Then one deeper, firmer brush stroke, one treat. Then two. And so on. You will have, in a few short sessions, a dog who you can brush deeply from head to toe for one small treat at the end. When the dog is comfortable about having his feet and nails touched in the veterinary-exam simulations, start touching his nails with the nail clippers. One touch, one treat. Do this until he is very relaxed. Then, do two or more touches for one treat. Then hold the toe in one hand while you pretend to cut his nail with the nail clippers in the other hand.

95

At this point, the nail clippers are not making contact with his nail, just with the air, but he is experiencing the restraint and sound of the clippers. Give one treat per nail until he is quite relaxed.

If you own a high-energy dog, you may want to practice this initially when the dog is already in a relaxed mood. When the dog happily lets you "air-clip" all his nails for one treat, try a real clip. Take off very little so you don't risk hitting the quick, which is very sensitive. The goal is not to get the nails clipped but to set the dog up for a lifetime of easy nail clipping, so be patient. One tiny clip, one big treat. At the end of the session, have a short play period. In the early days, it's a good idea to have grooming sessions be a reliable predictor of things high up on the dog's reinforcer hierarchy, like predatory game sessions, walks, training games or meals, along with the treats given throughout the session.

If, at any point in grooming or veterinary-exam training sessions the dog is reluctant or skittish, slow down and desensitize the anxiety-producing procedure more carefully. Dogs are often anxious about people looking in their ears, handling their feet and mouths, and pulling their coats (as when mats are removed). Invest time making the puppy comfortable about all these procedures. It's well worth it. When the puppy is highly groomable and easily examined, we call them "wet spaghetti" types because they are so relaxed and pliable.

Other things to practice are: grabbing the dog, patting, hugging and looming over him in scary ways. Make a game of these. Start off with slow, gentle grabs. One grab followed by one treat. Then grab faster, then faster and rougher, culminating in emergency grabs and wrestling holds, treating after each successful trial. Do things to the dog that you would expect a two year-old child to do. Grab an ear and pull. Give a treat. Grab the tail and pull. Give a treat. Particularly challenging are skin grabs: do plenty, escalating their severity gradually, with a high density of food reinforcement. Pat the dog the way children do: PAT PAT PAT. Loom over the dog like a monster and then give him a treat. Pretend he has a broken leg: lift him into the car. Your imagination is the limit. What might people do to your dog in his lifetime? When the dog is relaxed and enjoying every minute of these games, recruit strangers and kids to do them, under your close supervision. Let the kids give better goodies than you normally give the dog, so they can make a favorable impression.

It's worthwhile, if your dog will be regularly handled by a groomer, to visit the groomer a couple of times before the dog has to stay to be groomed. Bring him in, put him on the table and have the groomer feed him a bunch of treats or take a few minutes to play tug or fetch with the dog in the grooming room. Practice in and out of the cage placements. Let the dog explore a bit. Then go home. You can make similar visits to your veterinarian to make a strong, positive first impression. Needless to say, it's a good idea to find veterinarians and groomers who are gentle and willing to take a little time to hand-feed your puppy. And, last but not least, find a good puppy class and enroll.

If you have an existing handling problem, do the same exercises, focusing on the particular problem, however:

1) proceed more slowly and gradually
2) temporarily avoid the problem situation in day-to-day life at levels the dog hasn't yet achieved in training sessions

3) if the problem is severe or you feel like you're floundering, get yourself into the hands of a qualified trainer or behaviorist

Rehab of Aggressive Dogs

Aggression is like any other behavior: it can be elicited and it morphs with learning. Examples of likely aggression elicitors are: initiation or expectation of something painful, proximity of something the dog is afraid of, approach when the dog has some resource, body-handling and any rapidly retreating object. This last

97

trigger, where the dog chases and/or bites a squirrel, ball or squealing child, you now know is food acquisition behavior that, although topographically resembling aggression (involves biting living beings), is a whole other kettle of fish than the topic of this chapter: dogs that are motivated to make others back off when they are uncomfortable or guarding some resource.

It's useful to divide our thinking about aggression into two domains: 1) questions about ultimate causation – the evolutionary (adaptive) significance of the behavior, i.e. "why do dogs do that?" and 2) detailed information about immediate triggers, i.e. the who, what, where, how far facts about the eliciting stimulus. Sometimes information from the first category will inform technique choice and execution but more often than not the second category – trigger details – will have the greatest influence on the nuts and bolts of behavior modification.

The first domain, that of the evolutionary significance of behavior, helps people understand dogs and so, hopefully, better tolerate and even enjoy expressions of their doggie nature. One of the fascinations of having dogs in one's life is the daily cornucopia of a foreign species' repertoire. Empathy and expectation adjustments, however, shouldn't be confused with behavior modification techniques. I have some healthy skepticism of explanations of aggression that make authoritative statements about what dogs are "thinking" when they threaten or bite. It's barely a cut above "Pet Psychic" stuff to make unfalsifiable proclamations, but this etho-babble is common. Many aggression classification systems are seemingly based on "we're not sure how to fix this so let's spend a long time talking about it."

For example, if a dog growls and snaps when the owner leads him by the collar or restrains his head, you could spin yarns to your heart's content about the dog's thoughts on the matter, including his thoughts about your thoughts about his rank, your rank and the rank of his littermates[5]. Label him dominant, mid-ranking, rank-seeking, lacking confidence, lacking good temperament or whatever you like (the one I like, as you've seen, is labeling him uncomfortable). Or, condition him to tolerate and enjoy having his collar yanked and his head restrained. Many training systems do both. This is fine though less efficient than acknowledging that *we really don't actually know exactly why he does it* but we have a technique with a good track record at modifying it.

Similarly, if the dog is a location guarder, it's too late to agonize about some genetic predisposition or second-guess your breed choice. Your dog is growling at you. The most fruitful course of action is to condition the dog to enjoy being approached when he's dug in and to practice placement cues. And, perhaps most tragically, a dog who is timid, growly or "reserved" around strangers is not "selective," "loyal" or "a good guard dog." He is experiencing innocuous things like visitors to your home as threatening. That's not a fun way to be.

Even ideas that are on firmer ground than mind-reading and labeling don't usually contribute much to the development of rehab technique. Knowledge of the fact that resource guarding or neo-phobia were adaptive in the past doesn't suggest effective modification strategies. You can't undo the evolutionary pressures that were on the ancestors of dogs or the selective breeding of dogs that came afterwards. You can't change his genes (yet). There *is* one evolved module, however, that you *can* exploit to both prevent and resolve aggression problems: the capacity to learn, to change behavior based on experience.

Once you recognize that exploiting learning laws is the most fruitful avenue for building treatment techniques, your only task regarding the goings-on inside the dog's brain is to answer the following question when confronted with an aggressive dog: *Is this*

---

[5] The appeal of yarns about what dogs are thinking has yielded a cottage industry in dog body language interpretation

dog upset? In other words, is this dog anxious, worried, afraid or experiencing some unpleasant emotion or other? In the case of most aggressive dogs, the answer is "yes," but there are some cases – predation and bullying of other dogs for instance – where the dog is not.

If yes, it behooves the trainer to line up her Pavlovian conditioning ducks when designing the mod-plan. Pavlovian conditioning has the power to actually alter the emotional response, which in turn will affect the behavior. If there is no emotional response driving the behavior, the trainer can and should blast away at operant conditioning – manipulating consequences to alter what the dog is doing.

There is one way that aggression stemming from an underlying emotional response can be directly influenced by its consequences, and this is through the mechanism of negative reinforcement. If threatening and biting succeed at increasing the distance between the dog and scary person, you can bet money that this strategy will be used again by the dog in the future. This is in fact a common way for a fearful dog to learn aggressive behaviors.

Bite Threshold Model

One model of aggression in domestic dogs that helps organize eliciting stimuli, especially in those all-too-common cases where multiple stimuli combine to elicit a bite, is the bite-threshold model. All dogs have a threshold at which they will bite. This kind of breaking point also exists for you and me. There is a level of provocation at which you or I will blow and behave aggressively, probably by way of an angry and abusive tirade of words. There is probably also the point at which you or I would get physical, even though we have been instructed otherwise all of our lives and are aware that it is Against the Law. There may be the odd person for whom nothing, including things like babies held at knifepoint or personal physical assault would ever make them use physical force, but they are the extreme minority. There are

100

definitely people who seem never to get angry and who often end up with problems like depression or psychosomatic illness instead. The point is that absolute passivity is not the yardstick we use to describe "normal" human behavior. There are no doubt dogs for whom no amount of abuse would constitute grounds for self-defense, but these are not normal animals. The Walt Disney ideal, however, would have us believe that absolute pacifism is the norm for dogs with the exception of extreme provocation. Announcing that nice dogs don't bite and vicious dogs do is like saying that nice people never argue or get angry and vicious people do.

Real dogs have a bite threshold. They also have thresholds for other levels of threat, such as growling, snarling (displaying their teeth) and snapping (biting the air). Dogs also have triggers, which are the stimuli (things) that bug them. Typical triggers include: categories of people to whom the dog is not socialized, hands and/or being touched, approach, possession of food bowl or other guarded resources, and cues that predict aversives (such as a choke collar or a strap used to beat the dog). Whether any one of these triggers by itself would elicit threat or biting depends on how intense (how close, how invasive, how long a duration etc.) a stimulus it is and where that individual dog's particular thresholds lie. Triggers can be added together. Combinations of more than one trigger at the same time usually evoke a higher level of threat. This is the usual reason some dogs seemingly bite "without provocation" or "for no reason," possibly even without having ever behaved aggressively before. Some novel combination of elements pushes the dog higher than the elements on their own have ever pushed him previously. For any dog, a tentative profile can be built using the existing history.

For instance, hypothetical dog Zaphod has always been uncomfortable around strange men. His other major risk factor is that he freezes up on approaches to his food bowl. The owner has also noticed that he seems just a little bit more sensitive at night than during the day and not perfectly relaxed with hands or when approached. These last two, by the way, are in the profiles, to

101

some extent, of most dogs. One day, Zaphod bites a man who approaches to pat him. The owner is completely floored as Zaphod has never bitten or even growled at anyone before and there was no provocation from the owner's perspective on this occasion. As can be seen from his profile, however, Zaphod was a time-bomb which, unfortunately, went off. There is often a "suddenly and without warning" quality to dogs whose growl, snap and bite thresholds are sandwiched close together like Zaphod's are. A stimulus that would evoke growling is almost at the bite threshold in these dogs. To say there were never any warnings, however, is false. The warnings were always there in the form of his being uncomfortable about all those things. His owner simply bought into the "nice dogs don't bite" myth. Zaphod would probably also have bitten any strange man who went near him while he was eating. He is still, by the way, a nice dog.

Another dog, Maggie, growls at children but has never, ever made contact. She is uncomfortable about having her nails clipped and has numerous other predictable minor bugs in her profile. What is insidious in this case is that her owner is convinced that Maggie would "never bite." After all, when a child approached her in her bed one day she still "only" growled. As you can see from her profile, it wouldn't take much more to push her into inflicting an actual bite. But the owner was sure her dog would "never bite" unless severely provoked. For Maggie, the items in her profile *are* provocation. Note that she probably would never be observed to snap as it would be too closely followed by a bite. It could very well be, by the way, that some individual dog has one or other of these threats omitted in his or her profile. Not all dogs give protracted warning before biting. Each dog has his own threat signature: the types of threat behavior, order of their appearance, and how low or high their respective thresholds are.

To treat dogs who behave aggressively, all the risk factors must be teased out and worked on separately and safely. Each bar in the graph of Zaphod and Maggie must be made as low as possible so that, even if many are stacked up, they don't get up to the bite threshold. This means remedial socialization, resource-guarding, approach and handling exercises. What the dog missed out on as a puppy has to be installed now. This is slow, painstaking work. The moral of the story is to prevent all this by actively intervening with young puppies before these problems develop.

Prognosis

When dealing with adult biters there are three options. You can treat the problem, manage the problem or execute the dog. I say execute rather than euthanize because a biting dog is not suffering and does not need or want a merciful death. He is killed because of transgressions he has committed against humans. That's what an execution is for. The tragic part is that the dog, in most cases, is behaving normally, for a dog. Socialization and anti-aggression exercises were simply either omitted or insufficient and/or the gene team co-conspired to drop the ball.

Management refers to physically preventing the problem. If the dog is not socialized to kids, the dog is kept away from kids for the rest of his life. If the dog is a food-bowl guarder, the family stays away from the dog while he's eating. If the dog bites when his nails are clipped, he's muzzled and held down by two people whenever his nails are clipped. No attempt is made to get the dog over the problem. Sometimes, management is the best option. Some dogs, especially those with a narrow enough problem, can live a full, normal life and be successfully kept away from their triggers by astute, caring owners.

Treatment means changing the dog's behavior, using some combination of operant and Pavlovian conditioning. Management for the duration of treatment is still necessary if one opts to treat. It compromises any desensitization program to confront the dog with something he can't handle. The dog ends up with another rehearsal of his aggressive behavior rather than a therapeutic experience. If, for instance, the dog is afraid of men with beards but has been desensitized to the point where he will approach and take a food treat if the man is sitting still, it is counterproductive for some bearded man to walk up and try to pat the dog. The dog will eventually get to that stage with careful training, but is not there yet. Better management would consist of the owner keeping bearded men from approaching until the dog is up to that point in the program. The softer the dog's mouth and the more compliant and committed the owner, the better the prognosis. Dogs with softer mouths do not have the ruinous prospect of another offense looming over them should there be a management lapse, and compliant, committed owners will have fewer instances of management failure, do the homework, and bounce back better from the occasional regressions along the way.

Chapter Four
It's All Chew Toys to Them

Empathy 101

Imagine you live on a planet where the dominant species is far more intellectually sophisticated than human beings but often keeps humans as companion animals. They are called the Gorns. They communicate with each other via a complex combination of telepathy, eye movements and high-pitched squeaks, all completely unintelligible and unlearnable by humans, whose brains are prepared for verbal language acquisition only. What humans sometimes learn is the meaning of individual sounds by repeated association with things of relevance to them. The Gorns and humans bond strongly but there are many Gorn rules that humans must try to assimilate with limited information and usually high stakes.

You are one of the lucky humans who lives with the Gorns in their dwelling. Many other humans are chained to small cabanas in the yard or kept in outdoor pens of varying size. They have become so socially starved that they cannot control their emotions when a Gorn goes near them. Because of this behavior, the Gorns agree that they could never be House-Humans. They are too excitable.

The dwelling you share with your Gorn family is filled with numerous water-filled porcelain bowls, complete with flushers. Every time you try to urinate in one, though, any nearby Gorn attacks you. You learn to only use the toilet when there are no Gorns present. Sometimes they come home and stuff your head down the toilet for no apparent reason. You hate this and start sucking up to the Gorns when they come home to try and stave this off but they view this as increasing evidence of your guilt.

You are also punished for watching videos, reading certain books, talking to other human beings, eating pizza or cheesecake, and writing letters. These are all considered behavior problems by the Gorns. To avoid going crazy, once again you wait until they are not around to try doing anything you wish to do. While they are around, you sit quietly, staring straight ahead. Because they witness this good behavior you are so obviously capable of, they attribute to "spite" the video watching and other transgressions that occur when you are alone. Obviously you resent being left alone, they figure. You are walked several times a day and left crossword puzzle books to do. You have never used them because you hate crosswords; the Gorns think you're ignoring them out of revenge.

Worst of all, you like them. They are, after all, often nice to you. But when you smile at them, they punish you, likewise for shaking hands. If you apologize they punish you again. You have not seen another human since you were a small child. When you see one on the street you are curious, excited and sometimes afraid. You really don't know how to act. So, the Gorn you live with keeps you away from other humans. Your social skills never develop.

Finally, you are brought to "training" school. A large part of the training consists of having your air briefly cut off by a metal chain around your neck. They are sure you understand every squeak and telepathic communication they make because you sometimes get it right. You are guessing and hate the training. You feel pretty stressed out a lot of the time. One day, you see a Gorn approaching with the training collar in hand. You have PMS, a sore neck and you just don't feel up to the baffling coercion about to ensue. You tell them in your sternest voice to please leave you alone and go away. The Gorns are shocked by this unprovoked aggressive behavior. They thought you had a good temperament.

They put you in one of their vehicles and take you for a drive. You watch the attractive planetary landscape going by and wonder where you are going. The vehicle stops and you are led into a building filled with the smell of human sweat and excrement.

106

Humans are everywhere in small cages. Some are nervous, some depressed, most watch the goings on from their prisons. Your Gorns, with whom you have lived your entire life, hand you over to strangers who drag you to a small room. You are terrified and yell for your Gorn family to help you. They turn and walk out the door of the building. You are held down and given a lethal injection. It is, after all, the humane way to do it.

Top Ten Behavior Problems of Pet Humans on Planet Gorn

1) Watching TV

2) Use of porcelain bowls filled with water as elimination sites

3) Listening to music other than Country & Western

4) Talking to other humans

5) Smoking or drinking

6) Sitting on chairs ("How can I get him to stop sitting on CHAIRS?!")

7) Tooth brushing

8) Eating anything but (nutritionally balanced) Human Chow

9) Shaking hands to greet

10) Smiling

This nightmarish world is the one inhabited by many dogs *all the time*. Virtually all natural dog behaviors - chewing, barking, rough play, chasing moving objects, eating food items within reach, jumping up to access faces, settling disputes with threat displays, establishing contact with strange dogs, guarding resources, leaning

107

into steady pressure against their necks, urinating on porous surfaces like carpets, defending themselves from perceived threat - are considered by humans to be behavior problems. The rules that seem so obvious to us make absolutely no sense to dogs.

If someone tried to punish out behaviors you knew were necessary for maintaining your well-being or earning a living, would you cease doing them altogether or would you try to figure out when it was safe to do them and when it wasn't safe? How would you feel about the punisher? What kind of credibility would he have? It is as inherently obvious to dogs that furniture, clothing and car interiors are good for chewing as it is inherently obvious to you that TV sets are good for watching. If I reprimand you for watching the TV, your most likely course of action is to simply watch TV when I'm not around. And you're a large-brained, conscience-laden human.

We smart, moral beings do this kind of discriminating all the time. Take speeding on highways. A lot of people get tickets. What's the actual effect of this hefty punishment? An immediate suppression of the behavior: you slow down right after you get the ticket. You're angry and upset. But what happens over the next few hours, days and weeks? Most people start speeding again, although they will tell you that they fully understand that speeding is against the law, that it is potentially very dangerous, and that they understand the penalty if they are caught. Those last four words are the key: if they are caught. What is typically obtained with punishment is finer discrimination: you get better at smelling out speed traps, at knowing where and when you can speed. This is a typical result obtained with punishment. We are subject to the laws of learning. So are dogs, but with less incentive from understanding the potential harm of their behavior. Dogs cannot have moral failings as they cannot knowingly act against the common good. They therefore never self-punish with guilt and self-recrimination as we do. This doesn't make them morally inferior. It's just how they are. We take far too personally phenomena that are simply products of animal learning laws.

108

Similarly, burning your mouth on pizza makes you check the temperature of the pizza next time before digging in but doesn't stop you from ordering it again. This is because pizza tastes good and you know this. An organism will always look for a way around the punishment to get to the reinforcer, if there is one. It's useful in fact to think of punishments as obstacles to overcome on the way to reinforcement. Likewise, a dog will rarely find it "wrong" or quit cold turkey his habit of digging in the azaleas although he may learn it's dangerous to do so when you're there. What else could a flowerbed possibly be for, to a dog? Whenever you punish, you're the cop giving out the speeding ticket to a not very sophisticated and amoral being who really wants and maybe even needs to speed. Oh, he'll stop for a while if the fine is hefty but he'll sooner or later be back to speeding and he'll be better at avoiding speed traps.

Division of Matter in the Universe

HUMAN	**DOG**
FURNITURE	CHEW TOY
FOOTWEAR	CHEW TOY
CAR	RETREATING OBJECT
CAR INTERIOR	CHEW TOY
CARPET	TOILET
DOG FOOD	FOOD
HORS D'OEUVRES	FOOD
KLEENEXES	FOOD

CELLO	CHEW TOY
BOOK	CHEW TOY
CAT	RETREATING OBJECT
SQUIRREL	RETREATING OBJECT
PLASTIC WRAP	FOOD
HI-FI SPEAKERS	CHEW TOY
HI-FI SPEAKERS	TOILET (INTACT MALE)
ROCK	FOOD (LABRADOR)

Housetraining

Remember the Gorns? If one of them leapt out of the bathroom cupboard and yelled at you every time you sat on the toilet to defecate, it would still feel pretty obvious that toilets were the "right" place to go to the bathroom. You may, however, start checking the cupboards before going to make sure the attacker wasn't there. You would also be pretty reluctant to defecate in any other location if you-know-who was standing around. This isn't spite. It's eminently sensible.

Owners interpret dogs who "refuse" to eliminate on walks and then go on the carpet when the owner leaves the room to answer the phone as "getting back at them." Absolutely not so. The dog has simply learned to go to the bathroom on an obvious toilet - the carpet - when the attacker is not present. He behaves obsequiously on the owner's return to try and turn off the punishment that inevitably occurs when certain context cues (owner plus poop on rug) are present. It is clear from his terrified, submissive posture that the dog would dearly love to avoid that punishment if only he knew how. If someone punished you in a certain circumstance,

110

you would beg for mercy too, regardless of whether you had any clue as to why they were about to punish you. It's Orwellian what we do to dogs.

The reason owners are stymied by the housetraining process is that it is too inherently obvious to *them* that the indoors/outdoors discrimination is the name of the game. Dogs, on the other hand, although capable of making this discrimination, don't necessarily leap to that conclusion based on the information provided by the owner. Owners also assume that the dog can learn right-wrong when what he really learns is safe-dangerous. It's "proto-morality." When a dog is learning how the world works, there are many different pieces of the puzzle to assimilate. Let's look at a typical housetraining effort: the first dozen urination attempts of Henry, a newly adopted dog:

HENRY'S BEHAVIOR	CONTEXT CLUES	RESULT to HENRY
Urinates in hall	Braided rug, owner absent	Relief
Urinates in living room	Thick carpet, owner present	Yelling
Urinates in yard	Grass, owner present	Relief Praise
Urinates in living room	Carpet, owner present	Attacked by owner
Urinates in hall	Braided rug, owner present	Attacked by owner
Trip to yard, no urination	Grass, owner present	Taken in

111

Urinates in yard	Grass, owner absent	Relief
Urinates in bedroom	Carpet, owner present	Attacked
Urinates in dining room	Under table, owner absent	Relief
Urinates in dining room	Rug in corner, owner present	Serious Attack
Trip to yard, no urination	Grass, owner present	Taken in
Urinates in basement	Sofa, owner absent	Relief

From the owner's perspective, there were only three mistakes: the first one in the hall, the one under the dining room table and the one in the basement. All the other attempts were caught and punished or occurred in the desired location, the yard. But what has the dog learned? It's possible that the dog is learning that all indoor locations are dangerous and that the grass is safe. It's equally possible that the dog is learning that bedrooms and living rooms are dangerous, dining rooms are dangerous if you're not under a table, and grass, sofas and basements are, so far, safe. *The one sure thing is that it is never dangerous when the owner is absent and dangerous almost half the time when the owner is present.* If you were the dog and had to play the odds, you might start holding on when the owner was with you, including in the yard, and then nipping down to the basement to pee in order to play it safe. You would be proven correct. It *is* always safe to go when you're alone.

What's missing from this housetraining example is a **solid history of reinforced trials in the desired location**, the yard. This establishes the owner's presence and the location as both safe and reinforcing. Subsequent punishments would therefore have a narrower possible interpretation: the *location* must be unsafe. This solid foundation is usually missing. Owners start to assume learning after two or three correct trials, which is only a drop in the bucket.

To guarantee success in housetraining, rule one is: catch performances by the dog with timely feedback. Rule two is: be the good guy most of the time. In order to give feedback *and* be the good guy, one must arrange for elimination to occur outside and be present with treats in hand or pocket. Rule three is: prevent any mistakes indoors. Each and every instance of elimination that is prevented inside the house is one saved up for the right place - outside -, another opportunity to condition outside elimination through reinforcement and be the good guy at the same time.

This is the major thrust of the housetraining. The minor addendum in housetraining is, later in the process, to catch mistakes indoors with well-timed interruptions. You don't even need to punish at all.

Crate Training

To get an uninterrupted reinforcement history, the dog has to be prevented from even attempting to eliminate in the house. This can be achieved using a dog crate and frequent trips outdoors at likely times. Most dogs will do their utmost to hold on and not eliminate if closely confined. This makes the crate a valuable tool. Reams of material exist on the subject of crate training. It's astounding that the concept is still resisted in the name of being humane. The alternative to crate training is a possible early punishment history that will not only stress the dog but may derail the whole process. People get the job done in other ways but the wear and tear on the dog is considerable.

Before using a crate as a training tool, take the time to make a good first impression. Make it comfy with a nice crate pad or pillow and blanket, situate it in a high traffic area like the kitchen and, whenever the dog isn't looking, drop a couple of treats at the back. Let the dog discover the Wonders at the Back of the Crate on his

113

own. Feed him meals in there, always with the door open. Using heavy string, tie an attractive stuffed chew toy to the rear inside so that the dog must lie in the crate in order to chew on it.

After a few days of this, start teaching the dog to enter and exit on cue. Say "into bed" or "into the crate," then throw in a treat, praise as the dog goes in and eats the treat and then order him out with the cue of your choice. Encourage him to come out and, when he does, praise him (no food treat for exiting). Repeat this a few times and then change the order of events slightly: instead of throwing the treat into the crate after you say "into bed," wait for him to go in on his own before dropping in the treat. If the dog doesn't enter on cue, simply wait. Do not cue him a second time and do not crack and throw the treat in. You can encourage him in with hand gestures but even this is riskier than simply waiting. If he doesn't go in, end the training session without comment. Try another session in a little while, still withholding reinforcement until the dog goes in on his own. When he does (and they all do eventually so hang in there), give him a double or triple treat, do a few more reinforced reps and then end the session. Always leave the dog wanting more.

When the dog is going in and out on cue, practice closing the door for a few seconds and feeding treats through the front bars. Then open, invite the dog out and repeat. After you've practiced a session or two like this you are ready to try the first lock-in. Rent yourself a favorite video and stuff a couple of chew toys with something extra-special. Set the crate up right next to your comfy movie chair and, just before you sit down to enjoy the movie, invite the dog into the crate. When he goes in, give him the chew toys, close the crate door and start the movie. Leave a few times to get popcorn, a drink, but always come back within a minute or so. The first experience being locked in the crate must be an overwhelmingly easy and good one. Ignore any noise, agitation or tantrum from the dog.

At the end of the movie, if the dog is quiet and settled in the crate, simply open the door and let him out. Under no circumstances will you open the door to the crate if the dog is misbehaving, otherwise you are conditioning that behavior. If you do not like it, do not reinforce it. When you do open the door, don't gush and hug the dog. Make the exit an anticlimax. Behave very neutrally. All the good stuff should happen while he's IN the crate, behaving nicely. Once he's out, practice a few in and outs for food treats before you finish your training/movie session. If he refuses to go in, do whatever prompting it takes to get him in, reinforce him and get your in/out exercise polished up again.

Now spend a few days locking the dog in the crate for moderate durations (up to an hour or two) when you're at home, going about your usual business. Ignore any noise and provide interesting crate puzzles (i.e., chew toys) each time. When the dog is going in without fuss and no longer distress vocalizing, you may start leaving the house. Voila. Crate training.

There are dogs who are not inhibited by crates. They merrily urinate and defecate. They may have early histories of being caged for long periods, forcing them to eventually eliminate. They lose their cleanliness instinct. Sometimes it can be nursed back by keeping the crate and dog immaculate, removing porous bedding that might elicit urination, and getting them out often enough so they never get close to being full, and thus eliminating, in the crate. For dogs who continue to eliminate without reserve when closely confined, the crate is less valuable. The principles of housetraining are the same, however: arrange for a lot of right responses and reinforce each one. Interrupt wrong responses. For crate-impervious dogs, this means close supervision. Sometimes they can be stretched to hang on longer by using an "umbilical cord" when you're home: a short tether from dog to your waist.

Keep careful track of whether the dog is "empty" vs. "full." Freedom in limited dog-proofed areas of the house can be granted at empty periods: in other words, you have just witnessed and reinforced the dog for doing both functions outdoors so you know you're safe for a short while. When the dog is full, you have two choices: 1) he can be in his crate (being "stretched") or 2) outside at the elimination area with you, liver in pocket in case the dog guesses right and performs. You must time reinforcement precisely.

Housetraining Procedure Review

1) Establish a reinforcement history by taking the dog out to the same place at frequent intervals and reinforcing all elimination in that spot with both praise and a food treat. The food must be in your pocket so that you can give it within one second of his performance. Praise as he's going and reinforce immediately after. In order to reinforce immediately, you must be present: sending the dog into the yard through the back door while you watch from the window may result in a dog peeing or pooping in the yard but there is no training effect without the immediate reinforcement. You also may not know whether he's gone or not when he comes back in. You are also setting the dog up to prefer going out of your presence, which can be problematic. This is because when the mistake interruption phase comes, the dozens of times he has been reinforced for going in front of you while outside will make the interruptions more tightly associated with the location, which is exactly what you want.

You may also reinforce the dog by taking him for a walk after he has eliminated in the toilet area. When he learns that the walk starts *after* he eliminates, he will tend to eliminate more quickly. We love this. Most people train it backwards: they walk the dog in hopes of stimulating him to eliminate and then end the walk, taking the dog directly home, as soon as he's empty. The dog learns that eliminating ends walks and starts to delay going to the bathroom in order to extend the walk. This is not a plot by the dog, but simply the laws of learning in action again. In my house, the rule with border collies was: Empty dogs play Frisbee. They loved Frisbee and learned the game never started till they were empty so they

116

emptied themselves with a fair amount of urgency. Again, the take home message is to focus on providing consequences, not to focus so much on trying to manipulate behavior with elicitors. More on consequences and elicitors in chapter five.

2) <u>Free periods</u> are for empty dogs. When the dog has just urinated and defecated outdoors in front of you and has been reinforced, he may then and only then be loose for thirty minutes or so in a dog-proofed area. If he is perfectly chew-trained, you may choose to give him the whole house. This is a moot point as most dogs who require housetraining are probably untrained in other areas like chewing as well. If it's a new dog or puppy, don't presume he's okay because he has not yet taken out the dining room set. Presume he will chew virtually anything at any time so don't let him discover his love of oak or rugs. If he occasionally produces an addendum (pees or poops again within half an hour of being completely emptied), don't take the chance of this happening again: crate him for a couple of hours to get him to stretch and to prevent any accidents. Every accident inside is 1) one you weren't able to reinforce *out*side and 2) one you failed to catch inside which gets that habit rolling or 3) one you caught inside, but which might set *you* up as the bad guy. Avoid mistakes indoors in early training at all costs.

3) <u>Crate the dog except during supervised empty/free periods</u>. Make the crate comfy and give him plenty to do in there in the form of chew toy puzzles. If you must leave the dog alone for more than a few hours on a regular basis, you cannot in all conscience crate him. It's hard to advise here, given that someone with so little availability has gone and acquired an unhousetrained dog, but here are the damage control measures. The dog will have to be left in a dog-proofed room with a toilet area at the opposite end from the sleeping and eating area. The room should have a hard floor, like a kitchen floor and the toilet area should be something porous like a good thickness of newspaper or, even better, turf. All this will maximize the likelihood of the dog

choosing the right place when he needs to go. It in no way guarantees this, with no feedback happening every time.

When you are home, you will do the reinforcing as usual at the selected outdoor toilet location. Crating overnight is fine. I do recommend putting overnight crates in your bedroom. Sleeping en masse is very much a dog thing. I am grateful to the Monks of New Skete for pointing this out. If the dog wakes up early and whines, simply do not respond until both of these conditions have been met: 1) it's your rising time or later and 2) dog is quiet in the crate. Dogs learn quickly that there will be no action before a certain time (they estimate time very well) and that noise doesn't work.

4) Interrupt and redirect mistakes when a reinforcement-history is well established in the outdoor toilet area. This means setting the dog up to make mistakes indoors so you can be alert and ready. Usually an adequate reinforcement history will be indicated by the fact that the dog will almost reflexively start eliminating as soon as he reaches the chosen site. Think in terms of two or three weeks, provided you have not been allowing mistakes to occur indoors during this period. Sometimes, if you have been diligent with the reinforcement part, the dog never even makes a boo-boo and you're off scot-free. In many cases, though, although the dog now has a preference for the toilet area, alternative toilets, like carpet, have not necessarily been ruled out yet. To rule them out cleanly and efficiently, you must catch the initiation of the act. If the dog has completely emptied his bladder or bowels by the time you interrupt him, it is far less clear. If you are two behaviors late, i.e. the dog pees on the carpet, walks away and sighs and then you try interrupting, you have, you guessed it, caught sighing. It is not inherently obvious to dogs that there is anything emotionally charged about urinating on carpets as opposed to sighing so stop thinking it's obvious. If you wish to modify behavior, you must keep up with the flow of behavior change.

If the reinforcement history was well executed, it will usually take just a few indoor interruptions to finish the job. That is, if those are

118

two or three in a row. If the dog sneaks one in which you don't catch, count on a more protracted struggle. This whole thing has nothing to do with dog stubbornness or other emotional content, it's a raw, unadulterated conditioning procedure. That goes for marking[6], unhousetrainable breeds and any other classification you feel exempts your dog from the laws of learning. To be conditioned, all the animal needs is a spinal cord and brain stem. For dogs that mark, the complicating factor is double motivation for urination: full bladder, like all dogs and marking elicitors such as novelty, the scent of other dogs, certain vertical surfaces etc. The procedure is the same, though: establish a reinforcement history and prevent mistakes to condition a habit and then and only then rule out wrong options. Once the dog has it down, reinforce outdoors occasionally. At this point, you may now consider sending the dog out rather than taking him out, as well as gradually extending his free periods in the house. Note: gradually.

Training Regressions

People are terribly mystified by any change in their dog's behavior and go on a lot with the "why? WHY?" as though there should never be any variability whatsoever in this living organism's behavior. Training regressions are a frequent occurrence and no big deal. It is so important to remember that behavior is always in flux, constantly subjected to whatever contingencies there are in the environment as well as being influenced by unknown internal events. In the case of behavior problems, there are three main reasons for behavior that had seemed to be "fixed" to break down again:

1) Undertraining: the behavior was never that strong in the first place
2) Contingency change: the behavior extinguished or another one was trained by the owner or environment

---

[6] Marking refers to the depositing of a smaller amount of urine, usually on vertical surfaces and usually by males

119

3) Failure to generalize: the behavior falls apart in a new location or context (Karen Pryor's "New Tank Syndrome")

These three reasons are really variations on the same theme, undertraining. It is extremely difficult in a real life setting to reinforce enough trials to get the response strength most people expect (i.e. perfection for life). It is also hard to keep on top of changing circumstances to maintain training and get responses generalized across new contexts.

Remember the first twelve urination attempts of Henry? He was headed for reverse-housetraining. Let's say Henry's next couple of dozen trials continue in similar fashion. Let's also say the door to the basement and bedrooms have been kept closed and Henry is crated when the owners aren't home. This arrangement might yield a Henry that appears trained to only go in the yard. But how trained is Henry? His safe options are currently limited to the yard, which he has been consistently using. After a few weeks, the owners successfully leave Henry alone for brief periods uncrated. They are out of the woods they think. One day, Henry's owner happens to go out to water a plant in the garden when Henry goes out in the morning. The owner's presence nearby inhibits Henry from going in the yard so he comes back in with a full bladder. The owner wasn't paying attention and goes about his business. When he leaves the room, Henry urinates on the baby blanket, the only porous surface available. No one says otherwise so Henry assumes this is okay. A new habit is born.

This simple case of undertraining may be seen by the owner as jealousy of the baby or any number of interpretations. This case, in fact, wouldn't qualify as a training regression at all because the dog was never trained. This phenomenon of a masked problem is at the root of a lot of punishment directed at dogs who supposedly "know" what they should do. People have a strong tendency to assume a very thorough knowledge on the part of the dog based on observations of some desired responses. The dog's understanding of contingencies is usually quite different from the owner's. What's

120

the solution for Henry then? 1) A solid history of reinforced trials in the desired location, 2) prevent mistakes until #1 is accomplished, 3) rule out mistakes with set-ups when #1 is accomplished and 4) maintain behavior with occasional reinforcement. Be ever ready for regression if contingencies or contexts change. No magic potion. Housetrain the dog.

Contingency Change: Inadvertent New Rules

A contingency change might look like the following. The dog has learned that it's safe and often reinforcing to urinate in the yard and dangerous in most places he has tried in the house and so a fairly solid yard habit is in place. The owner has become upset about the yellowing of grass from dog urine and has decided to limit the dog to eliminating in one corner of the yard. The owner takes the dog on leash at elimination times for a couple of weeks, always going to one corner and praising the dog for urinating. The first couple of times the dog goes out off leash, she urinates in the wrong area. The owner punishes the dog. On the third day, the dog will not urinate in the yard. The owner sees this and takes the dog for a walk. The dog has a very full bladder and finally urinates and is praised by the owner. The owner likes the idea of the dog urinating on the walk rather than in the yard and starts taking the dog around the block to eliminate, which is successful and keeps the yard urine-free.

A few months later, the owner is in a rush to prepare for guests arriving so lets the dog into the yard to pee while finishing the cooking. The dog does not urinate in the yard and comes back in full. When the guests arrive, the owner puts the dog on leash to calm one of the visitors who is afraid of dogs. The dog urinates on the Persian rug. The owner thinks the dog sensed that one of the guests didn't like her and urinated to demonstrate her resentment. In fact, the dog has learned to urinate when on leash only, based on the new contingencies inadvertently set up by the owner. Dogs aren't into big agendas. They just need to know where and when it's safe to pee.

121

Elimination on Cue

Dogs fail to generalize across many facets of dog training. In the case of housetraining, lapses will occur on visits to other people's houses simply because the dog has learned not to eliminate in the *owner's* house but has not generalized to all indoor locations. Location, surface, smells and whoever is around are the cues dogs attend to the most when it comes to housetraining. Some dogs are sensitive to weather as well. The fancy way around this is to put elimination on cue. People who frequent dog shows have learned this trick because they must get dogs to eliminate in new locations and on odd surfaces on a daily basis. To teach this, first observe the dog for a few days to get a precise idea of when he does which function and, specifically, the intention behaviors that immediately precede elimination. Then start training as follows.

Just before the dog reaches the place where he demonstrates intention behaviors, give a urination cue, wait while the dog urinates and reinforce afterwards as usual. Do the same for defecation, using a different cue. If the dog is thrown for a loop by your speaking just prior his elimination precursors, don't sweat it. Work to a nice sequence of cue-intention-behavior-reinforcement. This will result, after enough trials, in a dog who will urinate or defecate on cue.

In early training, don't risk giving the cue unless you're sure he's likely to go, because this results in a missed association. You need a sufficient number of trials under your belt before the cue will actually trigger any action. The key to this technique is being able to predict when` the dog will go. This technique also works without reinforcement (through straight Pavlovian conditioning). The best method is to selectively reinforce any eliminating that was preceded by the cue. When he goes without a cue up front, simply thank him without giving a reinforcer. This will strengthen on-cue elimination in preference to off-cue. Taken to the extreme, this could produce a dog who has a hard time eliminating without the cue, so watch out.

122

Dogs' underdeveloped ability to generalize can come in handy. For instance, dogs can be easily taught that it is okay to lie on this sofa and that chair but not the other sofa and the other chair. This makes "consistent" no-furniture-at-all rules unnecessary. I don't mean this as a value judgment in any way: if you don't want dogs on any furniture, it's fine to provide a comfortable alternative for a dog who demonstrates a preference for furniture (otherwise the dog will likely learn it's safe to lie on the sofa when you, the radar trap, are gone). It's just that it's not unfair or difficult for the dog to assimilate that some furniture is okay and some is not. Dogs discriminate tiny differences with great ease. In fact, they discriminate so well that it greatly complicates training in those instances where you *want* generalization. In all this, it's important to remember that the dog is not learning he "should" or "shouldn't" do something, or anything to do with right and wrong. He's learning about contingencies, i.e., the immediate results to him of doing this, that or the other thing. Repeat to yourself, as a mantra: dogs don't learn right vs. wrong, they learn safe vs. dangerous. This doesn't make dogs less sophisticated or valuable than if they moralized about it. It's simply how they are.

Non-static nature of Behavior

People get very shirty about training regressions. Once the dog has demonstrated understanding of a rule or gotten into habit A, many people presume some deeply personal motivation must be at the root of a breakdown. The truth is that behavior falls apart all the time. Often you will never know why. This goes for carefully trained in behavior or behavior that seems under pretty tight environmental control. Professional figure skaters quite regularly fall on their butts without a frenzied inquisition into why. Agonizing about whywhywhy a dog makes a boo-boo is interesting over coffee but doesn't solve the problem. Behavior is in constant flux. There is never a finished product. Retraining or touch-up training is part of the process. Experienced trainers understand this and take dips in stride. A useful tip is to not take long-established behavior for granted. Even long-trained adult dogs need to hear at least an occasional congratulatory mumble when they make wee-wee in exactly the right place yet again.

Barking

Dogs bark for a variety of reasons.

1) <u>Watchdog Barking</u> serves the dual purpose of alerting other pack members that there is an intruder or change in the environment and warning the intruder that they have been noticed. Dogs bark much more than their ancestors, wolves, who hardly ever bark. In domesticating them, we have selected for more barking[7]. The predisposition to watch-dog bark varies among breeds and individuals. The modifying principles are the same, though, whether you're trying to coax a little more barking out of a couch potato Newfoundland or tone down barking in a hair-trigger German shepherd or miniature schnauzer.

2) <u>Request Barking</u> starts off as a behavioral experiment by the dog, kind of a "let's see what this produces." Typical requests include opening doors, handouts from your plate, invitations to play, attention, and being let out of a crate or confinement area. This behavior is a problem not because the dog tries out the experiment but because the experiment usually succeeds: the owner reinforces the barking by granting the request and a habit is born. Dogs zero in on whatever strategy works.

3) <u>Spooky Barking</u> occurs when the dog is fearful or uncomfortable about something in the environment. It's the dog's way of saying: "Back off - don't come any closer." This is much more serious than garden-variety watchdog barking because the dog in question is advertising that he is afraid and therefore potentially dangerous if approached.

---

[7] Barking may be a trait that was selected for or it may have come along for the ride when other, possibly morphological, traits were selected for during the domestication of dogs

124

4) <u>Boredom Barking</u> can result when the dog's daily needs for exercise and social and mental stimulation aren't met. The dog barks compulsively. This is very much like pacing back and forth, tail-chasing or self-mutilation. Chained dogs and dogs left outdoors in yards are at high risk.

Controlling Excessive Barking

Aside from any bark-reduction training, it's also crucial to address, if present, any underlying socialization deficits, lack of exercise, and impoverished environment (i.e. inadequate mental stimulation). In the cases of spooky barking, barking secondary to separation anxiety and boredom barking, where the barking is a symptom, resolving the underlying cause is the principle intervention. Here are training instructions.

<u>Watchdog Barking</u> The goal is to teach the dog the meaning of the words "bark" and "quiet" (or any word you want to use as an "off" switch). First, you have to teach the dog to both bark and then stop on cue for treats. To elicit the barking the first few times so that you can practice, you need something you know makes the dog bark, like the doorbell or a weird noise outside. You may require a helper for this. Arrange the following sequence of events:

1) you cue "bark!"

2) doorbell or other prompt

3) dog barks

4) you praise: "good! wonderful!" after a few barks

5) you cue "quiet"

6) you show the dog the treat (to prompt quiet)

7) the dog's (eventual) distraction from barking by the treat

8) three to five seconds of quiet during which you praise: "soooo gooooooooood!"

9) you furnish treat after the three to five seconds of perfect quiet

10) repeat with less and less visibility of the treat prompt (you still furnish after perfect quiets)

11) repeat with longer and longer durations of quiet before furnishing the treat

12) practice with pretend visitors a few times

Do it over and over till the dog knows the game. It may take a few sessions so hang in there. How do you judge whether he knows the game? He knows the game when he barks on the cue and doesn't need the doorbell anymore, and he quiets on the first quiet cue without having to be shown the treat. You still *give* him one from your pocket or from the cupboard if he quiets on cue, you just don't show it up front anymore. If he ever interrupts a quiet time with even a muffled bark or two, give him a no-reward mark such as "oh! too bad" and start counting the quiet time from the beginning again. He has to know that barking during the quiet time was a mistake that cost him his treat.

You have to acquire the ability to yo-yo the dog back and forth reliably between bark and quiet in training sessions before you try out your quiet cue in real situations. Barking is strongly motivated for many dogs and you've got to build them up to actual visitor trials. The most common mistake is trying to use the quiet cue before it's well enough conditioned in training sessions. Think of quiet on cue as a muscle you're making stronger. The more practice, the stronger the muscle.

When you can turn barking on and off anytime and anyplace (you've conditioned a strong muscle in other words), you may now start practicing quiet on cue when the dog barks on his own in real

126

life situations. The first couple of times, the dog will respond poorly to the quiet cue so you have to be ready. Have really good treats handy and go temporarily back to showing him the treat up front if necessary.

A good adjunct for fuel-injected, turbocharged barkers is to teach them down-stay as well as quiet. To earn their treat, they must hold a stay on a mat near the door and keep their mouths buttoned for the full duration of the quiet period. The hardest thing about bark training is how futile it seems the first couple of times you try, either in a training session or during your first real life dry run. It's also the most interesting thing about this training because, no matter how bad it seems to go the first time or two, it gets better rapidly if you persevere. Many people never get over the hump. The best thing to do is thoroughly understand the instructions and simply practice with a Zen-like resolve. This procedure works if you give it the critical mass of training.

You can also do the down-stay on its own, without putting the considerable effort into teaching the "quiet" cue. This is a great solution for those dogs that can't bark while lying down. If the dog is nuts about toys, another variation is to cue and prompt the dog to fetch a favorite. He may not be able to bark and carry the toy. At the very least, it will serve as a muffler. Tennis balls make great mufflers.

Finally, you can teach the dog that barking after being told to "quiet" gets him an instant time out away from the action. Most dogs find front door goings-on sufficiently fascinating that it really bugs them to be banished to a back room. Timing is important, as usual. Once you've issued the quiet cue, the very next bark needs to meet your instant "ooh! Too bad for you" and quick escorting to the penalty box.

A minute or two in the penalty box is plenty but don't release him until he has been quiet for at least several seconds. Time-outs for watchdog barking can elicit a watchdog-request barking hybrid

127

(residual excitement plus "let me out of here"). Don't panic. Wait for your five to ten seconds of quiet. Keep the flow chart clear.

If your dog has a very low threshold, "going off" for the smallest sounds and changes in the environment, it would help the cause to get him better habituated. Take him out more and invite the world in to visit more often. Expose him to a wider range of sights and sounds. It's not particularly fun to be on chronic DefCon II the way some of these dogs are.

Request Barking When they want something, dogs will experiment with various behaviors to see if any of them work. Barking usually gets instant results from humans so is conditioned in short order. The first rule to get rid of it is this: if you don't like barking, *stop reinforcing it* with attention, door opening services, releasing from crates etc. Period. No buts.

Rather than the dog telling *you* when to take him out, take him out at regular intervals, always making sure that none of them are preceded by barking. Never let a barking dog out of a crate or confinement area. Always wait for a lull of at least five or ten seconds. Ignore dogs who bark at you to get stuff. Keep in mind that if you have been reinforcing it for a while, the barking will get worse before it goes away. You're changing the rules and the dog will be frustrated at first. The behavior going away from cessation of reinforcement is called "extinction" and the intensifying of the behavior before it goes away is called an "extinction burst."

We have extinction bursts all the time, too. When your demagnetized credit card doesn't function when the store clerk runs it through the machine, she doesn't give up immediately and start manually punching the number in right away. Instead, she runs the card through a few more times, usually each time more vigorously than the last, or else runs the card through at different speeds or even varies the pressure against different parts of the machine. The radical shift in behavioral strategy, in this case to tedious manual dialing, occurs after the card-running behavior extinguishes, with a

128

typical extinction burst. All that vigorous swishing of your card and its variations was the extinction burst. Likewise, your dog will not immediately abandon barking as a strategy, not without a fight anyway. Like the store clerk who has a strong history of being reinforced with completed transactions by running cards through scanners, your dog has had a history of being reinforced for barking. He will bark harder before he switches strategies.

One of my favorite extinction burst scenarios is button pushing. Imagine stepping into an elevator. When you push the button for your floor, the button should light up, the door should close and the elevator should start moving. Your button-pushing behavior gets a nice, boring reinforcement history. What happens, then, if the light doesn't go on, the door stays open and the elevator remains grounded? Do you immediately leap out and take the stairs? No. You push the button again. Harder. With rapid-fire bursts. With a battering ram if you have one on you. Then you take the stairs. So, when dogs escalate their barking when you stop reinforcing it, say to yourself: "He's pushing the button harder before he switches to the stairs."

What makes this a bit more wrinkly is that, very often in real life, variations in intensity or delivery offered during the extinction burst are reinforced either deliberately or by chance and end up getting trained in. This is a tragedy of large proportions for dog owners. Rather than just having crate barking now, you might have crate screaming or crate barking with digging-in-corner. When you use extinction as a tool, be fully conscious and prepared to make Rover go cold turkey: wait for a strategy shift that you *like,* such as lying quietly, before reinforcing with freedom.

Above all, start noticing and paying attention to the dog when he's quiet, something we all forget to do. Failing to do so is also using extinction, but this time to get rid of our favorite behavior: dog lying quietly providing doggie ambiance. Dogs find out that a strategy shift to laundry-stealing or pawing guests - or barking - gets attention much more reliably. Teach your dog that there are pay-offs for lying quietly, chewing his own chew toys and refraining from barking. Everyone could stand to cultivate a "you are soooo gooooooooood" reflex for those instances where the dog might have barked but didn't.

Barking when alone was discussed in alone training. Providing separation anxiety has been ruled out, it can be thought of as a common form of request barking: the dog is requesting that you come back. To summarize how to get rid of it: Baby-gate him in various rooms away from you to practice "semi-absences." Ignore any barking. Practice several brief absences every day. Go out and come back in in a matter of fact way. Keep departures and arrivals low key. Never make an entrance when the dog is barking. Wait for a ten second lull. Increase mental stimulation in the form of training and predatory games. Make him work for his food. Hide it around the house before you leave or stuff it into Kongs and hide those. Tire him out physically before long absences. Make him bring a toy to you when you come home, then play together with it.

Spooky Barking In this case, it is imperative to get the dog better socialized. Prevention is the easiest: socialize puppies extensively to as wide a variety of people and dogs as possible. You cannot overdo it. Expose them to plenty of places, experiences, sights and sounds and make it all fun with praise, games and treats galore. Find and attend a positive reinforcement-oriented puppy class.

If you missed the boat socializing the puppy, you'll have to do remedial work with the adolescent or adult. Whatever your dog is spooky about must now become associated with lunch. This is how undersocialized dogs work for their food. If he doesn't like strangers, meals need to be given to him in the presence of strangers until he improves. If he's spooky about traffic, hand feed him his meals on the sidewalk, one handful each time a car passes. Start on quieter streets and progress to busier streets as he improves. It takes a while to improve spooky adults so be patient. Above all, prevent problems by blitzing it with puppies.

130

<u>Boredom Barking</u> If you don't have time for a dog, don't get a dog. If you have an outside dog, do whatever housetraining, chewtraining and manners training it takes to make him an inside dog. There are very few guarantees in behavior but one is surely this: dogs chained out in yards self-condition to bark, dig and/or lunge at passing stimuli. Boredom barking is just a symptom of gross understimulation. What's needed is a radical increase in interesting stuff in the dog's life. Increase training, walks, socialization and predatory games. Only when that is accomplished would you do a bark and quiet protocol as is described under watchdog barking.

Jumping Up

A classic culture clash example is greeting rituals: in most human cultures, we shake hands or bow. In dog culture, they buzz around excitedly, lick and sniff each other. The origin of jumping up is in infancy. Wolf pups will jump up to lick the corners of adults' mouths, triggering the latter to regurgitate food that the puppies can eat. This jumping up and licking is retained into adulthood as a greeting ritual. It's extremely common in dogs though its root has faded: only a minority of adults regurgitate. Greeting may become exaggerated when dogs live with humans because the social group is continually being fractured, then reunited: we leave and come back a lot, necessitating constant broad rituals. We're also vertical: the dog wants to get at our face. We also tend to let tiny puppies get away with it and then change the rules when they grow larger.

The main reason dogs jump is that no one has taught them to do otherwise. I'm not talking about punishments like kneeing dogs, pinching their feet or cutting off their air with a strangle collar. This sort of abuse has been the prevailing "treatment" but is inhumane and laden with side-effects. Imagine yourself being kneed in the diaphragm or pushed over backwards for smiling or extending your hand in friendship. It's not the fault of dogs that their cultural norm is at odds with our greeting preferences.

131

The key to training dogs not to jump up is to strongly train an alternative behavior that is mutually exclusive to jumping. The dog cannot jump up and sit at the same time. Nor can he dig through walls while working on a chew toy, lie on a mat and annoy dinner guests, or hold eye contact while chasing cars. The applications of this technique - DRI (differential reinforcement of an incompatible behavior, or "operant counterconditioning") - are limitless.

The same logic applies to child rearing. Rather than simply punishing toddlers for throwing Wedgwood off the coffee table and again for writing on the walls with magic markers and then once more for putting a pencil in the dog's ear, we give them things to occupy them and keep the Wedgwood out of reach till they're trustworthy. The message is "please color in your coloring book," "be gentle with Buffy," "watch Sesame Street," or "play Nintendo" rather than a never-ending series of "don't." It is a given that children need something to pass their time or else they're going to get into trouble, and it's exactly the same with dogs. Dogs are also much more likely than kids to guess wrong about what are appropriate pastimes and ways to behave around humans because they are an even more foreign species than two year-old kids are. Which is saying something.

The behavior you choose as your competing behavior must be one that physically cannot occur at the same time. Don't teach barking to replace pawing at the dinner table; it will probably result in a dog who now solicits food with barks. Instead, teach down-stay away from the table instead. You often have to practice the new behavior to a reliable level in a few training sessions before trying to bring it into real-life context. In the case of a strong compulsion like jumping up, the dog should have at least a rudimentary sit and stay before attempting to use this to pre-empt it. So, first practice sit-stay for food reinforcement in a variety of locations, especially those places where the jump-ups take place such as the front door area and on the street. Details on how to teach cues are in chapter six. When the dog is an ace at sit-stay in low distraction, you will now teach him to sit in real life contexts, using both treats and facial proximity (i.e. bend) to reinforce successes.

Food Stealing

Dogs are programmed to be opportunistic: if it's edible and within reach, hell, eat it as fast as possible. This is annoying to most people and, in some cases, dangerous. Operant counterconditioning is the technique of choice. Let's look at jumping on the kitchen counter when food is being prepared. The only priming necessary would be a fast session or two of down-stay on a designated mat in the kitchen; then go ahead and train during meal-preparation times for subsequent sessions. The first few would be extended preparation times - because you're training - but worth it. The dog learns that the best way to score a tidbit is to hold position. Reinforce every two or three seconds the first few trials, then every five, ten, twenty, thirty and so on. You can use his own dinner. It sure beats giving it to him for free in a bowl. Every time he leaves the mat, pin a no-reward mark ("oh, too bad!") on it, then prompt him back to the mat. Beware of building a pattern of the dog breaking in order to get you to prompt him back to the mat in order to get reinforced. Lower criteria – reduce duration – if you get more than a couple of mistakes in a row.

The timing of no-reward marks makes a big difference in how quickly you'll make progress. Catching him after he has risen, left the mat and walked several steps is light-years behind catching the first muscle contraction or intention to break the stay. An experienced trainer can do this while do a reasonable job preparing the meal. A green trainer will need to budget a lot of attention on the dog. This is why, for a few days, meal preparation times will be extended. The dog learns: if he breaks the stay he'll be put back anyway but if he *holds* the stay he is reinforced. When the dog has it down, he will stay the entire meal preparation time for his one reinforcer at the end. A good investment.

You may need, after this initial bout of training, to add a sting if the dog makes a go for the counter when you leave the room. Bear in mind that there is no big agenda on the part of the dog: he's simply learning the safe-dangerous discrimination, just as we learn the safe-dangerous speed-trap discrimination when driving on the highway. You will only make yourself miserable if you agonize about him "knowing" that it's "wrong" etc. Teach him that it never works to try going up on the counter. To achieve this, it really helps to catch the first down-stay break when you're absent. So, rather than having him spontaneously spring the behavior on you when you're not ready with your very best timing, spring it on *him* by setting him up. Once your down-stay on the mat is nicely conditioned, deliberately leave something tempting on the counter and exit the room nonchalantly. But you're spying, you're ready, you're Clint Eastwood saying: "Make my day." As soon as the dog contracts a muscle to leave the mat, give the no-reward mark and re-prompt your down. If you do this a couple of times, the dog simply incorporates the clause that Big Brother is always watching so his best chance of scoring reinforcement is by staying on the mat whether you're in the room or not.

The dog will not generalize your kitchen counter regime to hors d'oeuvres on the coffee table, ice-cream cones in kids' hands etc. so be prepared to work these a bit too. Each successive "grab attempts don't work" lesson will come more and more easily as the tasks are similar.

It's perplexing to trainers the way many dog owners wait until they have an entrenched problem before doing anything. The reason is the misguided expectation that "good" dogs don't do things like steal food or jump up. This thinking has to go. It is a cultural norm for dogs to engage in many of our most despised behavior "problems" and therefore the onus is on us to educate dogs.

TOP TEN PREDICTABLE BEHAVIORS OWNERS CONSIDER PROBLEMS YET RARELY DO ANY PREVENTIVE TRAINING FOR

1) Pulling on leash

2) Jumping up to greet

3) Indiscriminate chewing of all matter

4) Eating any food within reach ("food stealing")

5) Distress vocalizing when socially isolated or freedom restricted

6) Interest in members of own species

7) Cannot be handled or groomed easily

8) Fear of strangers/biting strangers

9) Resource guarding

10) Chasing and biting moving objects/rough play with children

Chapter Five
Lemon Brains
But We Still Love Them
How Dogs Learn

Everything you would ever want to know about how dogs learn has been available for decades in the countless papers and books on the topics of operant and classical conditioning in animals. It is astounding how little use has been made of this information in an arena of such obvious direct application: dog training. It's not simply an example of the predictable lag between scientific understanding and practical application of theory, either: many dog trainers are at least *fifty years* behind. Partly, it's that the love affair between dog owners and Walt Disney has been too tight to allow behaviorism in. We've been clinging to the wish that dogs just might have big, convoluted melon brains like humans, and have a natural desire to please. The fact of the matter is dogs have little, smoothish lemon brains and are looking out for number one. I personally still like them.

The resistance to adopting flat out behaviorism in obedience methods is also partly due to the reality that existing training models have, with all their weaknesses, enabled a sufficiency of dog owners to muddle through with a species that is relatively easy to train. Marine mammal trainers, by contrast, have had no choice but to adopt more sophisticated training methods because their subjects won't tolerate the abuse dogs do. Yet another reason behind the reticence of most dog trainers to bone up on behaviorism is that it is not necessarily easy to translate all that theory and knowledge about rats and pigeons in perfectly controlled environments to basset hounds coming reliably on cue. Every obedience school has tales of psychiatrists and people with PhD's in psychology who are unable to get their Labrador to down-stay in class.   Evidently, frowning about "dominance" is a lot simpler.

Operant conditioning is, quite literally, the conditioning of operants. Conditioning just means strengthening. An operant is a class or category of behavior, like "sitting" or "grabbing laundry" or "biting people." Operants get stronger through conditioning the same way muscles get stronger through physical conditioning. When the dog sits at any given instant, it's called a "response," an individual example of the operant "sitting." An individual response in weight training is usually called a "rep" or repetition.   One instance of a response plus reinforcer or of a cue plus response plus reinforcer or of a boo-boo is called a "trial." A series of (usually 5 – 10) trials is called a "set." A series of sets on any one occasion is called a "session."

So, if you're conditioning an operant, you're making it stronger: raising its probability or frequency of occurrence by reinforcing responses. If a dog gets a cookie whenever he sits, the operant "sitting" gets stronger and becomes more probable. There isn't a magical moment where the dog has a flash of insight and "knows" sit. This is where people need to start revising their thinking. The dog either has a strong sit, weak sit or perhaps nonexistent sit. Training changes probabilities; it doesn't transmit "knowledge." Your quadriceps doesn't "know" or understand that the weight lifting has the goal of making it stronger, it gets conditioned through training. And, remember, this doesn't make the dog an input-output machine or any less an important member of your family. It is simply the best model to explain how he learns. It's also one of the principle ways we learn too. Operant conditioning is like a window of communication between species.

Operant conditioning also encompasses the use of aversive stimuli to change response probabilities.   Aversives are things that motivate by signaling to the animal impending injury or death. I've grown wearier and wearier over the years of the rhetoric in support of the everyday use of aversives in dog training, and will not elaborate here on comments made in earlier chapters regarding their routine use.

Classical conditioning is the strengthening of the predictive power of something that previously had none by consistently putting it ahead of something else, usually something important. Tip offs to important events, both good and nasty, allow animals to prepare themselves for the inevitable. Contrast this with operant conditioning, where animals can *change* what happens by responding in a certain way.

For example, food has intrinsic meaning to dogs, as it does to all animals. Cookie jars have no meaning on their own. Dogs quickly learn that the sight and sound of cookie jars predict cookies. The same phenomenon explains why dogs get excited when you put your coat on and take the leash out of the cupboard, or get depressed when you put on your coat and grab your briefcase.

Dog training always incorporates elements of both kinds of conditioning. Because behavior is under the control of its consequences, we deliberately manipulate consequences to control the dog's behavior. Operant conditioning. Because we are invested in whether dogs like rather than fear or dislike certain things, we try to make them predictive of goodies. Classical conditioning. If all of the preceding seems too tricky, don't worry. You don't need a perfect understanding of learning and motivation to train dogs, although the more you know, the easier it is to train. You do need to drop some of your baggage like "he knows, he's just stubborn/mad/too excited/the wrong breed etc." and start thinking like a trainer. You also don't need to be a forceful, dominant personality the dog will "respect." You just need to know a few of the basic rules.

Important Rules to Know

1) Dogs do whatever works (behavior is under the control of its consequences: law of effect)

2) There are four kinds of consequences:

    1 - good thing starts (positive reinforcement)
    2 - good thing ends (negative punishment)
    3 - bad thing starts (positive punishment)
    4 - bad thing ends   (negative reinforcement)

3) All these consequences must be immediate

4) The good and bad consequences will end up being associated with other things present at the moment of the consequence as well as affecting the probability of the behavior: these are the classical "side effects" of operant conditioning

5) Dogs are experts at reading the environment to know which consequences are likely for which behaviors in any given situation

Let's look at these rules as they apply to dog training.

Obedience Training

Because behavior is under the control of its consequences, obedience training is about providing consequences to the dog. Life is a never-ending series of: "If you do this, this happens, if you do that, another thing happens." There are two kinds of things that happen in life, good things and bad things, so there are four kinds of consequences: good stuff can 1) start and 2) end; bad stuff can 1) start and 2) end. Your dog is constantly trying to start the good stuff, end the bad stuff, avoid ending the good stuff, and avoid starting the bad stuff. He's playing his entire environment, including you, this way. If you can recognize this and exploit it, voila! Control of the dog.

As it happens, you have tremendous control of the starting and stopping of all the good and bad stuff in your dog's life. You simply may not have been making much use of it. You may be insufficiently aware of what the "good stuff" and "bad stuff" are and may be inadvertently installing through conditioning exactly what you don't want, as well as missing valuable opportunities. You might even feel that your dog's controlling you. This is because your behavior is governed by the same principles. You want to start good stuff, end bad stuff, avoid ending good stuff, and avoid starting bad stuff. Every living organism with a brain stem is doing this. And, because the dog provides consequences too, you may come under doggie control. Brings new meaning to the term "dog trainer." Luckily, you have the bigger brain and can get one step ahead of this game by boning up on operant conditioning. Your dog can't. So read on.

You have control of your dog's access to everything he wants in life: food, the outside world, attention, other dogs, smells on the ground, play opportunities. You can make toys come to life by throwing them or initiating tug games. You have opposable thumbs that can open doors and cans. A lot of people don't make any use of this. A lot of people recognize this but expect the dog's obedience out of some sort of gratitude: because they are providing all these things, they expect obedience in return. The system only works, however, if you make the dog do his part of the bargain first *in each and every exchange.* This means that feeding him faithfully for a week, taking him for walks rain or shine, and providing exercise and games every day has little bearing on whether he will return the favor by walking through doors nicely or coming when called in the park. You must arrange it so it appears to the dog that, whenever he wants park privileges to continue or the front door to open, he must do obedience first. Always make the dog do his part of the bargain first, then provide your end. The dog will see obedience as the way to get things he wants, rather than something that is interfering with getting him what he wants.

Take control of the goodies the dog wants in life - stop always handing them out for free. Nothing is "free" anyway: you are always reinforcing something when you open doors, put din-din down, initiate walkies or play sessions, or let him out of his crate.

141

This is because the dog is always doing something and that something gets reinforced whenever one of the goodies is initiated. All you're going to do now is become aware of this process and select the behavior to reinforce rather than simply reinforcing whatever the dog happens to be doing at that second. You must also be prepared to withhold reinforcement if the dog doesn't comply. Put your money where your mouth is.

Reinforcers tend to become more potent after a period of deprivation: hungry dogs work harder for food than satiated dogs, dogs who haven't been out for a while are more eager for the walk to begin, etc. A common example is the urgency with which dogs seek to make social contact with other dogs on the street. The majority of domestic dogs live relatively socially-deprived lives, especially when it comes to their own species. When trainers deliberately use deprivation to increase motivation it is an example of what's known as an "establishing operation." Food is established as a reinforcer through deprivation. When trainers really need maximum motivation, they will "close the economy," i.e. not provide *any* nutritive reinforcement for free. This applies to us as well. For most people, a huge gourmet meal is an enticing reinforcer. Think now for a minute about how you feel about a huge gourmet meal presented within minutes of overeating at Thanksgiving, or when you have the stomach flu. Food in this context is not motivating and may even be an aversive. And, just as food must be established as a primary reinforcer, signals like clickers and praise must be established as secondary reinforcers. Establishing operations are like pre-training measures to make sure training will be effective.

Dogs and humans learn to recognize when any given good or bad consequence is likely because, naturally, different situations call for different behavioral strategies: environmental clues let you know when any given behavior is likely to be successful. Putting money into drink machines will get you a soft drink. Putting money into garbage cans doesn't. Putting money into slot machines usually gets you nothing but occasionally gets you something and, rarely,

142

gets you something really, really good. So, humans put money into soft drink machines, never put money into garbage cans and may get addicted to slot machines, sometimes putting in their life savings. Your ability to discriminate between a soft drink machine and a garbage can enables you to be successful with your coin-inserting behavior. "Successful," in animal learning terms, means that the behavior was reinforced. It turned on something good or turned off something bad. In other words, it worked. Behavior that works gets stronger. This is a law that applies to all animals. It's a law like gravity: apples fall down, reinforced behavior increases in frequency. This is the essence of dog training - memorize it. All that has to be accomplished is to teach the dog "if you do this, this happens, if you do that, that other thing happens" and how he can recognize which flow-chart is operative at any given time.

Behavior as Experiment

The environment is training the dog all the time, expertly. Sofas reinforce dogs for lying on them by being warmer and more comfortable than the floor. Sofa-jumping goes up in probability. Squirrels reinforce dogs by fleeing. He's more likely to do it again tomorrow if he comes upon a squirrel. If the dog moves towards a mailbox it doesn't flee, so that behavior never gets rolling. If the dog stares at the fridge it never opens, so he doesn't do it for long, even though it's where all the good food is kept. The behavior dies: it doesn't work. Neither does scratching on the fridge. It may be done as an experiment but it probably will die quickly unless it works. Staring at the owner when he's eating sometimes works, so that behavior lives. If he scratches at the back door, a human opens it. That behavior works, so it will live to occur again tomorrow or the next day. If it keeps working it gets stronger and stronger until it plateaus out at some elevated frequency. This is not simply anybody's opinion: this is a law.

An important thing to understand is that the dog is not working this out logically in his head: "hey, maybe he'll give me some sandwich

143

if I look hungry enough" any more than he thinks "hey, maybe the sofa will give me some warm and comfy if I jump on it and lie down." The dog will do whatever works. If putting one paw over the other and sighing while lying in the bathtub got him bits of sandwich, he'd do that instead of staring. Dog behavior is like a never-ending experiment. Zillions of hypotheses are thrown out every day, such as rushing mailboxes, staring at fridge doors, scratching fridge doors, and coming when called. The animal's hypothesis list – the behaviors they will be inclined to try in various situations - is influenced and constrained by genetics. Cows never try chasing squirrels and dogs never (okay, rarely) try munching hay.

When a tried behavior dies from lack of reinforcement, it's called extinction. Extinctions like mailbox chasing, fridge door food soliciting and coming when called happen so fast that the owner is usually unaware that the dog is even trying anything out. It's all extremely efficient and highly organized: no animal on Earth would have evolved by continually wasting time in dead end behaviors, behaviors that didn't somehow contribute to keeping him alive to reproduce and pass on his learning ability.

This is usually where "what about desire to please..." crops up. We really need to put this one to bed once and for all. Although praise can function as a reinforcer for many dogs, especially when there is absolutely nothing else around to compete with it, the human obsession with trying to use it as the exclusive motivator gets in the way of training dogs. Normal, trainable dogs have been marginalized and needlessly punished as a result of human weakness for the DTP thing. It bogs down our brains when we need every brain cell we've got to train correctly, so let's get over it. Your dog is a magnificent example of his species without this.

Hard-Wired vs. Installed Behavior

A few behaviors are hard-wired, requiring little or no learning to be carried out to their fullest: dogs chase and bite moving objects,

144

distress vocalize when alone, go for any available food, compulsively greet all novel people and dogs, bury things, pee away from their sleeping area, etc. without conditioning histories. The rest of their behavior is the product of contingencies in the environment. Owners have nearly total control of their dogs' environments: where they live and sleep, if and when they may go outside and which limited pockets of the galaxy they may visit, when, where and what they eat, if and when they will ever see a member of their own species, the nature of their toys and activities, and even whether they live or die. Owners who feel like slaves to their dogs need to understand this. You have total control; you've just never demonstrated it to your dog. It's we humans who have the opposable thumbs, the big, convoluted melon brains and the roomfuls of information on animal learning and motivation. Lemon-brain can't help but get trained.

As it happens, most of the behaviors that we want to tone down come hard-wired. We must replace, finesse or redirect chasing, rough play, distress vocalizing, eating whatever is in reach, etc. And, most of the behaviors we *want* to install – sit, down, stay, come, heel (all on cue) - don't come with the package, and are useless, silly and irrelevant behaviors from the perspective of these social predators. That is, unless you make it worth their while. The way you do this is to get the little dumpling motivated. Compile a list of all the things he wants in life - it's a finite list for any dog - and start using these as prizes the dog wins by providing you with correct responses, by being obedient. This means no more free food, attention, walkies, dog-dog play etc. This is an attitude shift for the owner: rather than relying on a built-in desire to please (which doesn't exist in the first place), you are now proceeding to *build* motivation by exploiting your control of the dog's environment. Once he's a believer, once you have proven to him that he must play his cards right with you in order to get all the Important Stuff For Dogs, he will look like he has desire to please. Not because you're wonderful, although you may very well be, or because he worships you, but because it's in his own interest to please you. It's how he gets what he wants. Everybody wins.

Once this attitude shift is done, you need just two things, in this order: 1) a way to communicate to the dog how he's doing on winning the prizes, and 2) teaching and naming all the different things he has to do. This process is done absolutely backwards by hack-trainers. They start trying to name behaviors (i.e., give cues) they haven't yet conditioned, and in an animal who's not even playing the game yet, i.e. no motivation.

The dog, when presented with a signal like the word "sit," first must identify whether the signal means anything and then, very important, work out whether doing the behavior is a good use of scarce energy. To make this call, he'll consider whether this behavior has worked in the past, and the cost-benefit in terms of effort expended performing the action and likelihood and value of the prize compared to the other current behavioral options and their respective prizes. Dogs do not, of course, perform statistical analyses in their heads, but they behave exactly as though they do (so, maybe they do). There is a behavioral efficiency mechanism in animals that ensures they will, most of the time, engage in behaviors that work to their net benefit.

The difference between someone who knows about training and someone who doesn't can be summarized most easily as follows. Answer the question: "What makes a trained dog sit?" Someone who doesn't know about training thinks "the command" makes the dog sit whereas someone who knows about training would answer that the prior history of reinforcement for sitting makes the dog sit. The "command" is merely a signal, which is why we call them cues.

So, how does it all work? First, let's review the reinforcers we've been wasting on a daily basis.

Things That Are Likely Reinforcers for Dogs

- ✓ Food
- ✓ Access to other dogs: investigation and play[8]
- ✓ Access to outdoors and interesting smells on ground
- ✓ Attention from people and access to people, especially after isolation periods
- ✓ Initiation of play or other enjoyed activity: fetch, cuddling, tug of war, keep away

Those are the big five, although individual dogs will have other exploitable quirks. Like most reinforcers, these are always more potent after periods of deprivation. All you need to train a dog is to get control of his favorites and start doling them out only when he does what you want. If the dog is keen on all these things or extremely keen on a couple in particular, he's an easier dog to train than one who is extremely laid back and not very into any of them. Yet, most pet owners would love to have the latter dog, who doesn't food steal, is never excited around other dogs, doesn't sniff the ground on a walk or pull on leash towards the park or dog run, doesn't jump on people, never distress vocalizes when alone, doesn't steal laundry or bug you to pat him all the time. Very hard dog to train though. He doesn't want any of the prizes you're offering, so why should he play your game?

Contrast such a dog with the prototypical, adolescent golden retriever who immediately consumes any organic matter he comes across on the coffee table, ground or gutter as though he had never eaten, gives you a rotator cuff injury when he sees another dog

---

[8] Sex is, of course, right up there, and from an evolutionary perspective, the reason there is a dog in the first place - to move genes through time - but is too clunky to dispense for much incorporation into training

across the street, knocks you over when you come home from work, urinates on guests from sheer excitement, chronically leans against you and paws you until you wear the fur on his head thin from stroking, and grabs your kid's stuffed animals so you'll chase him all over the house. This is the dream dog for trainers. You've got his number. Explain to this dog, through training, that there are now new ways to obtain all that stuff, and then watch the dog fall into line. Trainers love reinforcer-junkie dogs. Dogs that are hot for moving object type reinforcers (tug and fetch junkies) are called "drivey" or "high drive" dogs. Trainers love these guys especially, though they rev rather high for pet owners.

In most practical training, we do the bulk of the reps with one or two easily dispensed reinforcers, notably food and tug toys, and use the rest as consolidators when they crop up in normal day-to-day living. This is because the access to other dogs, attention after absences, and many of the other motivators are hard to recycle repeatedly for the multiple trials necessary for efficient installation of behaviors. But be aware of them and use them when the opportunity arises because 1) they are potent, 2) varying motivation gives a stronger response, 3) what a waste not to, 4) it will make you train under a wider range of circumstances and 5) it will ensure you're not inadvertently reinforcing some other naughty behavior with these things. You will become conscious. For example, you can train sit for a cookie all you want, but if jumping up gains attention and facial proximity when guests arrive, your sit will not kick in in that situation. You must make the attention and greeting contingent on sitting.

Feedback: Formal Conditioned Reinforcer

To train well, you need a communication system, ways of telling the dog the exact instant when he has gained something good and ended something good. Signals are important because 1) the timing has to be so precise, and 2) sometimes we want to reinforce or punish (non-violently, i.e. by ending something good) behaviors at a distance. The reinforcement signal is called a conditioned reinforcer or bridging stimulus. The conditioned reinforcer is so named because it becomes associated with the real ("unconditioned") reinforcement through classical conditioning. It's sometimes called a bridging stimulus because it bridges the time gap between the behavior you liked and the actual reinforcement. It's like saying to a child: "This report card has earned you a fudge sundae!" The link between the sundae and the report card and even the hard work for the grades that got the good report card is made hours or more later. Dogs are nowhere near the league of kids when it comes to making these links. With dogs, you have to provide the real reinforcement, the piece of liver, as soon as physically possible after the signal "that sit earned you a treat," otherwise other intervening behaviors will be reinforced by the liver and your signal will start to lose its charge.

The signal you choose marks the behavior you wish to reinforce. Many trainers use clickers as reinforcement markers, rather than words or phrases like "good" or "yes," because the clicker is a very brief, crisp, consistent and distinctive sound whereas a word or phrase will always have small variations in intonation and volume, not to mention all kinds of pre-existing associated baggage. Words like "good" and "yes" also come up in regular conversation and thus may lose some of their charge. A clicker is basically a children's toy that fits easily into the palm of your hand and makes a cricket noise when you press the mobile part. The occasional dog will be spooked initially by the sound of the clicker but this is far from a prohibitive obstacle. The trainer can gradually desensitize the dog by muffling the sound with either layers of fabric or distance, and then reduce these as the dog gets used to the sound and as it gains strength through its predictive ability. There are also now softer sounding clickers available. The clicker itself is not supposed to be inherently reinforcing; remember, it's what it will come to *mean* that counts. It is certainly worth persevering with spooky dogs because of the timing advantage that clickers give to your training.

Charge your clicker by giving the dog a series of reinforcers always preceded by the click. Click-treat, click-treat, click-treat. Vary the interval between pairings. The click will become a PREDICTOR for the dog of the treat. For this reason, make sure the click always comes *before* the treat and make sure the click is always followed by the treat. Otherwise it is not a reliable predictor. In fact, it may lose predictive value if you always commence reaching for the treat before or during the click. The goal is for the click to be the very best tip-off that reinforcement is about to be dispensed. One way to commence clicker charging is to hand-feed the dog a couple of meals, one kibble at a time, or use tiny dog treats like sliced hot dogs or freeze-dried liver. If you want a powerful charge on the clicker, vary the reinforcer it precedes: sometimes it's kibble, sometimes it's cheese, sometimes it's a walk, sometimes it's a tummy-rub, sometimes it's liver, sometimes a new chew toy. Make this association dozens of times.

At this stage of the game you're not training any behaviors. In fact, you're deliberately refraining from training any behaviors, and this may take some care. The reason is that, as soon as the click gets any charge at all, you will be reinforcing something every time you click. There's a real risk that the dog might self-train to do some odd thing like take a step backwards if this got reinforced by chance a couple of times by the click-treat. He then might start doing it more and more. The next thing you know, the dog behaves as though the backwards step is *necessary* to get the click to happen. It's called superstitious learning and happens frequently in day-to-day dog training.

The efficiency of behavior will work for you in the long run. If you want to minimize the risk of getting anything too trained in while you charge up your conditioned reinforcer, make a conscious attempt to randomly vary the behavior occurring at the time of the click in those early charge-up sessions. This isn't easy because "looking at the trainer" behavior will quickly get conditioned. This is not such a bad bit of baggage though so you may want to let it

150

get rolling. The dog will, however, have to get unhooked from it if ever you train something requiring him to stop looking at you.

You will also want to vary the time interval between click-treat instances as well as between the click and treat. Varying the time between click-treat trials is insurance that you're not being too predictable. It is easy to fall into a rut of doing click-treat trials every 5.8 seconds and the dog will tune in to this. If he does, the clicker is no longer the sole predictor of the treat - the time interval is (an example of overshadowing) - and so is not as well charged. You want the click to be the only thing the dog has to go on that he's about to get the treat. Varying the lag between the click and the treat in an individual trial helps the dog better tolerate lags later when you're employing the clicker as a feedback tool. It's like saying to the dog: "Don't worry, even if you don't get it in half a second, it's still on the way." Do this within limits, especially early on, because you are trying to make the click a reliable predictor of food. Other things to vary include your body posture, orientation vis à vis the dog and the distance between you and the dog. This is easily accomplished by wandering around as you randomly click and give or throw treats to the dog.

The most efficient way to get the dog clicker conditioned is to do a couple of sessions of ten minutes each, perhaps in different locations and separated in time by twenty-four hours. The twenty-four hours canonic break between training sessions is more to guarantee a period of sleep between than to achieve that time period per se. Usually by the end of the second session – and often the start - the dog will demonstrate an "expectant look" when you click and/or charge you to collect his prize. Now you can start using it as a tool. When you use the clicker as a tool, you still provide a primary whenever you click. To not do so teaches the dog that the click is not a good predictor anymore. This is like a battery losing its charge. Remember, there is nothing inherently reinforcing about the click, or about a praise word: it must remain associated with the real reinforcer.

151

And, if you are reinforcing established behavior on an intermittent schedule – let's say, one out of five times - you click only on the trials you will be dispensing a tangible reinforcer on. The click-treat relationship is a classical one, where there are no "schedules," only partial/weaker conditioning. The intermittent schedule concerns numbers of behavior per reinforcer (click/treat pair). The click and treat are an inseparable pair.

Feedback: Low-grade Reinforcers

In formal animal training such as marine mammal training or conditioning exotics in zoos to facilitate their handling for medical or maintenance purposes, the use of conditioned and primary reinforcers is pretty well all that is used. In dog training, this is the most important feedback tool but there are others as well. This is where praise comes into its own. It can function as a signal to the dog that he is *on the right track* towards getting a click and primary. It can "prop up" a long duration behavior in order to increase tolerance of duration between primaries, as well as allowing faster gains in parameters like distance, distraction-proofing and multiple-choice behaviors. Dogs do learn that praise means they are "getting warmer."

Shaping

Shaping was discussed in the section on retrieving so I will reiterate just the main points here. Every animal and person has a repertoire of behaviors that they have performed at least once. If any of the behaviors in this repertoire are reinforced they will start increasing in probability. This is the foundation of training. However, some behaviors we would like to have our dogs do are never offered. These behaviors are described as not occurring "at the operant level." There are never any responses to reinforce. In cases like this, it becomes necessary to build the behavior from scratch by using shaping. Here's an example.

Lying down is a behavior that does occur at the operant level in dogs. To train it, simply click and treat when the dog lies down and the dog will start doing this more and more often. When it is occurring with great and predictable frequency, you may add a cue to the process to increase control over when the dog does and does not perform a "down." Although you could opt use a prompt such as a food lure to obtain instances of down, you could simply wait for spontaneous occurrences, which will sooner or later occur. All dogs lie down.

Spinning in a tight left circle is a behavior that tends not to occur at the operant level in dogs. There is no use waiting for it so that you can click and reinforce it when you see it. The dog never gives you one. If you'd like to condition it, it is necessary to first reinforce some *approximation* of the behavior that does occur at the operant level. In other words, what's the closest thing the dog is already doing at least occasionally? This may be a head or body turn toward the left. Select such a behavior by clicking and reinforcing it whenever you see it. When it goes way up in frequency there will inevitably be variations that the dog does which are an even better approximation of a tight left circle. So, start selecting those for reinforcement. This gradual raising of the standard until, sooner or later, you are reinforcing your original target behavior is called shaping. Shaping is a skill that takes a great deal of practice.

Reinforcement Schedules

Up to now, we've been talking as though every correct response is reinforced with a click and a treat. This is because, if you're a good trainer, in the early history of any behavior, you can and should reinforce every instance of the behavior you're trying to install. Each reinforcer, in early training, is a valuable piece of information to the dog on what it is you are after. Failure to select an example of the behavior (i.e. not reinforcing it) goes toward creating doubt in the dog: is that what you want or not? Reinforcing the behavior over and over makes the trend emerge more readily. Each and

153

every time he lies down, for instance, he is reinforced. Lying down must be the target behavior.

Later on, however, things are different. When the behavior plateaus out in frequency, you can stop reinforcing the behavior each and every time it occurs. Try reinforcing most, then half, then sometimes. The dog is absolutely sure now that this is the target behavior, so withholding reinforcement does not make him change strategies immediately. It is, therefore, now, safe to start withholding. This intermittent reinforcing of an operant is called putting the behavior on a "reinforcement schedule." The reasons for doing this are:

1) behavior on an intermittent schedule is more resilient – harder to extinguish
2) it facilitates the shaping process
3) you get more for your money

Resistance to extinction goes like this: If an animal is too used to getting reinforced every time, there will be an abrupt, behavior-crushing contrast when reinforcement ceases. The behavior goes into extinction; it stops happening because reinforcement has stopped. By contrast, if the animal is used to not being reinforced every time, it will take a lot longer for him to "notice" that reinforcement has ceased. The most common analogy is the comparison of soft drink machines and slot machines. You expect reinforcement in the form of a drink every time you put money into the soft drink machine. If the machine stops producing drinks, you will not put money in more than a couple of times before your money inserting behavior extinguishes and you try another strategy, such as calling some authority or body-slamming the machine (arguably an extinction burst rather than a "strategy").

When you play a slot machine, however, the rules are different. You expect to not be reinforced every time and so put money in again and again in the hopes that the next one will be the one that is reinforced with a winning combination. The programming of slot

154

machines has been done with the laws governing reinforcement in mind: schedules of reinforcement designed to maximize money inserting behavior per reinforcing payoff are always used. People can actually get addicted to them because human nervous systems are subject to the laws of learning. And, so are dogs'. This means, once a behavior is acquired, you have the option of putting it on a schedule if for no other reason than to obtain this resilience to extinction.

Reinforcement schedules can sometimes facilitate the shaping process when you feel stuck at a level without much variation from which to select the next criteria level. Let's say you're shaping the dog to open the refrigerator door. One of your goals may be to get the dog to grasp the handle of the fridge in his jaws. This isn't happening at the operant level so you decide to shape it. You click and treat every time the dog approaches the fridge, inching him closer and closer until he's walking directly to the fridge over and over again. You start orienting his nose to the door handle and start getting the occasional nose prod. Then you hit a nose prod plateau. He nose prods again and again in a stereotypic way, offering no variations that are any closer to nibbling or biting. This is where the schedule comes in. You start reinforcing every second or third nose prod, then every third or fourth. The dog, as though trying to discover what you like about the particular nose prods you are reinforcing, experiments with variations on the nose prod theme. The frustration of not being reinforced every time can even lead to faster and more vigorous responses, like a mini extinction burst. Now you have something to choose from and you can inch him toward more vigorous prods, nibbling and eventually grasping the handle in his mouth.

When you use a variable schedule to vary behavior, by the way, the dog, trainer and third-party observers might, if interviewed, have completely different conceptions about what the current criteria for reinforcement is. This is because during the transition from old to new criteria, the old behavior will "feel like" it's on an intermittent schedule and the new behavior will "feel like" it's getting

155

continuously reinforced. This is why trainers have so often heard the maxim "put the behavior on a schedule before raising criteria." This happens automatically, actually, if the trainer does not put the old level on a schedule but selects new criteria from among (varied) behaviors the dog is already offering at the old level. It's when variability is lacking at the old level that the trainer consciously puts the behavior on a ratio.

The third reason to consider employing reinforcement schedules is obvious: you get more for your buck. Rather than getting one sit for one treat, why not have an obedience routine lasting several minutes for one treat? There is a breaking point at which the schedule of reinforcement gets too "thin" and behavior tends to fall apart. Sometimes this has to do with the type of reinforcement schedule used and sometimes it is simply biological mathematics.

Schedules in Dog Training

There are four main kinds of intermittent reinforcement schedules. These are: Fixed Interval (FI), Fixed Ratio (FR), Variable Interval (VI) and Variable Ratio (VR). An animal whose behavior is on an interval style schedule has an opportunity for reinforcement every X amount of time on the clock. Ratio schedules provide reinforcement for every X number of discrete instances of a behavior. Knowledge about interval schedules and their features is good for doing well on undergraduate animal learning courses but not as relevant in dog training. Ratio schedules, on the other hand, can come up with some regularity.

A fixed ratio reinforcement schedule means that the dog is reinforced every X number of instances he performs the behavior regardless of how long this takes. In real life, this is called piece-work, or commission: you get X amount of money for every fifty widgets you produce. A variable ratio reinforcement schedule provides reinforcement for every X number of correct responses *on average*. This means, when training paw raises on a VR5 schedule, the dog may get a click and treat after six paw raises, then after

156

two, then after four, then after eight, then after three and so on. A variable ratio schedule produces a steadier rate of responding than a fixed ratio schedule. Remember the nose prod plateau in fridge opening? Reinforcing the dog "every two or three" nose prods is an example of a VR2.5 schedule.

In dog training, we frequently use differential schedules. As soon as a behavior is put on the VR schedule, we select the best examples of the behavior for reinforcement. In fact, many of the things we train dogs to do are not all-or-nothing type behaviors. Sits, recalls and retrieves can be faster, straighter, cuter, better, or amid more challenging distractions. This permits the trainer to reinforce differentially and thus perpetually crank up the quality of performance. How stringent the criteria are on a differential schedule is a trainer's judgment call. The ideal is to obtain an optimal rate of improvement without ever losing the dog's interest.

Good trainers have a good sense of schedules as well as a good eye for reading how thin a schedule is appropriate for any given dog in any given training situation. This is part of the art of training. Before you can develop the art, however, be sure you are crystal clear on the science. This is exactly what has been lacking in traditional dog training.

The ability of intermittent schedules to maintain behavior has been co-opted by trainers in the trenches to help sell the concept of reinforcement to sometimes stingy owners ("when can I stop giving him so much FOOD"). The dangling carrot of "more for less" down the road might encourage premature and overly low rates of reinforcement that make everyone frustrated. My hope is that the prevailing culture will continue to loosen up about reinforcement, eventually to the point that trainers won't be painted into this corner quite so much.

Bob Bailey, who has trained thousands of animals of a dizzying array of species, and to an impressive level of reliability, has gone on record that intermittent schedules are not quite what they're

157

cracked up to be in applied operant conditioning. In fact, he and his training staff most often maintained behavior on continuous reinforcement! This is as credible a source as there is on the subject, so I'm extremely inclined to sit up and take notice.

Prompts

In dog training, we have the luxury of being able to work up close to the subject and this opens the door to a variety of shortcuts to obtaining the actions we wish to reinforce rather than simply waiting for them to happen. These shortcuts typically take the form of luring movements with our hands, food or toys, vocal enticement, use of targets, and physical placement with hands or leashes. Rather than simply waiting for the animal to do, or *emit,* the behavior you wish to reinforce, you coach or *prompt* him to do it. A prompt is anything which helps manufacture the behavior you are looking to reinforce. Clapping and crouching tend to make dogs approach, and so are often used to prompt recalls.

Perhaps the most valuable type of prompt in dog training is luring. Getting the dog to target a food treat with his nose is an example of luring. Once control of his head movement is thus obtained, an amazing amount of behavior can be manufactured. If the treat is moved up slightly and backwards the dog will probably sit in order to continue comfortably targeting. If, as you're sitting on the floor, the treat is drawn under your leg, the dog will probably lie down to continue targeting the treat through the tunnel created. If the treat is held at your hip the dog will probably walk at your side. To avoid the dog becoming dependent on the prompt, it's used sparingly – at most a few times in a row – and then faded gradually to a reduced version or else dropped outright.

Luring is infinitely preferable to old-style prompting, which consisted of clunky, coercive physical manipulation and leash tugs. Not only is it aversive to squish dogs into sits and downs, strangle them into heeling, and jerk them towards you with leashes to obtain approaches, the dog is made a passive victim of the training rather

158

than an active participant, and so learning is slower. It is furthermore more difficult to wean these kinds of prompts. We have Dr. Ian Dunbar to thank for spearheading a revolution in dog training that started in the 80s, away from pushing and pulling and toward these efficient prompt-fade methods.

Early training sequences of any behavior will be one of three patterns:

1) cue
2) prompt
3) response
4) reinforcement

1) prompt
2) response
3) reinforcement

1) response
2) reinforcement

Which one to use depends a lot on what you are trying to train. When you are employing behavior shaping as your technique, you will always use the last sequence because you cannot add the cue until you have shaped the behavior to its final incarnation. Although shaping is usually described in strict response-reinforcement terms, you may use prompts to initially elicit various rungs on your shaping ladder.

It is somewhat risky to use the first sequence, the one with the cue in it, because you are gambling that your prompt is going to work to produce the response. If it doesn't, you have a missed association. You have uttered the cue, but it failed to be associated with the behavior because your prompt didn't work. This whole area is very difficult for beginner trainers to understand. They are obsessed with "the command": the all-important one word maxim, the tone of voice to use, whether it should be a hand signal or

159

verbal, etc. The command is a red herring. In early training, you should have one obsession: the response-reinforcement part of the sequence. Obtain and reinforce the behavior as many times as possible. This is a terrific selling point for advocates of clicker training for beginners, by the way – reduce the number of tasks. Rather than demanding that a green trainer utter a cue ("once and ONLY ONCE"), prompt with some finesse and then deliver a well-timed click/treat, the neophyte only has to observe and deliver the click/treat.

Perhaps because it's a superior system, perhaps as compromise necessitated by the marketplace – "We want commands! We want commands!" – and perhaps because of the relative ease with which simple behaviors like sit or down can be successfully prompted, beginner classes featuring cue-prompt-reinforcement styles seem more prevalent than add-the-cue-later regimes. There is also some spirited debate among dog trainers regarding the relative merits of prompting at all vs. shaping without prompts. In fact, the mother of modern dog training, Karen Pryor, argues relentlessly to let the dog discover the behavior while Ian Dunbar, the father of modern dog training, advocates the use of lures for its elegant simplicity. Many trainers alternate and combine them depending on who is training whom to do what.

In any case, the eventual goal with any of these is to get the following sequence:

1) cue
2) response
3) reinforcement (intermittent optional)

In order to get to CRR (cue-response-reinforcement) using the first early-training sequence, all that must happen is for the prompt to be reduced until the dog responds to the cue only and for the final behavior, if the trainer wishes, to be put on a reinforcement schedule. To get to CRR when you have started training using the second sequence, you must, when the behavior is reliable enough,

160

add the cue at the front, fade the prompt and, if desired, put it on a schedule. With the third sequence, CRR is achieved by adding the cue before the behavior when the latter is highly likely to happen.

Prompts vs. Reinforcers

The most important thing to understand about prompts of any sort is that they are not an end in themselves: they are valuable because they manufacture reinforceable responses, which you *must* then reinforce. Missing this point is a very common and ruinous mistake. The trainer claps and backs away, the dog approaches, and the trainer thinks the recall is being trained. There is a very real possibility that the recall is actually being extinguished by this procedure. If the response is not reinforced, it will start to die. A good prompt will buy you a few responses but, in the long run, the behavior is conditioned by its consequence: did it get reinforced, yes or no? Owners constantly muddle the manufacturing of a response with the reinforcing of that response. The most important act is the reinforcing of the response, whether it occurred spontaneously or was obtained by prompting.

The reason reinforcers get lost in the shuffle is that prompting is so reinforcing for owners: it seems to work all by itself ("he did it!"). But it is not training: training is the manipulation of the *consequence* of the dog's actions. You must reinforce the individual response you create if you want to condition the operant. If you don't, your prompt will sooner or later become meaningless and cease to work. At that point you will probably switch prompts and maybe buy yourself a few more responses, but it is all for naught if you fail to reinforce those responses when you get them. I've seen countless people kill their recalls by exhausting every prompt in the universe and then announce that their dog is stubborn because he clearly "knows" how to come (after all, they witnessed those correct recalls the first time they used one of the prompts). This is an example of a technical problem being mistaken for evidence that some particular individual dog has a character defect. Remember, behavior is an experiment. Think of the prompt as a

161

suggestion to the dog ("this might work..."). You are only helping the cause if you prove to the dog that it *does* work. Some dogs will even stop targeting food lures if it is proven to them that the behavior doesn't work. Dogs are not obedient to prompts, cues or "commands"; they are obedient to the laws of learning.

Start planning a removal strategy - fading or dropping – for any prompt you use as soon as it's gotten the behavior a couple of times. For example, after luring a few sits or downs, make the gesture more stylized or even dare to do it empty-handed, immediately supplying a reinforcer from your other hand when he does it. Many trainers, in anticipation of this process, use as their choice of hand signals gestures that have some resemblance to the original prompt used to help install the behavior. Sit hand signals are sweeping motions up. Down signals sweep downward. Verbal cues are much harder to train because they have no relationship to the original manufacturing prompt and are thought to be less attended to by dogs than are hand signals and gestures.

In the case where the cue has been given before the prompt in early training, even if the prompt is not faded deliberately, a sufficient number of trials will usually result in anticipation: the dog "jumping the prompt" and performing the behavior as soon as he perceives the cue (the mechanism is classical conditioning). Once this becomes regular, you may start selectively reinforcing him for this type of performance and withholding reinforcement when you also have to prompt. The dog will tune in to this new contingency and become extremely attentive to the cue.

This process is not always cut and dried. Variations in training context will usually cause regressions. If the dog repeatedly fails to make the new standard (i.e., reinforced only for unprompted performances), you must drop the standard and prompt a few responses to get him back on track. If you don't drop the standard and let him win some reinforcers, he will lose interest or become frustrated. This willingness on your part to relax criteria goes for all training endeavors, by the way, not just prompt removal.

162

Whenever the dog seems to fall apart, don't agonize about whywhywhy, simply drop the standard temporarily so that the dog has a reasonable chance at succeeding at being reinforced again. This keeps him in the game. You will be able to get up to your previous standard and beyond in no time if you are disciplined and drop criteria. If you don't drop the standard, sooner or later you will end up with a dog who dislikes training and would rather do anything else. Remember, the environment is competing with you for your dog's behavioral dollar: he will play the best game in town.

One useful trick for thinking about micro (small shift) criteria in the thick of training is to ask yourself this question between trials: "Do I need a winner or a loser?" Do you want to push criteria up slightly on the next trial, stick with the same as the last trial or drop? If the dog quits after two losers – two unreinforced trials – drop after one loser. If the dog can tolerate more losers in a row, you can stick for longer without losing the dog (whether you should just because you can is a source of debate). After a certain number of winners, you can (and should) push. Regardless of whether you're attempting to train error-free or how many winners and losers you've deemed optimal, a useful way to marry your ideal with a particular dog learning a particular behavior is to keep track of whether you're on thin ice with a too low rate of reinforcement (need a winner) or spinning wheels efficiency-wise by not raising the standard (need a loser).

Food Lure Addiction

Food is a special case as it is used as both a prompt and a reinforcer. As a reinforcer, food has the invaluable fringe-benefit of becoming strongly associated to the giver, i.e. you. Because food is so effective as a lure, however, owners can have particular trouble weaning off it. Firstly, make the distinction very clear in your mind between food as a lure, the prompt or target used to elicit the behavior, and food as a reinforcer, the thing that comes after the behavior but is often the same piece of food. If you hold a piece of food in your hand, allow the dog to sniff it and then back

163

away, you have prompted/lured his approach. When you give the food after his approach, you have employed it as a reinforcer. Two distinct roles. Problems arise when the dog learns that the food in its role of reinforcer is only likely when food is present in its role as lure. This is why it is so important, as soon as the dog is performing a lured behavior with any fluency, to reverse the contingency by performing the following exercise in a low-distraction environment, such as at home.

Start by teaching the basics of a behavior, such as basic position changes - sit, down and stand - using a lure. After several repetitions, the dog smoothly follows the lure for each behavior. Now do the following. Without a lure, i.e. with an empty hand, signal a sit. Wait, frozen. As soon as the dog sits, dispense a generous food treat hidden in your other hand (held behind your back if necessary to keep the dog off it). Repeat. Then signal a down, again empty-handed. If he doesn't go right away, wait a few seconds, frozen with your hand at the end of the down-signal trajectory. As soon as he downs, praise and reinforce. If he doesn't go at all for these empty-handed attempts, lure a few more without reinforcing, then try again. Don't crack too readily, however – if you don't have much competition, let him sweat it out. The goal is for the dog to learn that *not seeing a lure is more predictive of reinforcement than seeing a lure.* Teaching the dog that absence of a visible lure is better, from the perspective of reinforcer density, is the first step in making the dog a believer.

People drone on continually about how their dogs only obey when they have food in their hands. What they don't realize is that they have actively trained this in over the dog's lifetime by constantly supplying reinforcement when the reinforcer was visible and almost never supplying one when the reinforcer was not visible. Why not simply teach the dog that is not how the universe operates? Remember, he is obedient to the laws of learning, which specify that he will do whatever works. Dogs learn early in life that performing when no reinforcer is visible means that performance will not likely be reinforced. They innocently and merrily (and like the exquisitely-designed living organisms they are) simply don't do a behavior when it has been proven again and again that the chances for reinforcement are too slim, in fact possibly none. To teach dogs otherwise, it only requires a little artful hiding of reinforcers.

The same can be used for heeling. Initially, to get the behavior at all, the dog is targeting the food lure held against your pant leg. When the dog follows tightly and for long intervals between reinforcement, start selectively removing the lure for a brief instant just before giving him the food. By doing this, you are teaching the dog that *the removal of the visible lure predicts reinforcement.* With practice, he will be able to tolerate longer and longer stretches of lure removal because he has learned this is very good news: the reinforcer is imminent. He will, in fact, come to *prefer* heeling without a visible lure because this behavior works better than following lures. In this specific exercise, it can help to substitute another prompt such as a stream of enthusiastic praise or verbal coaching on the first few lure-free steps. You can also develop nice momentum by walking briskly.

For people who don't mind prompting behavior well into training rather than dropping or fading it ASAP, you can still rely on the dog eventually jumping the prompt. For example, if training the dog to watch your face while heeling, or simply to look at you on cue, the first training sequence, the one with the cue at the beginning, is a reasonable choice because watching is such an easy behavior to prompt.

First, say "watch," then prompt the dog to watch your face while he sits in heel position by moving a tasty morsel from his nose up to your face. Reinforce as soon as his head is up and his eyes make contact with yours. If you repeat this sequence, sooner or later the dog starts anticipating and watches before you have to supply the prompt. Once the dog has started jumping the prompt regularly enough, this now becomes the new standard. If he watches on cue he is reinforced, if he does not, you prompt the behavior but

165

withhold reinforcement. You can then proceed to gradually add features like duration, movement and distractions.

Training Parameters Separately

When you do things like adding duration, movement, distractions etc. to an exercise, you are adding parameters. Sit-stay, for example, has the parameters of:

1) distance: how far is the handler from the dog

2) duration: for how long must the dog hold the stay between reinforcements or even visits from the handler

3) distraction: how distracting is the environment in which the dog is performing.

When training sit-stay, criteria raises on these parameters should be done separately before attempting to combine them. Failure to do so is extremely poor training – you would lose the dog over and over racking up loser trial after loser trial. Both trainer and trainee must agree on what the criteria for reinforcement are and this is unclear when there are multiple parameters being trained at the same time.

For instance, if you are in a distracting environment and you ask a beginner dog to sit-stay at thirty feet for two minutes, he will probably break the stay. Somewhere in there, however, is a single parameter to train, such as "holding the stay at all amid this amount of distraction": try a one second sit-stay from two feet away and reinforce a few of those. Or, if you're in an undistracting environment, you may choose to play around with distance by leaving the dog at gradually increasing distances for one second at a time, bouncing back in as though attached to the dog by a bungee cord to reinforce him as soon as you reach the target distance. Then, on a separate occasion, gradually increase the length of time of the stay (from two seconds to five to ten to fifteen etc.) never going more than a few feet away, reinforcing after successful

166

intervals. When the dog has mastered each of these things separately, you may begin combining them, first two at a time at modest levels, then three, only increasing difficulty if the dog is successful.

Training several variables at the same time is the hallmark of an inexperienced or "hack" trainer. They appear to be getting away with it at times but this is usually at very great cost. Training this way will, sooner or later, blenderize the dog's brain. It may seem tedious and hyper-systematic to break down exercises into individual parameters but, interestingly, training progresses much more quickly this way because you remain at each level only briefly before moving on and you seldom lose the dog's interest. Because it is clear to the dog what standard he must make to be reinforced, he complies more readily. Pushing is a false economy.

Feedback: No-Reward Marks

In our communication system so far, a click means the dog has won reinforcement, and praise means the dog is on the way to winning reinforcement. Another signal, called a No-Reward Mark (NRM or "mark") functions as a conditioned negative punisher: a signal that the dog has just lost a reinforcer or that his chances for reinforcement dipped to zero with the behavior he just offered. When dogs learn what a NRM means, this signal can stop a behavior dead in its tracks. Dogs are very good at abandoning dead end strategies. This is why so many dogs fail to come when called, by the way: it has proven to be a dead end strategy. Approaching the owner in the park when she calls leads either to nothing in particular, maybe a bit of praise or, worse, the leash being put on and an enjoyable run ended. It is not surprising dogs do not come when called. In fact, any fun-ending could and should be paired with a no-reward signal rather than the "come" signal.

The NRM acquires its meaning through repeated pairing with a clear-cut removal of expected reinforcement. This is efficiently accomplished by training a simple behavior such as sit-stay or

167

"don't touch." If you hold a tasty treat at dog nose level a foot or two in front of a sitting dog, the dog will immediately move towards the treat. This is plan A, targeting. The instant he does, simply say "Too Bad!" or "AH!AH!" then snatch the treat away into oblivion. Then re-cue the sit and repeat the same thing. If your timing is good, the average dog will make the same mistake two or three times before changing strategies, i.e. not moving, lying down, barking or some other behavior besides targeting the treat. This next strategy would represent Plan B. If the dog opts to simply freeze and stare at the treat, immediately reinforce. His freezing compels your treat hand to his mouth. Repeat the exercise several times. You are now on the way to conditioning the behavior sit-stay as well as installing a NRM signal.

As soon as the dog gets two or three right in a row, change something so that he will make another mistake. Usually a simple change in your position in relation to the dog is enough to make the freezing behavior fall apart. Remember, when you hold a treat at nose level, plan A is almost always to target the treat: this is how we were able to lure sit, down and heel position after all. It is extremely obvious to dogs to target food, so the switch to plan B, i.e. not moving, will fall apart frequently. For some dogs, freezing may be plan C or D. This is okay: you want a lot of mistakes so that you have more opportunities to pair your NRM with the snatching away of the lure. It's not okay if the dog gives up and stops trying. If you lose him it means the rate of reinforcement dipped too low. You need more winners. You must either increase your speed of trial delivery (i.e. work faster – as soon as you NRM and snatch, commence another trial), drop your standard or both, until he is playing your game again. (A good way to drop the standard at this juncture is to "dangle" the treat a bit higher, i.e. less within dog striking range.)

Changing the picture in early, up-close stay training works nicely to create default lure-targeting errors for NRM conditioning. If you were standing to the left of the dog, now stand to the right and dangle the treat again, always ready to give your NRM and snatch

168

away the treat when he breaks the stay, which will almost inevitably happen. The reason the dog falls apart when you change sides is that dogs do not generalize very well. "New picture, new exercise" is the maxim. The dog will also fall apart for a trial or two if you place the treat on the floor, change the type of treat, try the exercise in a new room or change trainers. Cover all these variations to make this fledgling sit-stay more solid and to give you grist to charge up your NRM by repeated pairings with reinforcer removal.

The choice of NRM depends on the dog and the context. You may choose to have more than one installed in a given dog. "AH!AH!," for instance, when said quickly and with any intensity is inherently aversive to some dogs. For them it is not only a conditioned negative punisher. It functions as a primary positive punisher as well. "Too bad" or "wrong" are more neutral. One of these latter NRMs is preferable for extremely soft dogs. Choose NRMs that roll easily and comfortably off your tongue because you will have to use them with precise timing in the heat of training.

Use of Aversives

The tools we have discussed so far are: positive reinforcement, conditioned reinforcement, low-grade reinforcers (praise), prompts, reinforcer termination (negative punishment) and no-reward marks (conditioned negative punishment). The tools we have not discussed much yet are those that employ aversives. There are two ways to employ aversives – applying them and terminating them. This is parallel to giving and snatching away of reinforcers, except that what's being given and stopped is painful, scary or otherwise kicks off the animal's "Red Alert – Danger of Bodily Harm" system.

Negative reinforcement is the turning off of painful, scary or unpleasant things when the dog responds a certain way. The dog *does* something to turn off the bad sensation. Positive punishment also employs an aversive but this time it's the start of the aversive (rather than its termination) that functions to stop or reduce a behavior. The dog *stops doing* something to avoid turning on the awful thing. Negative reinforcement is the termination of an aversive and positive punishment is the initiation of an aversive. Negative reinforcement increases the likelihood of a behavior and positive punishment reduces the likelihood of a behavior. The same aversive on the same occasion will have two "ends" if it has any duration. In other words, if it works as a negative reinforcer, it is also, technically, a positive punisher when it first starts. If I'm twisting the skin of your arm until you say "uncle" and then I stop, your saying "uncle" was negatively reinforced. You are now more likely to say it again under similar circumstances. In order to terminate the arm-twisting to train uncle-saying, I had to start twisting at some point. Whatever behavior you happened to be doing the instant I *initiated* the twisting on your arm would be punished.

Aversives are common in human society. I think we do it because it has been done to us, and come up with the rational sounding explanations and justifications later. It's one of those alligator-brain level copying legacies. Religions also tend to have strong punishment themes in their attempt to keep behavior in line. Yet in spite of this, we seem to keep sinning a fair amount, especially considering the size of the consequence: eternity in hell, the ultimate late punishment. Given this cultural context, it is impressive indeed how the revolution in dog training has resulted in an explosion of methods based on positive reinforcement. More and more training styles have abandoned aversives altogether with great success. So what role, if any, is there for aversives in dog training?

Negative reinforcement, the termination of an ongoing aversive, is a slippery technique to do well. Furthermore, even done correctly, its use is morally unjustifiable for the training of stylized behaviors like retrieving (remember the ear pinch?), for which it is a popular technique. For behaviors that are lifesaving or strongly impact quality of life, the water is muddier. When all else fails with a

170

predation problem, one of the toughest things to fix, and the dog's life or quality of life hangs in the balance, I personally still might employ negative reinforcement to train a recall. But this is a very specific corner to be backed into. "All else failing" means all else well planned and executed, not "I tried this a bit and that without much know-how and now I'm fed up."

The other "end" of the aversive is positive punishment. Examples of positive punishment in dog training are: verbal reprimands, swatting, spanking, hitting with rolled up newspapers, throwing things, spraying with water or citronella, shaking by the scruff of the neck and the ubiquitous leash jerk. These interventions typically have to be used over and over - in the case of leash corrections probably thousands of times in the course of the dog's lifetime. To better understand all this, let's take a look at what makes a punishment work.

Years ago, the rules for administering effective positive punishment were laid out in an excellent book by Dr. Daniel Tortora called "Help! This Animal is Driving Me Crazy." In order for a punishment to have even a temporary effect on the future probability of the punished behavior, several conditions must be met:

1) The punishment must be immediate – i.e. it must interrupt the start of the behavior. This is to avoid the collection of any reinforcement by the dog.

2) The punishment must be sufficiently aversive to avoid adaptation. If you start small in an effort to be kind and then scale it up, you will build a "punishment callous," which will toughen the dog up. Never start small and get bigger: start big right off the bat.

3) The punishment must follow each and every attempt at the behavior and be associated only with the behavior: there should be nothing else to tip off the dog that he's about to

get punished. When the dog is punished for behavior that has been unpunished up to now (and also has been reinforced otherwise it wouldn't exist in the first place), it is as though the dog asks himself "what's different this time?" If it is the fact that you're in the room, his question is answered in spades. He learns to avoid doing the behavior when you're there. If the punishment is not delivered on a continuous schedule it's a matter of time until the dog discriminates when the punishment does and does not happen.

If you have the timing, availability and stomach for this, the punishment will likely buy you a temporary suppression of the behavior. You're also likely to have a dog that's too upset to do much of anything right after a punishment. Punishment is like carpet bombing. The behavior you wanted to target gets hit but so can a huge portion of the dog's whole repertoire. Dogs who are punished a lot behave a lot less in general. What's insidious is that that is exactly what a lot of dog owners want. They want a general toning down of the dog. It is a sad comment on the human-dog relationship when we claim to love dogs and then attempt to behaviorally lobotomize them with thousands of leash jerks in the name of "obedience." The bland, behaviorless animal many people bond to can scarcely be called a dog. It is the ghost of what once was a dog.

This makes punishment in many peoples' minds a virtual synonym for "training." If you walked into an obedience class twenty years ago you would see dogs marching around in a circle receiving leash jerks scores of times in the course of the lesson. Even today, when many people ask how to stop the dog from doing something, they expect to be told what particular flavor of punishment (or "discipline") is "best": yelling, hitting, throw-chains, booby-traps, electric shock etc.

There are two immediate gratifications for people who punish. One is that toning down of behavior. The other is a cathartic release of anger and frustration. For many people, trying to control dogs is maddening. And so we are up against these motivations when we try to help people opt for more benign training techniques.

One thing that can sober people up about aversives is pointing out the collateral damage they very frequently cause. One well-known side effect of aversives is defensive and pain-elicited aggression. Stories about dogs "turning on their masters" are pathetic attempts to turn into high drama a dog defending himself, often after a history of punishment, from his owner. Any dog, or human for that matter, has a breaking point. The most placid among us might resort to violence to save oneself from perceived threat.

Another longer term side effect is the development of conditioned emotional responses – Pavlovian or classical side effects. Let me give an example. A dog has been jumping on and mouthing the kids. This is fun and reinforcing to the dog because it burns his predatory gasoline and elicits nice shrieks from the prey objects. Mom first tries saying "no" in a firm tone of voice but the dog quickly habituates to this sound and there is no impact on the behavior. She may as well be saying "harder! rougher!" in a firm tone of voice. Dad, the first time he sees the dog do this, picks the dog's entire front end up off the ground by the scruff of the dog's neck, growls into the dog's face "NO!" and gives the dog a nasty backfist under the chin. The dog slinks off to mull this over. He doesn't mouth the kids for several days but then the behavior, like a phoenix, rises from the ashes. It had only been stunned by Dad's well-timed, highly aversive punishment. What is the dog's likely course of action now? Right. Never mouth the kids when Dad's around. The dog now mouths the kids during the day when it's safe and refrains in the evening when it's dangerous. No substitute behavior has been trained in to fill the gap, so the original one emerges whenever it's safe. Now for the side effect. The dog also is more worried and appeasing around Dad and is slightly afraid of his hands, especially when they move in a certain way. And this from one trial.

The classical side effects of aversives are enough to keep me away from them. These are typically associations to the scary, awful aversive of other elements in the picture at the time of the punishment, such as the father and his hands, above. Side effects are a good bet even if the timing of the punishment is perfect. We tend to punish our dogs interactively so, even if it's well-timed, i.e. the dog is "caught in the act" you risk a good part of the association being with you, the punisher. This can lead to innumerable problems in other areas, most notably fear and aggression, and getting the dog to come when called. Side effect likelihood goes off the charts if the timing is poor. The punishments themselves, if delivered more than a second or two after the intended act, are basically abuse and the imperfect timing undermines the dog's ability to avoid the punishment through learning. The result is that the only accurate predictor of the punishment is not a behavior but the punisher. The desperately submissive behaviors of dogs who have experienced lots of these punishments - incorrectly interpreted by owners as guilt or worship - are indeed sickening to behold.

Chops

Operant conditioning works perfectly in theory and in behavioral science labs. It's messier in the real world. A trainer's mechanical ability to apply operant principles in real life human-dog interactions is called training "chops." A lot of people have chops with little acquired knowledge; they are just good natural animal trainers. Most of us have to build our skills, but luckily for us and for dogs, chops are acquirable. So what exactly are "chops?" In the early 90s I videotaped young dogs that had just enrolled in beginner level obedience classes being trained by two groups of people. The first group consisted of the dogs' owners and the second group consisted of professional or highly skilled amateur trainers. My aim was to get a handle on exactly what the difference was between a good, experienced trainer and a rank novice. All the participants were told the study was to do with learning styles across dog breeds so that they wouldn't change their training styles.

What I was most interested in was counting instances of attempted feedback from the handler to the dog. These included all examples of: verbal praise, food reinforcer, pat, offering a toy, reinforcer removal and no-reward marks, grab, strike, verbal reprimand and leash correction. The person who did the counting from the videotaped record did not know which people were the trainers and which were the non-trainers.

The impetus for this study came from years of observations in obedience classes. Dogs who behaved badly for their owners became "different dogs" when one of the class instructors borrowed them for demonstration purposes. This was all without any training history or priming. Once the dogs were given back to their owners, they immediately reverted back to misbehaving. What goes on, in the moment-to-moment interaction between dog and trainer that makes the difference? My hunch was that trainers give dogs a lot more consequence-type information per unit time. The difference in the amount turned out to be even greater than I had imagined.

The owner-handlers delivered some kind of feedback to the dog every twenty seconds on average for a rate of attempted feedback quotient (RAF) of 2.8 per minute. The trainers gave feedback about every six seconds for a whopping RAF of ten per minute. Trainers praised and gave out food reinforcement three times as often as non-trainers but they also doled out more punishments, mainly in the form of leash corrections or no-reward marks ("AH!AH!"). It was as though the trainers used the punishments to "slam doors" on behavioral strategies they wanted the dog to abandon so that the dog would be more likely to offer something they might be able to reinforce. They were opening temporary voids.

They also timed reinforcement better. Reinforcers came fast and furiously because it appeared the trainers had a mental image of what they were after ahead of time and never hesitated to reinforce it when they got it. This got a roll going. In short, the trainers

175

defined a tighter envelope or narrower range of behavior by marking or punishing deviations, so the dog, with a narrower range of options, offered reinforceable responses, which the trainers unfailingly reinforced. They ended up getting many more reinforceable responses than the non-trainers because:

1) they prompted for them relentlessly

2) they punished lunging and pulling very quickly

3) they set reasonable criteria for reinforcement

4) their timing was excellent: they never missed a reinforcement opportunity

5) their training delivery was fast: they took no coffee breaks

These qualitative differences were even more striking than the RAF difference between the two groups. Trainers were good "slot-machines" for the dogs to play, much better than the other available things, such as the floor, doorway, other people or dogs in the room. When one views the videotape, the fastest way to tell whether you are observing a trainer or a non-trainer is to simply look at what the dog is "playing." If the dog is playing the handler, it is likely a trainer. If the dog is playing the floor or something else in the room, it is likely a non-trainer at the helm.

The non-trainer group could be characterized as "trees." They supplied little in the way of feedback to the dog for either good or poor responses; from the dog's perspective it must have felt like being tied to a tree. Dogs tend not to interact much with trees when they are tied to them.

The non-trainer feedback was:

1) Stereotyped and perfunctory: regardless of whether the dog did something utterly brilliant or only slightly better than

176

average, the same reward was dispensed. For instance, one owner would say "good dog" and give a scritch behind the ears each and every time he wished to reward the dog. Trainers were much more varied in their feedback: they used a huge range of feedback "tools." (All participants had identical too, kits issued to them.)

2) Non-contingent or slow: slow feedback was just that: slow, often two or three behaviors late. For example, when the dog would sit, by the time the handler had perceived the sit and dispensed any kind of reinforcement, the dog had stood, lunged and sneezed. Sneezing ended up being reinforced.

Non-contingent feedback was an interesting non-trainer phenomenon. Quite often when the dog was absolutely gone, either lunging or playing the floor or watching the doorway, the handler would offer praise in an apparent effort to get the dog's attention. This kind of prompting, incidentally, was counted as attempted feedback for the purposes of the study, which inflated the RAF for non-trainers. Their feedback density was therefore even worse than the numbers suggest. Interestingly, a couple of dogs used in the study were "ringers" (trained dogs with obedience titles) and they too ended up tuning out the non-trainers by halfway through the allotted time, in spite of a lifetime of training. Their offers of great responses were quick to extinguish, and they ended up playing the floor as well.

When you think about it, it's not surprising that there is such a gulf between people who make dog training their passion and people who like dogs and buy them as pets. Just because someone loves dogs doesn't mean they love animal training or have any training skills. Likewise, there are probably a lot of great latent animal trainers out there who will never own a dog because they don't particularly like them, or at least not enough to own one. Those who become good at training usually love training on top of the fact that they love dogs. They may or may not start out with any natural gifts. Their love of training, however, will make them better at it over the long haul because they will end up logging a lot of training time and pursuing knowledge. But most owners are not in this group: they love dogs, not animal training. It is pretty astounding the way we have developed dog training skills in these well-meaning people. We have taken them and what have we done? They have, quite naturally, no conception of how to set criteria (i.e. they don't know what a reinforceable response looks like much less how to reinforce it), no timing and almost no experience at prompting. What tools have we given them to commence learning these very basic skills? We have given them their own completely out of control adolescent pet and a strangle collar. It's like teaching sixteen year-old kids to drive by giving them a formula one car and putting them on the autobahn.

Think for a minute about the implications of this. The fundamental skills of training are: the ability to recognize a reinforceable response (criteria setting), the ability to obtain that reinforceable response (prompting and shaping) and the ability to immediately reinforce it once it's obtained (timing). These are not easy tasks. The animal we want trained is a dog, typically a young dog, a dynamic animal with a relatively high rate of behavior change who actually may be trying to maul (playfully) his owner during the session. If a dog owner, with virtually zero development of any of these skills, is issued an aversive tool like a choker, what happens? The answer is random punishments with the owner as the principle discriminative stimulus. The dog learns slowly, necessitating more and more leash jerks and the result is either adaptation to the collar or a zombie-like dog who has had huge amounts of behavior veritably wiped out. We would never condone this anywhere else but in a dog obedience class.

Let's say you are a novice violin player or a novice pole-vaulter. You are going to start learning your new skill. Every time you make an error, a six month-old dog gets a small electric shock. How many errors do you estimate you will make in your first week of learning to pole-vault or play a musical instrument? How many

178

in the first month, the first year? What is the effect on that dog of all those shocks? Is that okay? Now, how many timing or criteria setting errors is a novice dog trainer going to make in his first month of training? If the main training tool is some sort of aversives dispensing collar, that makes for quite a lot of poorly timed punishments. What has been making us think that this is okay? If someone can't deliver food reinforcers with any timing or skill, should we be arming them with devices that dispense pain?

A new way of developing basic training skills in dog owners is needed. It must identify the deficits dog owners bring to class. These are:

1) too low rate of reinforcement

2) failure to exploit naturally occurring reinforcers in day to day life – those vital consolidators

3) timing: reinforcement and NRMs are non-contingent or slow

4) they don't know how to set criteria

5) they don't know how to prompt

6) they don't know when in the sequence to prompt

The first breakthrough for many dog owners is recognizing that their principle role in obedience training is to supply consequences, as opposed to giving "commands." This speaks to the widespread fallacy in the dog owning public that cues, i.e. antecedents, drive behavior. The evidence for this is the endless quest people have for the right "tone of voice," the right number of words in the cue, the correct word to use, the correct hand signal. By now, of course, you know that cues don't drive behavior, consequences do. The main focus in early obedience training is manufacturing, recognizing and reinforcing those reinforceable responses at every

179

possible opportunity. They are like gold. The cue is merely a signal to the dog that an opportunity for reinforcement just came up and suggests which behavior he ought to try. You can't cue a behavior you have not yet trained.

Your own skill at training will start improving the instant you start installing your basic training tools, the conditioned reinforcer (the clicker) and your no-reward mark ("AH!AH!" or "Too Bad!") Then you need to get yourself as rapidly as possible into the hands of someone who knows what they are doing. A good instructor is invaluable for three reasons: 1) to coach you, 2) to provide a model or example of good training skills and 3) to provide sequences for the basic cues you want to install in your dog. Sequences you can find in a book like this one. The modeling you can get from hanging around and watching good trainers and from watching videos of good trainers in action. The coaching, however, can only be accomplished via feedback from a good coach. In The Academy, I do this via detailed video analysis of student technique. Without it, trainers risk rehearsing errors.

The skills of training and instructing are separate, by the way. A good trainer is not always a good instructor and vice versa. Ideally, in an obedience class, there will be one of each, sometimes in the same person but sometimes not. Try to find a school that has both an ace trainer and someone who can impart knowledge to others. Here are some pointers to get you started.

1) Never miss an opportunity to watch good trainers in action. Whenever I am in the presence of a good trainer, I shamelessly stare and soak in as much as I can. You may also want to consciously and deliberately avoid looking at poor trainers, even if you're aware that their example is a poor one. Humans are such compulsive imitators, you could be "infected" by their bad habits. Avert your gaze and only put the right pictures into your brain.

180

2) Stop giving the dog so much free food and start parsing it out to reinforce desired behavior. Exploit the most potent motivator in animal training. If you have puritanical misgivings about food as a reinforcer, get over them and fast. He has to eat anyway. I'm continually assaulted with the line "yeah, but if I give him food, won't he always expect something?" Firstly, no, not if you elect to employ intermittent reinforcement schedules. But, secondly, and I think this really addresses the root problem, this is like saying, "yeah, but if your employer gives you a pay check for working, won't you always expect one?" I often want to ask people who make that remark what exactly they thought this endeavor was about. I don't ask because I know the underlying assumption has to do with cues driving behavior and with DTP (desire to please). Suffice to say that you're shooting yourself in the foot if you deprive yourself of food training and expect to compete with the rest of the environment using your personal charm only. People must understand that food training in no way cheapens or ruins the bond you have with your dog. It enhances that bond by associating you with one of the most potent unconditioned reinforcers on the planet. The alternative to training with positive reinforcement is training with aversives. Choose and stop agonizing.

3) Use vocal intonation more. High-pitched or enthusiastic sounds - baby talk - are mild to moderate reinforcers for a lot of dogs in low distraction environments and can be established as "getting warmer" signals for all dogs. Reservations about behavior in public shackle many people when it comes to praising their dogs. This is yet another reason to get yourself into the hands of a good trainer. A good trainer will have very broad vocal tools, which will serve as a terrific, infectious model for you. Groups of trainers who train around each other a lot pick up each others' idiosyncrasies right down to individual words and phrases. Exploit this copying facility to good ends.

4) Become aware of your timing of reinforcers, NRM's and punishments. Were there any intervening behaviors between the one you wanted to give feedback to and your actual feedback? If so, tighten that up. If your timing is pretty good and you want to make it better, train fast-moving, "hyper" dogs, young, impetuous puppies and rodents. Train fleeting behaviors such as eye blinks, lip smacks or particular head tilts.

5) Improve your delivery. Delivery is inter-trial latency (as opposed to timing which is response-reinforcer latency). Good trainers are very efficient: as soon as a trial has ended (with a click, primary, praise, release or NRM), they immediately commence another trial. They have great "flow." The pay-off is in terms of efficiency. By boosting rate of reinforcement per unit time, the trainer can afford more loser trials (if that is your cup of tea) without losing the dog. Post-trial loss of the dog's attention is a common problem, necessitating time and energy to get the dog refocused before the next trial. Rapid-fire delivery solves this. In ten minutes a fast-paced trainer can accomplish more than someone with poor delivery can in an hour, even if their skills match up otherwise. Train intensely, having as your goal keeping the dog's attention on you for the entire session. Keep training bursts brief if necessary.

6) Be very cool-headed when you train. This will enable you to shift gears easily between NRM's and reinforcers. If you take everything very personally, you will be inclined towards low-grade, chronic aversives. This is something we humans do to each other all the time. We mope and brood and give dirty looks for hours or days to family members and colleagues who have wronged us. We elicit guilt. This kind of punishment may work on people. It absolutely does not work on dogs. It may make them behave very carefully if a crabby mood has come to predict

a higher probability of reprimands and Yucky Stuff for Dogs, but as a specific feedback tool, it's worthless.

Take, for example, a dog who lunges at another dog in an obedience class. The owner gets angry and starts glaring and seething at the dog. The dog then sits and looks up at the owner and is met with what? You got it: glaring and seething. The owner is now applying this mild punishment to ongoing behavior, including those beautiful sitting-and-looking-up responses. You must be able to shift gears with ever-changing behavior. For this reason, it will feel rather artificial for a while. Your reinforcements and NRM's have nothing to do with how you *feel* about the dog's performance. You are employing them as feedback tools to influence the future probabilities of the behaviors. If you do this based on your real feelings, you will be slow and inaccurate. Get into a detached, Zen-like frame of mind when you train. You will never be able to oscillate quickly back and forth between a no-reward mark and reinforcement if you get upset at mistakes the dog makes. Emotions will slow you down. Remember that your job when you are training is to condition behaviors, not moral goodness in the dog.

7) Get over any obsession you have with "commands" and start focusing on providing consequences. Cues are just signals that inform dogs which behaviors might earn reinforcement at any given time. You have to have a behavior first. If the behavior is weak, there is no point trying to signal for it. Same thing with elicitors or prompts. Like cues, these are antecedents of behavior, "the things that come before." Elicitors are like discriminative stimuli for behaviors that have been genetically selected for rather than selected for by training histories. They are subject, however, to learning laws and can become useless if the consequences of responding are not attended to. What all this means is that your primary goal, as dog

trainer, especially in the early stages, is to strengthen behavior by providing positive reinforcement as a consequence whenever you see the behavior you like. The manufacturing of the behavior, by eliciting, cues, narrowing of options by having other behaviors terminate reinforcement opportunities, or simply waiting for the dog to do it (to "emit" the response) is not the point. The point is reinforcing it when you get it.

8) Think about the criteria you are setting. Be aware of the standard, at any given moment in training, the dog must achieve to get reinforced. This standard can and should constantly change. Its fluidity is dictated by the dog's progress. It is never arbitrary. This is a common flaw in beginner trainers. Because the goal in mind is a dog who will hold a five-minute sit-stay as dinner guests arrive at the front door, the owner is frustrated because, although the dog can do a thirty-second sit-stay alone with the owner in the living room, he still jumps all over people and is oblivious to all cues when guests arrive. The frustrated owner needs to train with more gradual increases in the level of difficulty, culminating in the guest-at-the-door scene. Every level of difficulty is like a wall you are building. The first row of bricks, representing the first level of difficulty (sit-stay alone with the owner in the living room for a few seconds from two feet away) may be already laid down, but there are many rows to be laid down before you have your ultimate goal. Each row must be laid down solidly before laying the next. Build a training plan to give you the big picture: what are the different bricks you need in your wall? Duration? Locations? Various specific distractions? Finally, in the second to second heat of action - "micro" criteria setting -, use the "do I need a winner or a loser trial" question to optimize efficiency.

Chapter Six
Nuts & Bolts of Obedience Training

One way to think about macro criteria setting is to think about what "grade" the dog is in in a given subject. If your dog is in kindergarten or grade 1 on sit-stay, he will flunk a test at the grade 12 or PhD level. This is not malice, revenge, spite or stubbornness, it's just how animals learn. The following sequences for teaching sit-stay, down-stay, stand, come, heel, don't jump and don't pull are organized by increasing level of difficulty from kindergarten through to the college and PhD level. Before training any of these, charge up your clicker (conditioned reinforcer) as described above.

Kindergarten Sit

Put a treat in the palm of your hand and cover it with your thumb so it stays in[9]. Allow the dog to sniff this goodie. Ascertain if he is targeting the treat by moving your hand around. Does he try to follow the hand? If yes, he is targeting and you may now proceed to lure a sit. Move the treat slowly over the dog's head, high enough that he must crane his neck back to continue targeting but not so high that he jumps to target. Move the treat backwards over the dog slightly, maintaining the same height. Then just wait. If the dog jumps or backs up, remove the target for an instant and start over. Most dogs will eventually sit to make it more comfortable to continue targeting the treat. As soon as the dog sits, click and give him the treat. Imagine that the dog is training you to open your hand by sitting. Repeat this three or four times – the dog should sit with less and less effort from you with the target. Your

---

[9] The detailed sequences in this chapter use prompt-fade or prompt-drop procedures. For details on training prompt free and later adding cues, there is no better resource I have found than Karen Pryor's *Don't Shoot the Dog*

hand gesture can now be executed quickly with your palm facing up. This paves the way for the hand signal you're about to train.

Now, put a morsel of food in your pocket or in your other hand behind your back. You will now use your empty hand as a target by giving a broad, clean, confident hand signal to sit. The hand signal is an upwards scoop with palm open. Always conceptualize "sit" as an attempt to get the dog's head up rather than getting the rear end down. If you get the head up and back, the rear takes care of itself. When the dog sits, immediately click and give him the food reinforcer from your other hand or pocket. This stage is very, very important - it reinforces the notion that the dog's behavior produces the reinforcer and that this does not have anything to do with whether the reinforcer was visible or not as a lure. Our goal, in fact, is for him to learn that *not seeing a lure* is more predictive of reinforcement than seeing one. It is vitally important that the dog learn the blank hand is better than the one with the food in it. For the novice dog, this is like a leap into the unknown. Many initially sit for blank hands in a manner that looks as though they think "well, this couldn't possibly work but I'll try anyway." You have to make them believers by reliably reinforcing responses to empty-handed signals. This is contrary to the human inclination to dispense reinforcers that are already loaded into hands (as lures).

This is such a critical juncture in training. Failure to get reliable response with the reinforcer invisible sets you up for a possible lifetime of a dog who "only does it when I have food in my hand." Practice until the dog sits as reliably for the empty handed signal as he did for the original lure. If the dog balks at any stage for the blank hand, don't crack and put food back into it. Simply wait and reinforce the sit when you finally get it. You'll need to train in a low competition environment initially to achieve this.

When the response for the blank hand is very snappy, you may tighten the quality control if you like. Select the better sits. This may mean faster, cuter or neater. It's up to you. When the dog is still sitting enthusiastically exactly as you'd like him to when in

186

low competition environments (such as at home), go on to the next step.

The next step is to do some distraction proofing. Load up a zip locked snackie bag with ten or twelve food treats. Put it in your pocket ready to dispense and then go somewhere with the dog. It can be out on the usual walk, on a car errand to the grocery store, at Starbucks while reading the Sunday paper, anywhere except where there are dogs. Hang out at your chosen place until he stops swimming around sniffing the ground and checking out the sights and sounds. This might take a couple of minutes or possibly longer. Once he starts checking in with you or looking bored, practice sits with your empty hand signal, reinforcing each one, until all your treats are gone. Then go home. Do it again, in the same place, a day or two later. How did he do? Did he offer any sits before you started signaling? Did he get bored with the environment faster? You can also practice "cold" sits while on his regular walks. Load up your baggie with half a dozen treats and, at random times on the walk, signal sit, reinforcing whenever he does it. When he doesn't do it, stop walking and wait until he attends to you, then try again. Once he sits for the signal, dispense a treat and then continue the walk. This is a double reinforcer – he got a treat and he got you moving again. Very good for the "sit works" personal philosophy you're trying to build in him.

This deceptively simple exercise – taking a behavior on the road for location generalization – is gold. Most dogs get pretty sharp after just a couple of outings and can then be worked in progressively more difficult surroundings. You can include any places or contexts you'd like the dog to be responsive in, leaving the heavy competition – dogs and small furries – for later. If you want the dog to be obedient "everywhere," practice in as many places as you can.

Once you've done some preliminary proofing, it's time to associate the word "sit" to the behavior by saying sit before you give the hand signal. The word "sit" is the new part, so it will go first in the sequence. Go back to low distraction to commence this exercise. Proof it in your locations once he's reliably sitting on the verbal cue. Here's the sequence:

1) verbal cue "sit" (wait one full second...)
2) hand signal
3) dog sits
4) click
5) hand opens and dog gets reinforced

Be careful to say the verbal "sit" *before* you give the hand signal (as opposed to simultaneously as is most peoples' inclination) otherwise the known cue will block the new cue you are trying to establish. The new cue needs to stand in isolation for a full second before you define its meaning to the dog with the known signal.

After reinforcing several in a row this way, try the following. Cue "sit" verbally and wait, with the food treat behind your back or in your pocket. At first the dog may simply stand and stare at you, whine, bark, paw at you or try to target the treat in your pocket or behind your back. Simply ignore all this and wait for twenty or thirty seconds. If the dog sits at any point, click immediately and then give him a treat from your pocket or hand. Then do it again – cue the verbal and wait. If the dog does not sit after twenty or thirty seconds, do one reminder review: the verbal cue followed by hand signal and then reinforce when he sits. Then give the verbal cue for sit and try the waiting game again. With this stalemate, you are teaching the dog to attend to the verbal cue. Verbal cues are opportunities the dog will eventually learn to not miss.

Remain at this stage of training, reinforcing every response to the verbal cue, until the dog sits immediately after every verbal cue to sit. This will fall apart initially when you go "cold" – giving the verbal cue out of the blue rather than in the context of a training session. If you get nothing after a twenty second stalemate (or if you lose him at any point), do one review with verbal followed by hand signal, then repeat with just the verbal. If you get stuck in this pattern – the dog never performs cold for the verbal, and always

188

needs the signal review – do the signal review and praise the response without giving food reinforcement. Then, give food to reinforce the sit for verbal cue only. Then, make the next trial "cool" rather than cold. Practice a minute or two after the last successful sit-on-verbal trial rather than hours or days later but not immediately after as in a training session. This is a useful gray area between good response in a training session ("oh, this is the time when I sit a lot") and real life ("what?"). It is also the one exception to the rapid delivery of trials rule in operant conditioning: consciously have longer lags between trials for the express purpose of teaching cues.

When you get reliable sits on verbal cue, start reinforcing about 50% of the time. This simply means you reinforce about every second time the dog sits on cue. When you do this, by the way, don't do one reinforcer, one skipped in a fixed pattern. Randomize it more. Pick the nicer ones. These nicer ones – your new criteria – will actually be on 100% reinforcement. As soon as the dog is perfect again at this new criteria level (i.e. winner after winner trial), you go down to 50% reinforcement before making it harder with yet some other variation on how you want it done. When all the criteria have been added, you may wish to go for a maintenance schedule lower than 50%. For now, a thin reinforcement schedule is not necessary.

The Kindergarten sit is harder than you might imagine because, although staying is not expected yet, the goal is semi-stimulus control over sit (from a stand). In theory, stimulus control means that the dog always sits immediately whenever the verbal cue or hand signal is given, the dog does not sit in the absence of the cue, the dog does not sit when any other cue is given and the dog does not do any other behavior after the sit cue. In most practical pet dog training, what we're after is that the dog sits immediately whenever the cue or signal is given. As you'll see, there are a lot of pieces to the puzzle, especially when there are a lot of different cues and behaviors to be learned and the context is constantly changing. Dog trainers are like jugglers who have a lot of balls to

189

keep in the air. The best place to start this entire process is by teaching a good, solid sit.

At this point you have a dog who sits on both a hand signal and verbal cue. Soon we'll add more proofing. That is, we'll strengthen the responses to the sit cue while you increase competition and distractions, vary your orientation to and distance from the dog, and practice inter-cue discrimination. When you proof, you increase reliability. You are teaching the dog that the only ingredient necessary to set up the contingency for sit is the verbal cue or hand signal for sit. You do this by deliberately and systematically varying everything else to prove their irrelevance. A certain location is not necessary. Nor is it necessary that the trainer be standing two feet away in front of the dog. Nor does the dog have to be first standing. All that's needed is the word or signal for "sit." The dog does it anytime, anywhere, no special conditions necessary. The dog can tell the sit cue apart from all the others he knows. This is inter-cue discrimination. No matter in what order you throw cues at him, he always gets the sit right immediately on the first try. Until now you haven't practiced inter-cue discrimination because sit is the only cue your dog knows. Soon, inter-cue discrimination will be one of the balls you must keep in the air.

Before we get more into proofing, let's get those other basic cues up and rolling so that we can discuss proofing in a more general context.

Kindergarten Down

The first order of business, as it was for sit, is to repeatedly obtain and reinforce the behavior of the dog lying down. You could simply hang around and wait for the dog to spontaneously lie down. This avoids the prompt fade baggage. You can also prompt down as follows. Sit on the floor with a treat and bend one of your knees so that your leg makes a tunnel. Once the dog is targeting the treat, you will slowly lure him through the tunnel. He will have

190

to lie down to keep his nose/mouth on the treat. If you're struggling with the mechanics of this, an experienced trainer can show you the nuances.

As soon as he is in the down position, click and open your hand so that he wins the treat. Repeat this up to a half-dozen times. If the dog does not readily target the treat as you move it under your leg, you may be pulling it through too fast. Go slowly, especially for dogs who seem suspicious about crawling under your leg. Let him win a couple of treats for putting his head under before raising the standard to head and shoulders and finally an actual down. If the dog jumps over your leg to continue targeting on the other side, simply say "too bad!" and start over again. This behavior will fade if it never works.

When the dog is diving readily under your leg to make your hand open, see if he will go down without the tunnel. Sit on the floor (no tunnel now) with a treat in your hand. As soon as he's targeting the treat, move it slowly straight down, palm down, between his front paws with your fingers covering the treat so that it is between your hand and the floor. Then, just wait. He will probably worry at it, licking, gnawing, pawing at your hand. You are simply waiting for him to lie down. Ignore all the other behaviors. They will die if they do not work. Eventually the dog will lie down. Click right away and open your hand. Then repeat. The second and third time may still be fairly protracted but most dogs catch on in very few trials thereafter. The dog is simply becoming more efficient: worrying at your hand with mouth and paws has never worked, so he more rapidly cuts to the chase and lies down. Lying down, after all, keeps proving to be the best strategy to get that hand to open. Other strategies get ruled out through trial and error.

When the dog is instantly lying down as you place your target hand with the treat in it on the floor, you now have the task of dropping the food lure. Before doing this, with a treat in your hand, practice several "push-ups" using hand signals. Push-ups are sequences of sit-down-sit-down. If the dog has difficulty moving upwards to a

191

sit from the down position, simply move your target hand with the treat in it, palm up, up and back slightly and then freeze. The dog will pop into a sit sooner or later in order to continue targeting. When he does, you simply click and open your hand again. Don't use your verbal sit cue here as sit from a down is a whole new ball game from the sit from a stand you've been working on.

Through all of this, the dog is not only learning sit and down, he is learning how to learn. Inexperienced dogs must not only learn which behaviors you want and what the signals for these behaviors are, they must learn the concept that there is something quite specific that you want *at all*. Experienced dogs, the ones with great and instant responses to dozens of cues, learn much more rapidly because they know how the game is played. They try out and abandon behavioral strategies in a fast, efficient manner and pick up what the right option is often after the first click. This flies in the face of popular mythology about young dogs learning more rapidly than older dogs. Naive animals of any age learn more slowly than experienced animals of any age. It is prior education that counts. So, be patient when working on neophyte dogs. Each bit of training is money in the bank.

Once the dog is warmed up by doing brisk push-ups over and over with the target in your hand, reinforce these sits and downs 50% of the time over a set or two. Choose the quickest ones. Then remove the target and show the dog your empty hand. Have a treat ready in your other hand. With your empty hand, give your down signal, palm to the floor, the same way as you have been doing during the push-ups with the treat. Now, wait. If the dog stands, mark the mistake ("too bad!"), get him back into a sit and try again. Eventually, perhaps reluctantly ("this couldn't possibly work.") the dog lies down. Immediately click and treat. Repeat several times so that the trend emerges. Just as for sit for an empty hand, our goal is for the dog to go down as easily for the blank hand as he did for the food lure. When that is happening, you may start to reinforce less often, demanding two, then three or more complete push-ups per reinforcement. Then take your push-ups on the road.

192

When your dog will do smooth push-ups for an empty-handed signal in a few different locations, you are ready to add the word "down" to these proceedings. Go back to low distraction. Before giving the hand signal, say "down" and then give the signal as usual.

The sequence is:
1) verbal cue "down" (wait one full second...)
2) hand signal to down
3) dog lies down
4) click/treat

Your verbal cue will become a reliable predictor of the known signal. After half a dozen repetitions in a row of the sequence 1) verbal cue, 2) hand signal, 3) correct response and 4) reinforcement, try giving the verbal cue and simply waiting. As soon as he lies down, immediately click and furnish. Again, the first few trials might be painfully slow but you must live through this to get to the other side: a dog who reliably lies down for a verbal cue only. If you lose him, give the verbal cue and then hand-signal – try a smaller one, not as low to the ground as you have been giving - and reinforce to get him back in the game. If you haven't lost him but he stares interminably, blinking without a shred of a clue what to do, prompt the down with your hand signal and praise but do not reinforce with food. Then immediately start over – give the verbal and wait. When the down gets smooth for a verbal cue, take it on the road, giving the slightly nicer "road-reinforcers" every time.

Elementary School Sit & Down: Inter-Cue Discrimination

Inter-cue discrimination becomes an issue the minute the dog has two choices of response: sit and down. What do you, the trainer, do if you cue down and the dog sits? You have four main options: one is to mark the behavior ("oh! too bad!") and then bail the dog out by cueing down again and reinforcing it when you get it. The second option is to simply mark the behavior - "Oh! too bad!" - and

193

pause the training by looking away for a few moments or even walking away briefly before starting the next trial. If the dog is hooked on training as he likely is by this time, this will function as a negative punisher - interruption of opportunities for reinforcement. Only a correct response on the first try gets reinforced: "Try harder, oh dog." The third option is to mark the boo-boo, prompt the correct response but withhold the reinforcer since the correct response required this extra help. Again, only a correct response on the first cue gets reinforced. The fourth option is to simply wait, no click, no food, no praise, no mark, nothing...and then start another trial after a pause.

So, which option should you choose? Some are more costly to the dog than others. Knowing what to do in any given circumstance with any given dog is part of the fine art of training. These judgment calls are what separate the adequate from the proficient. Don't agonize about it too much. You'll get better with experience.

If you bail the dog out by first marking and then re-cueing the behavior, the dog is likely to guess right on the second or third trial, especially if the discrimination is between only two cues. This is okay for beginner dogs because it gives them another chance with little pressure on them. The game is kept easy to win. The disadvantage is that the incentive to not guess wrong in future is low. This comes into play when the discrimination task is harder, i.e. when your dog has many responses to choose from rather than just two. With this training style, if the dog gets it wrong, the worst thing that happens is the chance for reinforcement is delayed slightly by having to be re-cued after the mark.

The second option is tougher. The mistake is identified as such by the mark ("too bad!") but the dog is not given a second chance. The disruption in training delivery is a small time out. The idea is to motivate the dog to guess more carefully in future. The stakes are higher. Only correct first guesses are reinforced and thus keep the flow of training going. Use this option for non-novice dogs, keen dogs that guess a lot or if no improvement is gained using option one over two or three sessions. If you use it and the dog checks out – you lose him – go back to option one or crank motivation up and competition down.

The third option, to mark the mistake and prompt the right response but withhold the reinforcer, is even tougher. The dog expends calories every time, one way or another, but reinforcement is only given for those responses made on his own by guessing right the first time, as in option 2. If the dog is not keen enough, you will lose him fairly often by training this way. If you're not losing him, this is a nice penalty for guessing.

The fourth option, to simply do nothing if the dog guesses wrong works marvelously with very motivated dogs but has one drawback. When the animal is on an intermittent schedule, not every correct response is reinforced anyway. Ignoring wrong responses may feel the same to the dog as those unreinforced but correct responses. In early training this is hard on the learner. For this reason, it is good to praise the dog for the correct responses that go unreinforced so he can tell the difference. Praise helps the dog discriminate between a right response that is unreinforced because of the schedule and a response that is unreinforced because it is wrong. The praise is a signal that the dog is on the right track with that response whereas the silence means "dead end, no way that will ever be reinforced." The same result can be achieved by marking wrong responses ("too bad!") and ignoring correct responses that are part of the schedule. My advice is to experiment with all these communication options and discover what works best for you and your dog. It is good to have a grasp of all these options so that you can switch strategies if necessary during training.

All this talk about the dog "guessing" may have you wondering how the dog could possibly need to "guess" between two easy cues like sit and down. The answer is that, although dogs learn the behaviors relatively quickly, getting our semi-stimulus control, i.e. getting dogs to the level where they never guess wrong, is much, much harder than dog owners imagine. Dogs, when given a cue,

195

typically guess sit, or whatever the most prevalent behavior is, first. By "prevalent", I mean whichever behavior has received the most reinforcement in the training history to date (cumulative reinforcement) or was blitzed most recently (the "latest trick" syndrome). Dogs also seem to learn patterns of responses more easily than they learn cues. A classic example of this is a dog who, regardless of what cue is given, performs sit-give-a-paw-down-roll-over in a stereotyped sequence. It is as though order-of-events learning overshadows the content of the cues. If you want your dog to learn the actual cues, you must continually vary the sequence and penalize guessing.

It seems to be the policy of many dogs to notice that they have been given a cue, not tune in to what the cue was specifically, and proceed to guess their way through their repertoire until they stumble onto what the trainer wants. They approach responding to cues with a carpet-bombing mentality whereas we would prefer neat, precise "smart" bomb responses.

The only viable explanation for this is that inter-cue discrimination is taxing to them. You, the trainer, must therefore provide adequate incentive for the dog to attend to the content of the cues. This is a specific and relatively long-winded training task, especially when the number of responses you have trained piles up. Dogs struggle much more with random order sequences of multiple cues. They get better at it with practice, but only if a standard is set that demands they get each cue right the first time. This means it behooves you to use as tough a penalty regime for wrong guesses on sit-down discrimination as your dog can tolerate. Every time he gets it right for the verbal, reinforce. Do not go to a 50% schedule for this exercise, even once it starts to look good. Discrimination tasks are bettered by continuous reinforcement. The goal is for the dog to do either a sit or a down for the first verbal cue, with no more wrong guesses. Once he can, take it on the road. Now let's get the final position up and running so we can build a three-way cue discrimination, the landmark that, in my opinion, moves a dog out of the novice category.

Kindergarten Stand

As dogs stand up from a sitting or lying position, they almost invariably take a step or two forward. Your lure and, eventually, your hand signal will reflect this natural movement. The first step in teaching stand is, as usual, to obtain and reinforce the behavior. To do this without any prompt baggage, you can wait for emitted stands, capture them and then, once they're at very high frequency, add a cue. Here's my favorite MO, a prompt-drop procedure.

The dog is sitting and you have a food target in your hand. Hold the target near his nose and then move it smoothly away from him in a clean horizontal motion. To target the treat, the dog stands. Reinforce once he's in position – don't let him take more steps than necessary to get from a sit to a stand.

If the dog has had any "stay" training, he might not budge, as it might feel to him like a sit-stay proofing exercise. For these stay-savvy dogs, you must briefly press him to do another strategy shift: back to targeting the lure. There are three ways to do this: 1) a body prompt to stand, 2) "bigger" lures or extra verbal prompting, or 3) simply waiting for the reinforceable response. The body prompt is a gentle finger or two in the dog's groin area, gently lifting upwards. As soon as the dog stands, click and reinforce. Be sure to do the physical prompt after the signal. Usually only a few physical prompts are necessary to let the dog know that this is not a stay exercise. To verbally prompt, try your release word right after the lure or other encouraging noises to try to get him unlocked from staying. You can also tap your lure hand with your other hand. After a few repetitions, reduce the prompting and wait for the stand after the first lure, reinforcing every instance until it is solidly installed.

All this will, naturally, make a temporary mess of your stay (if it's started). Don't panic: the dog will learn to discriminate a stand cue from a sit- or down-stay and get better at this sort of task in the process. To do this, you may want to oscillate between "sit-stay" and "stand from a sit" trials to improve the dog's discrimination between these two cues. Then do the same thing with down-stay and stand from a down. If stay has not been started, the stand installation should go without a hitch.

Once the dog is standing readily from a sit for a food target, teach him to stand from a down. This is trickier than stand from a sit but is made easier by the fact that the dog has learned to stand from a sit already. Use the same prompts. When he's standing with great abandon from either a sit or a down, work to obtain this response for a hand signal only, just as you did for sit and down. The food lure goes back into your pocket or other hand. You may go back to physical and verbal prompting temporarily if the behavior falls apart. Reinforce every empty-handed stand until he's smooth at this. Then take it on the road for nicer treats.

When the dog performs stands without mistakes or hesitation for an empty-handed signal, cold and in your desired locations, you may start installing the verbal cue. You will probably have to signal or prompt quite a few after giving your verbal cue before weaning off these crutches. The sequence is:

1) verbal cue "stand" (wait one full second...)
2) hand signal and/or food lure for stand
3) dog stands
4) click/treat

Remember that stand from a sit and stand from a down are two separate exercises, so work on them separately. When the dog masters the stand with only a verbal cue from either a sit or a down, it's time for the three-way.

High School Positions: Three-Way Cue Discrimination

This is an important foundation exercise in obedience training. Can the dog reliably, on the first cue, perform a sit, down or stand from any position? Can he do it for verbal-only cues? The three-way exercise is harder than the earlier sit vs. down discrimination because, in that exercise, when the dog is already in a down, the next thing asked for is always going to be sit. If he's already in a sit, the next cue will surely be down. Dogs learn, in other words, to "do the other one." You can, in fact, avoid this by throwing in trick questions (cueing another down when the dog is already down). But it's much more efficient to simply add a third position. Adding that third position - the stand - changes everything. This is where dogs really get the concept that the cue means something very specific. And this is where the trainer gets good at acquiring semi-stimulus control.

Practice sit, down and stand in random order for verbal cues. Pause briefly between each cue to stymie anticipation – make him stick with his first guess rather than bombarding you with volume positions. Help with a hand signal when the dog does nothing or is incorrect, but deliver praise only (no food) when you have to help him. Fast delivery helps, as always. Reinforce only those responses where the dog guesses right first try, without the added hand signal. We're banking that the dog can tolerate this amount of penalty. You'll know if he can't. You will either lose him or his performance will get worse secondary to flustering or frustration.

Note weaknesses. Typical initial weaknesses are: the sit from a down, down from a stand, and stand from a down. These particular changes often need to be drilled on their own: practice the same change until it is performed smoothly and then reintegrate it into the random order exercise. This is fairly painstaking work but well worth it for the gains you reap in terms of the dog's understanding of basic positions and the "learning to learn" effect. This puts you in good stead for everything else you ever plan to teach your dog.

Once initial weaknesses are ironed out, many dogs will still perform seemingly at chance the first few sessions. Keep practicing. If you've got him motivated and he gets clearly above chance by the fourth or fifth session, all is well. If not, back off. Choose one change – sit from a down for instance – and do a few reinforced reps of verbal followed by hand signal. Then try with just the verbal. If he does nothing or guesses wrong, penalize this with a "too bad," pause in the training, and then try again. If he blows it again, signal the right response and reinforce when he does it. Then push again by penalizing guessing.

The right balance between pushing for the dog to get it right on his own and backing off on the standard to keep the dog in the game differs for every dog. The principle – to not hang out endlessly at the same level and to not lose or frustrate the dog – is always the same. An appropriate goal for a trainer is to keep progress going while never losing the dog. This means you've learned to drop the standard before you lose the dog and yet you keep inching up criteria for reinforcement. This will keep the dog playing the game and maximize progress in the particular exercise, all the while cultivating his growing addiction to the game itself. Making the game too easy results in a minimalist approach from the dog.

There can be some real legwork to training a reliable three-way position discrimination. Although some dogs seem to make dramatic breakthroughs in their percentage right, for many dogs the percentage of right guesses inches up gradually over the long haul. Don't try the distance work until the dog has a very first-guess-right-always three-way with you a couple of feet away.

College: Positions at a Distance

The change in picture when the handler is farther from the dog can cause massive generalization problems. We tend to do all our interacting with dogs, including training, at very close range. One of the key elements in the package is that most reinforcers are, quite naturally, transferred from trainer to dog up close. The

200

rcpcatcd association of closc to handlcr = high probability of reinforcement while far from handler = low probability of reinforcement, contributes to behavior falling apart when you get more than a few feet away. The dog is seeking both the familiar up close picture and anticipating the collection of reinforcers as has happened in the past: up close. This culminates in "creeping" – the dog edging toward you on each position change. The reinforcer collection anticipation "misbehavior of organisms" effect can be attenuated by frequently tossing primary reinforcers a distance from the dog (as described below) in early training.

Overcoming the distance obstacle is a major breakthrough in the dogs' generalization of any cue he has learned. It's as though he has the revelation: "Hey! You mean sit works at twenty feet, too? Amazing!" Getting there is like any other training task. You must set a standard that the dog can already achieve sometimes (so he can win the game right off the bat) and gradually crank it up, provided he continues to play the game and make progress. If you can get position changes at a distance, it paves the way for other behaviors you would subsequently like to have at a distance.

A good warm-up for this is to practice your three-way discrimination up close but with a varied cue "picture." During training, dogs attend to more than cues. The location of training, the trainer's distance, posture, body language and orientation are all salient elements in the stimulus package. Our goal is to vary everything except the cue itself. So, make him do position changes while you sit in an easy chair, flipping treats across the room for collection after the click, so he starts to get unhooked from the idea that being up close to you is necessary for reinforcer collection.

Practice position changes while he is in his crate. Practice with you lying on the couch or on the floor. Practice with your back to him, using a mirror to watch his responses. All of this helps the dog find out that regardless of how the "picture" changes, the cue always means the same thing: doing the behavior earns him a treat. If he gets stuck and starts cranking out losers, have the new, tricky picture predict a more familiar picture for a couple of trials. For instance, if he can't stand from a down when *you're* lying down and giving cues, give the cue lying down, wait a second and then prompt by sitting up and giving a stand hand signal. Reinforce this once or twice, push for him to jump the prompt by stalemating on the third trial.

When you've got these in the bag, distance will come much more readily. In spite of good prep, many dogs will still tend to creep forward in early distance training. I strongly suggest you prevent this mechanically. There are a number of ways to accomplish this. One is to work him while he is in a crate or ex-pen. After each nice successful run of reinforced position changes you take one step backwards. The dog learns that he can make you approach the crate or pen and reinforce him by executing correct changes on cue. Putting him behind some barrier, like a baby-gate or fence, is equally effective. You can work with him at the top of a flight of stairs or other natural inhibitor of forward motion. You can put him on leash and tether him to a post. This affords you the added generalization bonus of the dog doing changes with the sensation of the constant pressure of the tether. A lot of dogs initially fall apart when you do this: "I can't possibly lie down with this tether on" – and then learn after some training - "Well, hell, I guess I can."

Increase distance gradually and spend time working through any mental blocks, such as the tethering one. One wall you may hit usually occurs at around eight to ten feet, especially if you are working on hand signals as well as verbal cues. It could be that the signal looks different when you reach that particular distance or it might just be the distance at which the training "gravity" loses its hold and you are on truly novel ground. Who knows. Once you get past this, things seem to go more smoothly. The transition from ten to thirty feet comes much more easily than the transition from two feet to ten.

Whenever he's right, *go in and reinforce.* Failure to do so muddles the discrimination task *and* supports the "reinforcers are more likely up close" idea you're trying to weaken. If you've got a good arm, flip the treats behind him, which can further reduce the tendency to creep forward. When he guesses wrong or does nothing, approach to whatever distance you need to get the response. Praise these "repaired" trials but try to reserve food reinforcement for snappy, correct responses on the initial cue or signal. Avoid the habit of holding the signal or repeating the cue as this will lead to chronically sluggish changes. Randomize the order of positions so the dog can't latch onto a pattern, such as sit-down-stand-sit-down-stand.

Do not try this exercise without the physical barrier until he is truly acing the changes without hesitation. If you allow creeping in early training, it gets stamped into the exercise and will give you grief for all your distance work further down the road. Keeping creeping at bay is hard enough without good early training. Trainers are so eager to see what looks like a finished product that they naughtily try distance changes without their mechanical management too early. Do not do this. In fact, I quite like teaching the dog "back up" and then employing this between position changes. This can be captured by a good shaper, or prompted by crowding the dog slightly by walking into him. After you cue and then prompt, as soon as he takes one step backwards, click and treat. Build distance and fade the crowding prompt, and then stick back-ups consistently between position changes once you start teaching distance. His anticipation of the next "back up" cue puts Pavlovian anticipation to work for you.

Stays – Cueing in Early Training

In early stay exercises, it's actually pretty safe to use a hand signal – an open palm toward the dog like a traffic cop – and/or the word "stay" right off the bat because you are extremely likely to get good responses very early in the game. The cue also helps with the discrimination between targeting (stand) vs. not targeting (stay). When you teach stay, you are also teaching the dog an exception to the targeting rule: the dog is now told he is wrong when he targets the treat. The word stay will provide a nice discriminative stimulus that will take on the meaning: "Don't follow the treat." Until now in his training, it has paid off to do what is very natural - targeting the treat or the hand (i.e. follow it wherever it goes). Now you are asking for a strategy shift. This is not just a different behavior but a new approach to finding out what the behavior is! Targeting was his strategy before. Now *not* targeting the treat is the way to win it. The sequence is, therefore:

1) cue or signal to sit or down
2) dog sits or lies down
3) praise/reinforce[10]
4) cue to stay – verbal followed by signal
5) dog stays or breaks
6) reinforce a stay or mark a mistake
7) release stay or do another few seconds, if dog right; if dog wrong, repeat exercise or drop criteria

Be sure to say "stay" only once, then follow with your palm toward the dog. Novice trainers tend to fall into a mantra-like chant of "stay...stay...staaa-aaay..." to "remind" the dog. This is sloppy training. Give cues once and then sink into your main role of feedback provider.

Kindergarten Stay

For either sit- or down-stay, the first exercise is a repetition of the procedure described in the previous chapter for conditioning the no-reward mark. As soon as the dog is in the sit or down position, hold the treat a couple of feet away at dog height and snatch it away (just after your NRM) at the first sign of movement. Be sure to hold the treat at dog height, rather than high and out of striking distance. The whole idea is to tempt him to move so that you can

---

[10] If the rate for stay is high enough, the position change is part of a chain that leads to R+ and so does not need to be paid. If there are too many losers in a row, a legal way to boost rate is to pay the position too

204

mark this as an error and get a more *deliberate* attempt to not move. This is playing devil's advocate and really grinds home the concept of stay. Repeating this forces the dog to switch strategies to plan B, which is usually immobility. The first evidence of deliberate freezing must be immediately reinforced. The duration of the stay in this exercise is a second or so for the first few trials, the time it takes for you to notice that the dog "decided" not to move for a second. If he doesn't move, pay. Again, if you're struggling with the physical mechanics of orchestrating this with nice fast delivery (necessary because of the strings of losers), watch slick trainers do it to give you a picture of what it looks like.

Once the dog reliably freezes in spite of the devil's advocate treat, practice with your body stationed on the other side of the dog, and in front of the dog but with the treat lower and on the floor (be ready to cover it in case he breaks – breaking mustn't work). Then, start bumping the duration to two, three, five and then ten seconds by simply marking and removing the treat every time the dog breaks position. He learns that he can sit there and keep collecting at five to ten second intervals provided he doesn't move.

The down-stay can be harder than the sit-stay for dogs that pop back into a sit. The dog may assume the exercise is a push-up or three-way. This is another case of inter-cue discrimination. You wanted down-stay whereas the dog learned the pattern of alternating sit-down-stand. "Another position change follows down" might be his policy. This again underscores how readily dogs learn patterns: he only knows three cues and already it's a pattern. This tendency in dogs works against you every step of the way[11]. The dog wants to learn the right order but you want him to learn the right cues. The way out is through perseverance and exquisite timing: mark the instant the dog starts to pop out of his down and re-signal the down (drop your "verbal cue" criterion as you're after the duration component of the down here). Click all

---

[11] An exception to this tendency working against the trainer is performance of a fixed-order behavior chain where sloppiness doesn't matter (link merging) and speed of performance is a parameter

205

evidence of the dog holding the down-stay while you rise to standing position and/or move. As you did for sit-stay, work up to five to ten seconds on the down, with the handler standing in a normal posture.

Releases

In any stay exercise, when the dog has stayed for long enough, far enough and amid enough distraction - he has made the criteria for reinforcement, in other words - you may choose to release him from the stay, rather than reinforcing him while he's in the stay and then continuing the "same" stay (it's actually a new trial once reinforcement has been dispensed). A release is distinct from the reinforcing of the stay. The reinforcer is the treat. The release is a signal that the dog may now move again. Whether you reinforce a given stay or not, you must let the dog know when it's over ("you can stop staying now"). You may also wish to reinforce a stay in progress but not release it just yet. Most clicker trainers click to signal reinforcement, end the trial, and also end the obligation to continue the behavior (which is moot for behaviors where the dog can't collect reinforcers and continue the behavior at the same time anyway). In the case of stays and other behaviors where duration building is so critical (watching and heeling are two others), I favor installing a formal release word. It's handy to be able to reinforce along the way and have the dog collect reinforcement in the position. Most dog trainers use the word "okay!" said with some enthusiasm, but some argue that this word comes up too often in everyday use.

Practice this basic stay exercise in as many places as possible to get in some early generalization. Vary your position relative to the dog, vary the food reinforcer, vary trainers if you can and even try dropping the food on the ground by "accident." When you play this last game of chicken it is critically important that you are fast enough to prevent the dog from getting the treat when he breaks the stay. Dogs usually fall apart when you drop the treat: not targeting food in your hand is one thing but not targeting an obvious freebie on the floor is much, much harder. So, be ready. As soon as you drop the food and the dog breaks, mark the mistake ("AH!AH!") and snatch up or step on the bait. Re-cue the sit or down and repeat the same exercise until the dog freezes even when you drop the food on the floor. Reinforce this show of self-control immediately. The dog learns that the way to win even that piece of bait on the floor, once the word "stay" has been uttered, is to not move. When the dog is doing this correctly over and over, try it in a new location or with a different body posture or type of bait to get more generalization. You can also practice this exercise with meals and exits to the yard. Ask the dog to sit-stay before you put the bowl on the floor or open the door. The dog must hold position while you put the bowl down or open the door and wait until you give the release to begin eating or to exit.

Elementary School Stays

The goal is that the dog will hold a sit or down-stay for up to twenty or thirty seconds while the handler walks in circles around the dog. The dog must remain seated or down even if the trainer is moving. To start training this, cue sit or down, then cue the stay as in the kindergarten exercise and take a small step to one side. Keep your eye on the dog. Try to time your no-reward mark to the instant his butt starts to come off the floor. Also mark any lifting of front paws to rotate with you. If he holds position, pivot back in front of him and reinforce. Then try two steps to the side. If he breaks the stay, mark the mistake, get him back into a sit and then try one step again before attempting two. Remember that beginner dogs are fragile little learners: they need to win the game often. With a dog who is more experienced at learning, the trainer would probably take another stab at two steps after the dog's boo-boo rather than giving him an almost guaranteed success on the very next trial. More experienced dogs tolerate dry spells between reinforced responses better than greenhorns. When your dog is hooked on obedience, you can get away with more push in your training. For now, err on the side of being too generous and gradual. This is especially the case if your dog's attention tends to wander.

Work gradually up to the level where you can cue sit-stay or down-stay and, on the first trial, every time, walk around the dog without him breaking the stay. He is allowed to follow you by rotating his head, but body rotations or position breaks are no good. Many dogs find it disconcerting to have you move behind them while they hold a stay, so always be prepared to temporarily drop standards and reinforce easier reps if things bog down. For instance, if you have worked up to five or six steps to almost behind the dog but the dog breaks the stay whenever you take that seventh step to directly behind him, go back to the reinforceable five or six step exercise often enough to keep the dog playing the game. You may also insert an intermediate step like six steps plus a lean toward the seventh. If he can do that, reinforce it a few times and then try a half step after number six. And so on. Dogs fall apart because trainers lack the discipline to train gradually enough: we set arbitrary criteria, in other words. It is extremely presumptuous, if you think about it, to want to dictate what another being, let alone a being from another species, is going to find easy or difficult. You must always select something from the sample of responses the dog is already giving you.

When he can hold a stay while you parade around him, take it on the road. Expect the dog to regress in each new situation. Many people take it very personally when dogs regress or fail to generalize. They start searching for a reason: over-excitement, lack of exercise, malice, revenge, spite, stubbornness, breed. These are usually irrelevant. The reason is likely to be a competing motivator or a failure to generalize. If you've got him, i.e. you don't have competition, simply retrain, if necessary from scratch. The retraining will go more quickly than the initial installation, often with one trial per increase in difficulty (dog: "oh yeah, this again"). For now, avoid locations with strong competing motivation (e.g. running squirrels). You can try those later.

208

High School Stays

The goal is that the dog will hold a stay for a minute or two with the handler thirty or so feet away. There are two parameters here: one of duration (the minute or two) and one of distance (the thirty feet). These must be perfected separately before combining them. So, first, while remaining at very close distance, start increasing the length of the stay. You can walk circles around him, as in the previous exercise, or simply hang out in front. I like to mix it up. From thirty seconds go to forty-five then sixty and so on. If, at any duration, the dog falls apart, reattempt it once and, if he breaks again, back off to the last success and then inch up more gradually. For instance, if he breaks when you go from seventy-five to ninety seconds, repeat seventy-five and then try eighty. It may take a few sessions to get him up to two minutes or more in any location. When he is reliably doing a couple of minutes without breaking, tackle distance. For this you must work in a safe, secure area.

To train distance while keeping duration short, practice "bungee" stays. Pretend there is an elastic cord between you and your dog. Move away from him to an initial distance of, say, six feet. When you reach the six foot mark, immediately bounce back in to reinforce the stay. If the dog breaks at any point, mark the error and try again. If the dog breaks again, do an easier one, i.e. shorter distance. As for duration building, I suggest attempting the same distance one more time before lowering your standards. If you lose the dog, i.e. he loses interest and stops even trying, you need to drop standards faster, in this case after one mistake. Remember, *whenever you're cranking up the level of difficulty, be very sensitive to the animal's attitude to the training: his quitting or excessive frustration mean you're going too fast.*

The reason you can't initially combine the parameters of distance and duration is that both you and the dog need to agree on the criteria for reinforcement at any given moment in training. If you attempt twenty feet for one full minute right off the bat and the dog actually stays for forty seconds and then breaks, he missed the duration aspect but nailed the distance: do you reinforce or not? Criteria pile-ups like this can be very confusing and demoralizing for dogs. Choose one and train it, only combining it with others when they, too, have been trained separately. Not only do reinforcers then hit target but no-reward marks will also be more likely to hit accurately.

When you do start combining distance and duration, start modestly with something like ten feet for ten seconds, then twenty feet for ten seconds, then ten feet for twenty seconds. Crank the standard up gradually by raising one element and then, if successful, the other. Don't raise two things at the same time – in fact, drop one when you raise the other. Disciplined parameter juggling is the hallmark of a good trainer.

When the dog does two minutes at thirty feet, take it on the road. Drop back to modest distance for modest durations (say, ten feet for ten seconds) and build back again. Each location will, once again, probably cause a regression, which you will take in stride by dropping standards to get reinforceable responses and then gradually building again. This pattern should be starting to feel familiar now. Once you've got it in four or five varied locations, you graduate to College where you get into heavier distraction proofing.

College Level Stays

The goal now is for the dog to hold a stay in the presence of distractions such as other dogs milling around, a squirrel or tennis ball zipping past, or a wiggly child patting the dog's head. Each distraction needs to be worked separately and with distance and duration minimized at first. Go back to working up close to the dog doing three to five second distraction laden trials, reinforcing after each and every distraction refusal. It's important to understand what a distraction refusal is, because this is the reinforceable response in distraction proofing. A lot of people beaver away at manufacturing distraction refusals with gradual increases in intensity and beautifully timed no-reward marks but then fail to reinforce them when they get them! Have the picture clear in your mind before you start presenting distractions and reinforce without hesitation when he doesn't break. What makes it difficult in stays is that the reinforceable response is a non-event: the dog does nothing but hold his stay. This is a classic example of why you must think in advance about criteria.

Begin with some simple handler-movement distractions. Jump in the air a few feet from the dog. If he holds the stay, go back and reinforce. If he breaks, mark it and repeat. If he breaks again, assess. Was it a major break or was it an almost-stay. If the former, back off and do something easier. If the latter, try one more time. Needless to say, at every moment during distraction training, you will have your full concentration on the dog. It is critical that you catch the instant when your dog begins to break his stay. There is a saying: a mediocre trainer catches the dog after he gets up on a stay exercise, a good trainer catches the dog as he starts to get up, a great trainer catches the first muscle contraction. In distraction training, timing is even more critical because your best hope of stopping the dog from going flat out for a really attractive distraction is to interrupt early in the sequence. An extreme case will help clarify the point: imagine attempting a no-reward mark on a dog chasing a fleeing squirrel at the moment before his jaws make contact with the squirrel some fifty yards away from you. Now, imagine a no-reward mark when he's at your side and his ears go up when he sees a squirrel in the far distance. Your chances are better in the second case.

Whenever the dog gets two or three right in a row, escalate the distraction. Try a jumping jack. Try a twirl. Try Flamenco dancing. Try the twist. Try crouching down. This last one is tricky because, for a lot of dogs, crouching is a recall prompt. It is not, however, a cue so it's fair game for proofing stay. The dog will start to learn that the only thing that can end a stay is another cue or a release. Try faking a sneeze. Try drumming on the floor. Whenever he refuses a distraction by holding the stay, go back and reinforce. If he cracks, mark the mistake and repeat. Never escalate until you've had at least two perfect responses in a row with the same distraction. Try lying on the floor. Try rolling around on the floor. Try bouncing a ball. Try rolling a ball. Try throwing a ball. Try throwing several at once.

Now try touching the dog while he is staying. For a great many dogs, this is a whole new ball game. If your dog is jittery or explosively friendly when people approach or touch him, this "sit to greet" is so worth cultivating. Start doing a series of approaches and head touches yourself until the dog is sitting solidly trial after trial. Then try swishing him all the way from head to tail. Then do simulations of how people pat dogs. These will include the up and down pat-pats on the head as might be delivered by a young child and the two-handed grasp around the ears with deep scritching that many adult dog lovers administer.

When you can't get him to break the stay anymore, start getting other people to administer the pats while you watch and supply feedback in the way of reinforcers and NRM's. Instruct your helpers clearly to start with light head touches. It is critical that you do multiple repetitions, i.e. series of touches, rather than just one or two. (Please note: if your dog is not socialized to people, do not do this until he has had some remedial socialization, described in Chapter 3.) When the dog is solidly sitting for head touches, try the full-length swish by the same person. When this has been solid for several trials in a row, start the gamut of dog-pat styles.

You can have multiple people do the same level of exercise until the dog can't be stumped or you can stick with the same person and escalate difficulty, then start with another, whichever is more convenient. Be prepared for the dog to fall apart temporarily each time you introduce a new person. The magic moment is when you introduce a new person and whiz through the progression without any mistakes at all. This may be on person number three or person number twelve, but it will eventually happen. Make sure you've covered the major demographics, especially kids. When this is done, you have a nicely proofed sit to be patted.

When he will hold position confidently as you throw balls and squeaky toys all over the place, and as he's manhandled by any person, take your distraction training on the road. Each new location will compound the distraction problem with its unique combination of ambient distractions. This is above and beyond the fact that all new locations evoke a failure to generalize. It will therefore be necessary, as usual, to drop the standards and rebuild the sit-stay for each location. Take comfort in the fact that each subsequent retraining of obedience exercises will go faster and faster, culminating one day in a dog who you can teach even brand new exercises in highly distracting environments and who will almost instantly generalize that training to all novel locations. Such an educated dog is simply a product of extensive training, rather than some genetic endowment of either dog or trainer. Luckily, training is fun; so get involved with the process rather than obsessing about the product. You'll get there if you persevere.

Come When Called

Coming when called is high on the priority list for any pet dog to learn yet is usually mangled by the trainer if it is taught at all. The critical mistake, in many cases, is the attempt to use the cue before it has been installed. This premature use of the cue actually serves to undermine future attempts at training. The typical premature use scenario consists of the owner calling the dog over and then doing nothing in particular if the dog comes or else inadvertently initiating something unpleasant or ending a pleasant activity. The cue is presumed "known" because the owner had witnessed correct responses in the past. Sooner or later the behavior falls apart utterly and completely and the owner blames the dog for a moral failing. Underneath all this is the dangerous assumption that the dog will be "naturally" obedient. Let's look in detail at what's happening.

Most puppies have a natural tendency to approach when you call them, crouch, clap your hands or make enticing noises. They are compulsive greeters. They are also, as you know, perfectly obedient to the laws of learning. If you capitalize on this natural inclination for the puppy to rush at you for these prompts and then fail to reinforce these beautiful responses or, worse, apply either a positive or negative punisher, the puppy's days of coming will be numbered. The subsequent disobedience has nothing to do with rebellion, testing of authority or spite, but merely represents the cumulative effect of any and all deliberate and inadvertent training to date. What are the consequences to the dog of coming? Let's look at an example.

New puppy, Muffin, comes home to her new family. For weeks, Muffin toddles enthusiastically up to anyone who calls her, wagging and wiggling. This is compulsive greeting. Muffin's owners presume that she understands to come when she is called. She is, after all, doing it every time. She is, however, endowed with a brain stem and spinal cord, which make her what? Subject to the laws of learning.

After a few weeks, Muffin occasionally does not immediately rush to anyone who calls, especially if she is otherwise occupied, but this is not considered a big deal because she comes "most of the time." Her owners routinely call her over to give her affection, to come in from the yard outside when she has been let out to have a pee, to interrupt her when she is getting into something she shouldn't be doing, to groom her, to put her into her crate when they leave and, occasionally, to reprimand her for leaving a puddle on the floor or for chewing the baseboards. What is the cumulative effect of all this?

Sometimes Muffin gets reinforced for coming by the attention and affection. The rest of the time, when she comes on the cues "Muffin!" or "Come!" the result is either the initiation of an aversive (punishment for past transgressions, grooming – she's not a fan and hasn't been counterconditioned) or the ending of

214

something she likes (being in the yard, getting into stuff she "shouldn't" be getting into, being crated). When she is old enough, Muffin is taken to the park for exercise and called when it is time to go back home. The sequence used is 1) cue "come," 2) Muffin comes, 3) leash put on/freedom ended. She comes the first couple of times but then starts "refusing" to come. One day, when her owner is late for work, Muffin does not come at the end of her morning romp and plays keep-away for fifteen minutes. The owner calls an obedience school that evening and announces that Muffin is "stubborn." After all, she "knows" what come means and yet refuses to comply. But what does "come" really mean, to Muffin?

Muffin has learned, first and foremost, that "come," clapping and bribes very often mean the end of fun or the start of something yucky. She learns, as any normal animal would, to not approach when she hears that word or sees that picture. This is not related to some rebellious flaw in her particular personality. This is important to understand. The fatal flaw in the thinking of most owners is that they imagine the dog is a moral being who understands the owner's authority and is susceptible to guilt. When the owner demonstrates disapproval of the dog for not coming, this is presumed to be sufficient motivation to overcome the obvious animal learning implications: the initiation of aversives or ending of reinforcers for the dog contingent on coming when called. Dogs are amoral. If they have a concept of the word "should" it would tie closely into their pure sense of self-interest and perfect obedience to learning laws. In dog culture, when someone calls you, you *should absolutely not* come if that results in the ending of something you like or initiation of something you don't like.

The first mistake Muffin's owners made, long before punishing scores of recalls, was to presume that the dog was "obeying" a prompt: the calling and clapping. Prompts are merely elicitors. They tend to make behavior happen, all other things being equal. But these antecedents quickly take on the more powerful role of discriminative stimuli when they prove to predict contingencies of

215

relevance to the animal. *The consequences make all the difference.* The prompt, in the case of Muffin, wore out pretty quickly when "come" started to mean bad news. This is why a prompt might appear to work for a while and then cease to work anymore.

The way out of this common predicament is to bite the bullet from the outset and not only accept, but actively exploit, those laws of learning to which the dog will be perfectly obedient. Train in harmony with the principles of how animals learn. Stop trying to fight it. Stop trying to invent some mythical system, however appealing to human brains, that kind of/sort of exploits learning laws. Learn the actual laws. Each and every time the dog approaches, systematically reinforce him with affection, play and food treats from your pocket. Reserve the dog's name and the word "come" as sacred utterances. Never follow them with something the dog will not like or with the cessation of something the dog is enjoying. Have regular recall conditioning sessions, as you did for sit, down and stand. When in the park or dog run, teach the dog that come is simply a check-in most of the time: the dog comes, gets a pat and food treat and then is told to go back and play. Teach the dog that *failure* to comply, in the heat of fun, results in the ending of that fun. Stack the deck in your own favor. Here are some exercises.

Kindergarten Recall Exercise

Two or more family members take turns calling the puppy (or untrained adult dog) back and forth in the kitchen or down a long hallway. Every time the puppy comes to someone, he is told to sit, taken by the collar and then given a food treat from the caller's pocket or given a fast round of a tug game with a toy from the caller's pocket.

A variation on this exercise is hide & seek: the dog is held by one person while the other hides somewhere in the house. The dog is released right after the hidden person yells "Muffin, come!!" The dog is now on a search and rescue mission. When the dog arrives,

216

a greeting celebration ensues and a tug game is initiated. During this time, the other family member hides. The dog is then sent, after that person's cue, to make another find. The dog's impression of the word "come" shoots way up. You can also practice "random" recalls, for which you only need one person. Call the dog over at random times and reinforce him with a surprise treat or play session. In fact, why not precede all enjoyable activities with a recall so that the best predictor the dog has that something good is about to happen is the word "come."

When practicing recalls, the initial sequence of events should be:

1) cue to come
2) prompts: hand clapping, luring, squealing noises etc.
3) dog approaches
4) dog praised enthusiastically during approach
5) dog told to sit when he arrives
6) dog sits
7) handler takes dog's collar in one hand and
8) reaches into pocket with other hand to give dog a food treat or tug toy: whichever is most valuable (recalls are expensive and important behavior so this is no time to be stingy)

When the dog has had several brief sessions like this and thoroughly enjoys the game, phase out the prompting (#2) and then the "getting warmer" feedback (#4) so that the dog performs the behavior for the cue only. Try to practice in at least three or four different quiet locations before starting the proofing exercises that follow.

Elementary School Premack Recall Exercise

If the recall cue were a wall that you were building, you would have, with this kindergarten exercise, laid down the first row of bricks. You've started a foundation. To lay down the second row of bricks, you will teach the dog a controlled distraction exercise.

For this you need two people. One is the handler, and the other is in the role of distracter. The handler has nothing on her: no treats, no toys, nothing. The distracter has control of a top reinforcer: liver, cheese, or the dog's favorite tug toy. The distracter shows the dog that he has possession but without letting the dog have actual access. The handler, who has shown the dog that she has no reinforcers with her, goes a short distance away and calls the dog. In most cases, the dog will initially ignore the handler and "play" the distracter, the obvious slot machine at that moment. The distracter will simply ignore the dog's efforts. These might include pawing, jumping, whining, performing beautiful sequences of sit-down-stand, barking etc. The handler will keep trying to prompt a recall at regular intervals. Think of it as suggesting a strategy to the dog. There is no rush here because the motivator is well controlled. The dog is not winning anything but simply wasting his time with all his behavior directed at the distracter. He just does not know this yet.

Sooner or later, the dog's strategies to access the distracter's goodies will start to extinguish and he will experiment by moving towards the handler. Praise this with wild enthusiasm. If the dog abandons this strategy before arriving and goes back to playing the distracter, simply stop praising and go back to waiting. If the dog arrives at the handler's position, the distracter immediately runs over and relinquishes one big treat or gives the toy to the handler for a nice round of tug. Then the distracter back to his original position with the reinforcer, more than likely followed by the dog, and the exercise is repeated. The dog learns, over time, that the way to get what the distracter has is to do what the handler is saying. Obedience is the answer! Be advised: this takes time and patience the first few trials.

Once the dog can't be stumped and flies over to the handler (often before the recall cue is given – this is fine), switch to another reinforcer. If you were using cheese, try roast chicken. If the dog is a high drive type, use a hot toy. Once the dog is fluent at this, switch again. Keep rotating the motivator until the dog can't be

218

stumped on the first trial for a novel motivator. Then take it on the road.

Repetition is the key with this exercise. Some dogs catch on more readily than others. I'd bet this has less to do with learning rate than it does with how impulsive or emotional a dog is, as well as how well the dog has been primed with the basic, kindergarten recall exercise. It is a good idea to alternate roles of handler and distracter so the dog learns that the cue "come" is the key thing to attend to, not a specific person. Always rule out what's irrelevant.

To consolidate the concept and get some nice cold trials in, I suggest doing this exercise in day to day life whenever you have a controllable motivator. For instance, if the dog is all excited at the front door at walk time, move ten feet back from the door and call him. He will have to move away from the door in order to get you to approach and open it. You can make him do a recall in the opposite direction of anything he strains toward while on the walk in order to be granted access to sniff it. You can make him do short recalls away from dogs in order to meet them. You can make him do a short recall away from someone moving a favorite toy around in a tantalizing way in order to have it given or thrown. The more you vary the particular motivator and context the exercise is done in, the better generalized the concept of: "If you want something, believe it or not, the best way to get it is to go to your handler when called, not try to directly access it." This is such fabulous money in the recall bank.

High School Level Recall – The Speed Drill

When the dog is an ace at the controlled distraction recall exercise, it is time to bump the motivation up another notch. You will now teach the dog the game of running though your legs after a thrown ball or tug toy. This is putting the dog's predatory drive to work for you rather than having it as a perpetually competing motivation. If your dog is not very toy-driven, you can omit this exercise or else use something like a Kong stuffed with goat cheese that you let him

219

have for a brief time after every correct response. At first, use no cues. Simply get the dog interested in the toy by playing a quick round of tug or teasing him with it. Then, with your legs apart, lure him in close and, when he's focused on the toy, roll it through so that the dog goes through as well. Repeat this over and over to get the dog used to going through your legs. Some dogs are deeply suspicious about doing this. Big dogs will have to flatten themselves somewhat. All dogs can learn to do it and it is worth the effort.

When the dog is going through your legs without hesitation, put him in a sit-stay eight or ten feet away, set yourself up and, on the cue "come," send him through for the throw. Delay throwing the object until you are sure he is going to go through. Dogs quickly get into the habit of going around rather than through if the trainer allows a few of these scoot-arounds to be reinforced by premature throws. If the dog attempts to go around, withhold the throw. He must learn that he *has* to go through in order to get the toy. Keep your throws as horizontal as possible (rather than throwing upwards) to maximize the flat-out chase aspect. After each throw, have a vigorous round of tug of war. This makes the game even more interesting to the dog as well as giving him a reason to get the toy back to you as soon as possible after he catches it.

As he gets better at it, increase the recall distance. Do plenty from a sit-stay but also do it out of context of formal training sessions. Spring "come" on him when he is least expecting it (have your tug toy hidden on you). This can be the initiation of your daily tug/retrieve session with him as well as part of the obedience breaks during tug. The more the dog does this exercise, the more he learns to charge you with great intensity on the word "come." Harnessing predatory motivation exploits one of the most potent motivators around. For many dogs, it far outranks straight food reinforcement. When the dog will charge you at top speed from thirty feet away and reliably go through your legs every time, fade the prompts.

Up to now, you've been standing with legs apart and tug toy in hand. This picture is an important signal for the dog. It predicts what follows. What the dog must now learn is that the word "come" by itself is as good a predictor as that picture. The way to do this is to first hide the tug toy up your shirt or in your pocket, somewhere the dog can't see it, but where you can quickly access it at the key moment. Put the dog on a sit-stay and leave him to set up a recall as usual. When you get thirty feet or so out, stand normally, legs together and arms by your side. Tell the dog to come. What you will probably find is that the dog does not charge you with anywhere near the same zeal he did when you were doing the previous exercise through your legs. That's okay. When he gets halfway to you, whip the toy out from its hiding place, open your legs and do the recall throw as usual, just before he gets to you.

In a few repetitions, the dog will start charging again, even though you are standing normally. This is because your normal posture has started to predict the picture he has come to know and love, that of you with legs apart and toy in hand. You will work now to gradually delay the leg opening and toy appearance until the last possible instant. The goal is for the dog to learn that your regular recall cue and posture predicts the game as reliably as the open leg posture did before.

When the dog charges his recalls with you standing upright, it is time to put the sit back in. The goal now is for the dog to delay his decision on whether to sit or run through until the last possible instant. The way to accomplish this is to sometimes send him through and sometimes ask for a sit. You ask for a sit by keeping your legs together and cueing a sit. The first time you spring the sit on him after he has done scores of drills through your legs, be sure to unlock your knees or you could be injured. A good idea is to cue the sit well in advance on this first occasion, when the dog is, say, ten or fifteen feet away. Use a verbal cue as well as a broad hand signal. Practice a few sits in a row until he seems to anticipate the sit. Then send him through the legs a couple of times. Then go

221

back to sit. The idea is to keep him guessing so that his policy becomes to charge at top speed and then evaluate when ten feet away. This way you retain maximum motivation with deceleration delayed until just before recall completion. That's good juggling of the speed and sit elements. To reinforce recalls where a sit is the final product, whip the toy out from under your shirt and play tug after he sits.

Perfection of this exercise lends tremendous distraction-proofing to your recall by placing it at the top of the reinforcer hierarchy in virtually any situation. After all, the reason that dogs would rather play with dogs or chase squirrels or sniff through the underbrush rather than coming when called is that these activities are fun and exciting whereas coming is not. Your job is not to lament this, but to make use of the dog's addiction to fun by making recalls the most fun and exciting activity he gets to do.

College Level Recall

If you have successfully installed the High School speed-drill exercise, described above, you may find you don't need the College level exercise. In other words, the dog has a near-perfect recall in all situations. That is the power of predatory motivation. If you weren't instantly successful with that exercise, don't be tempted to give up early and try the next one in the hopes that it will fix competing motivation problems. Try harder to cultivate a speed-drill. Some dogs take longer to catch on than others. These are the unkeen retriever types, typically. It's worth loosening them up in any event, so I would encourage you to persevere.

The college level exercise is designed to convince the dog that you control access to competing motivators in the environment. It is a variation of the Premack recall you did in elementary school. Typical competing motivation is the dog interacting with another dog, deeply embroiled in some smell on the ground, or pursuing a fleeing object like a cat, squirrel or car. Please note that if you have a dog who is not conditioned, i.e. you have not diligently done

222

the kindergarten and elementary school recall exercises to the point of reliability in a variety of locations, you have no business trying what follows. It's not a Band-Aid to fix your "stubborn" dog who door-dashes every chance he gets or won't come in from the yard. No skipping ahead. There are no quick fixes here. You must pay your dues first.

Enlist a helper, someone who is good at agitating dogs with furry toys. Set this distracter up in an outdoor grassy location with an ordinary bucket and a novel furry toy on a ten foot rope. You are going to happen upon the scene fifty yards away, after your helper is already in place to best simulate a natural squirrel flushing. Your dog will be off leash. The idea is for the helper to run along with the toy dragging behind, which, if your dog is a squirrel chaser, has a reasonable chance of eliciting chase. If the vegetation is too high, the furry toy won't be visible when your assistant drags it along the ground so choose the location with this in mind.

Once he's spotted the furry and given chase, try your recall cue. There's a small chance he'll do it but a better chance he won't. That's fine. Once the dog ignores the cue your helper will quickly double back, put the bucket over the furry (open end down) and hold it down, waiting. The dog will arrive at the bucketed furry looking very keen. Try your recall cue again. Sooner or later the dog will do a recall. Once he does, have him sit and then say "GET IT!" Once you do, point out to him that the furry is on the move again – your helper will have unleashed it once your dog completes his recall. This time let him catch it. It's worth trying again even though the element of surprise – and the promise of a real furry – is gone. It's really worth setting this up on a few more occasions. The goal for the dog to learn that turning on a dime and completing the recall is the only way to get the furry. Then there's some chance it might kick in in a real situation.

Mastering this exercise doesn't produce a squirrel-proof recall on every dog. But it does sometimes. And, failing to master the exercise is extremely unlikely to yield a squirrel-proof recall.

If he has mastered the exercise as described and you want to live dangerously, try varying the point in the chase at which you give the recall cue, bearing in mind that the further the dog is from you and the closer he is to the object, the harder it gets and the more you squeeze your helper. Achieving a dog that turns on a dime at any point in the chase is graduating college with high honors.

Pulling On Leash

Dogs naturally pull on leash. There are a couple of reasons for this. One is that most dogs naturally ambulate faster than most people and the pulling reflects this discrepancy. The other reason is that the pulling so elicited is then reinforced by the owner in the form of forward movement. The dog continues to pull because pulling works. The other reason that has been put forward for pulling in dogs, even to the point of gasping for breath in obvious discomfort, is what's called an opposition reflex. As soon as they feel pressure against their necks or chests, they reflexively lean into it. An opposition reflex beefed up by selective breeding results in dogs like Huskies and Malamutes who really, really love pulling in harness. It is intrinsically reinforcing quite apart from getting where they're going.

So, given what you're up against, it is prudent to begin anti-pull training from day one, rather than waiting till the dog has an entrenched pulling addiction. The main pull prevention exercise, for puppies or dogs who do not already have a strong habit, is the red light/green light game. The rule of this game is that, while on a walk with the dog, you may only move forward if the leash is loose and jangly. As soon as the dog tightens the leash, you freeze dead in your tracks. The loose leash is the green light - handler moves forward; the tight leash is the red light - handler stops. Moving in the direction the dog wants to go is a potent reinforcer, which you must never give for pulling on leash.

The first time you play this game, the dog will likely do a bit of lunging and straining when you put the brakes on. Simply wait until, eventually, by chance, he slackens the leash. Then start moving. As soon as you do so, he will re-energize and, no doubt, hit the end of the leash, causing you to stop again. And so on. The dog requires some repetition to see the trend: tightening the leash grinds the walk to a halt every single time, slackening the leash makes movement happen. The dog does not learn to walk on a loose leash in one shot. What you get, rather, is a gradual decrease in attempts at pulling. So, keep it up. Timing helps enormously here. The more you can simulate a cause and effect relationship between behavior and consequence, the faster he'll learn. Clickers and NRM's can help here, though many people teach anti-pull without them.

If you already have an entrenched pulling problem, you will probably have to use heavier artillery than the red light/green light game. Your options are to 1) try the red light green light game anyway, 2) play the game but with bigger penalties, or 3) change equipment.

Playing the game with bigger penalties means that, rather than simply stopping when the dog starts pulling, you retreat some distance to make the dog cover the same piece of ground again. It's like a three yard penalty. A good motto is: "We'll keep doing this patch of sidewalk until you do it without pulling." The first few times out, the dog will likely have to do the same piece of ground many times in a row before he figures out that it's his pulling which is giving him the penalty. Once again, to sharpen up timing, mark the initiation of pulling with "Too bad!" This signals that he has just made things worse for himself in terms of his apparent goal of moving in direction X. When you retreat to re-try a piece of ground, make sure the leash is slack before commencing another stab at forward walking.

Industrial strength pullers can actually injure their human companions. If pulling has been allowed to blossom to this point, these dogs usually need new equipment. There are several "power steering" options available. Probably the most effective of these is the dog halter, which looks and works very much like a hackamore does on a horse. Halters move the leverage point from the neck to the muzzle. Now when the dog tries to pull, there is much less to lean into: the dog's head simply turns around. These sorts of devices allow people to control half-ton horses, so it's not surprising that they can give you a lot of control of an eighty pound Labrador. Halters for dogs are put out under a few different names, like "Gentle Leader," "NewTrix easyway collar," "Snoot Loop" and "Halti."

The advantages of halters are:

1) they greatly reduce pulling on leash in most dogs
2) they work without employing pain
3) they require very little expertise

The disadvantages of halters are:

1) many dogs fight them initially: there is an adjustment period or else the dog must be gradually desensitized
2) to the untrained eye, they resemble muzzles, which hurts owner compliance
3) the effects do not generalize well to when the dog is not wearing the device

Aside from the excellent reduction in pulling achieved, halters are also good tools for controlling lunging, aggressive dogs by virtue of the fact that the head can be turned away from the hot stimulus. They have not caught on as much as they should, in spite of their obvious efficacy, because of those first two disadvantages: people don't like the look and they don't like seeing their dog so obviously hating it the first few times it's put on. People who use them are asked over and over by passersby why their dog is wearing a muzzle. Halters are far from muzzles: while good control of the head and jaws is achieved, dogs can pant, drink, retrieve a ball and bite while wearing one. I personally think the look is cute. Dogs wearing halters look like little ponies. The adjustment period is over quickly if the owner handles the first few experiences properly. This means not giving in and removing the halter if the dog throws a tantrum. Gently raise the dog's head every time the dog lowers it and paws at the halter. Release the head and provide lots of praise and treats whenever the dog stops fighting it.

Another option is an anti-pull harness. These differ from pulling harnesses that are used for racing and drafting. Anti-pull harnesses, like halters, change the leverage point, so that the dog lists to the side when he attempts to pull, rather than being able to lean into the harness. Prospective users should test drive one on their own dog before buying. The advantages of anti-pull harnesses are:

1) very good dog and owner acceptance
2) good efficacy – pulling is significantly curtailed in most dogs
3) they take little skill to operate

The disadvantages are:

1) they don't work on every dog
2) the effect does not generalize when the dog is not wearing the device
3) they require some skill to initially fit correctly

These two products, halters and anti-pull harnesses, represent the evolution of anti-pull training. However, most people address their pulling on leash difficulties with another device, the choke collar. As its name suggests, this collar is designed to strangle the dog. It is probably the most widespread tool in dog training. There are chain link strangle collars, ones with wider links to preserve the dog's coat (not his trachea, mind you, his coat), fabric ones, ones with limited strangulation capacity, and ones with enhanced strangulation capacity (they clip on and sit higher on the dog's neck to increase the ability of the collar to cut off the dog's air). It is pretty amazing how much time and energy has been devoted to the design of strangulation devices for man's best friend. People avoid

227

halters in droves because the dog "doesn't like it" but think nothing of digging metal or a thin cord right into their dog's windpipe. It's a tool that, used as directed, can cause acute or cumulative injury.

One problem with strangle collars is that the aversive delivered is mild to moderate for most dogs. It doesn't hurt that much and so the dog habituates and pulling comes back, necessitating a more ferocious jerk or an upgrade to a prong collar. And, when it does kind of sort of work, rarely does the dog get one or two shots: a virtual lifetime of leash jerks is in store for dogs whose owners opt to use chokers to train. But while a strangle collar's capacity to *hurt* is iffy, their capacity to *harm,* i.e. to damage the dog is considerable. This is what is so insidious: it seems to have very little effect so owners escalate the number and force of leash jerks or switch to a more dangerous model when the dog habituates to the jerks. All the while, the dog's windpipe is being bent.

Another problem is the strength and coordination required to deliver an adequate leash correction. Many people are physically or psychologically unable to do the technique correctly. They end up simply putting on a choker and hoping it will do the work itself. The result is a dog straining on the end of a leash with his tongue turning a more obvious shade of blue.

So, why are they so popular? The answer lies partly in the historical traditions of dog training. The original trainers were military men training German-bred German shepherd dogs. This combo did okay with strangle collars though, I would argue, not half as well as they would have done with clickers and sliced hot dogs. But they got away with it. These were the prototype trainers whose methods trickled down to people who, after WWII, offered the first organized community obedience classes with their family pets. It kind-of-sort-of worked on enough dogs that, without critical scrutiny and without alternatives, the method stuck for decades.

228

The other part of the answer is probably our punishment-oriented mentality. These collars give the handler power to deliver punishments with all the attendant frustration displacement and temporary suppression of behavior (and eventual global suppression of behavior).

The last option for reducing pulling on leash is the prong or pinch collar. This looks like a medieval torture device, with double rows of blunt teeth which, when the dog pulls, dig into the dog's neck. This design makes it much more aversive than a strangle collar. Ironically, in spite of its fearsome appearance, it is self-limiting by design and therefore a much safer piece of equipment than a choker. Because of the increased aversiveness and decreased risk of harm, it is an infinitely better choice than a choker. However, in light of the availability of halters and anti-pull harnesses and of good, early training on plain buckle collars using red light/green light technique, prong collar use is hard to justify. It is even harder to justify as a tool to teach sit, stay, come or anything else apart from walking on leash.

Heeling

Heeling is defined as the dog walking at your left side (or right side - it doesn't matter unless you plan to compete in obedience trials) with his head or shoulder at your pant seam, never deviating from this position and sitting automatically whenever you stop. Teaching heeling and walking on a loose leash are two separate endeavors. Heeling is a complex behavior that will take many practice sessions before it is precise and reliable. Getting this behavior generalized from your living room to the great outdoors takes even more time and patience. And, because heeling is intense for the dog, don't expect it in endless quantities. Your main "gear" on walks will be loose-leash walking, not heeling. This way he has some freedom of movement to sniff the ground, the main highlight of walks for most dogs. Dogs need to investigate the urine and droppings of other dogs to gather important dog social data. They can't do this if they're heeling. The most important thing to remember is that walking on a loose leash and heeling are two separate enterprises. The heeling you will bring up to speed in training sessions before introducing it during walks, whereas walking on a loose leash will be trained on walks from day one.

Kindergarten Heeling

Kindergarten level heeling is simply teaching the dog to continuously follow a moving food target. The target is held against the left side of your body so the dog also learns to follow your body while he follows your hand. First, fill your pockets with treats. Load one hand, the one on the opposite side the dog will be on, with treats. This hand should also be your clicker hand. Don't load more treats into it than you can carry and also smoothly click your clicker! You can teach heeling without using your clicker but later on, when you've got longer durations between reinforcement, it will be useful to precisely select your moment of reinforcement.

Put one or two from your supply hand into your dog-side hand. Show this to the dog and then move the target to the side of your body, at your pant seam at your dog's height. Large dogs will end up with a target at hip level or higher and smaller dogs will need a target around knee level. This means, for the initial few training sessions, you will have to bend if you have a little dog. Some people are more comfortable using their hand nearest the dog for storage and reaching across their body with the other hand to lure. Experiment to discover which variation feels more natural to you.

If the dog attends to the target (i.e. snuffles), start moving forward. Encourage him to stay nice and tight with verbal chatter. Take a few steps and let him have the treat. The mechanics of this take a bit of practice so if you feel clumsy, don't worry. Keep practicing and you'll get better. Every now and then, stop walking. Right after you stop, give your hand signal for sit in a backwards direction, as though pushing the air directly backwards. Click and reinforce the dog when he sits. The point of this is to get the dog to sit straight, i.e. on a parallel track to yours and not turned inwards.

230

Dogs will tend to turn in towards your body because this orientation has, up until now, been the one associated with reinforcement. Your goal in initial heel training is to get the dog to associate the reinforcers he will be earning not just with the following but with the view he has of you from heel position on a trajectory parallel to yours.

You can do some extra reinforcing of just this "view" by simply standing there with the dog sitting in heel position and having him visually track a target from his nose all the way up the side of your body. If he is really keen to pivot to face you, do the exercise with him between you and a wall or other barrier, which will prompt him to sit straight. After praising him for watching for a couple of seconds, reinforce. You can even drop it to him: some dogs enjoy learning to catch. When you do this picture associating, make sure you keep your shoulders straight and not turned towards the dog at any point. Shoulder rotating changes the view to exactly the one you don't want.

After getting the hang of walking in straight lines, dispensing treats every three or four steps and reloading from your other hand while walking, practice turning in all directions: right, left and 180 degrees. When you turn 180 degrees, do so with the dog on the outside track. This means that if the dog is on your left, whirl around to your right. If your eventual aim is to compete in obedience, keep your left and right turns as square and military as possible and single track on your about-turns. This means that, when you do the 180, you are walking the same line in both directions before and after the turn, rather than executing a U-turn, which would put you in another "lane."

You will also have to learn smooth pace changes and decent footwork if you want to do well and look nice in the competitive obedience ring, so be sure to get yourself into the hands of a good, qualified instructor who can polish these things and teach you all the rules. For now, focus on improving your walk and reinforcement mechanics, and on getting the dog following reliably and turning as tightly in position as possible. Practice heeling in a few different low distraction environments before proceeding to elementary school.

Elementary School Level Heeling

The aim now is for the dog to heel with a faded target, sit automatically when the handler stops and keep attention fixed on the handler at all times. Before trying these exercises, be sure you've practiced plenty of lure following as described in the kindergarten heeling exercise. The dog needs to be a rabid targeter because this will ensure sufficient momentum for the fading and occasional removing of the target that you will be initiating now.

In a low distraction environment, warm the dog up with a bit of lured heeling. Now, do the following: for one second move the target up and away, from your hip to your chest. When you do this, chat to the dog enthusiastically. You want to convey to him that moving the lure further away is a good thing. After one second, if he's with you, make it an actual good thing by reinforcing him with the treat. Then, start off again with the lure in its original position. When he's following well, move it away again, keep him with you using enthusiastic chatter for one second and then give the treat. The criterion you are isolating for reinforcement is his *following the faded prompt*: the more distant lure.

Do the prompt-fade over and over just before reinforcing. The goal is for the dog to learn that the fading of the food target means reinforcement is about to occur. If you fade the food target and the heeling falls apart immediately, it usually means you have not done enough basic target-follow conditioning. It can also be that you are walking too slowly. Go back to kindergarten and practice some more and/or walk more briskly to develop sufficient momentum to get continued following on lure fade. Then try fading again. Make sure, also, that you prop up the heeling with the chatter the first few times you fade the target.

232

Practice this exercise until you see some visible brightening up or increased intensity when you move the target up. This tells you he's made the connection. Now make the lure disappear altogether for one second, reinforcing immediately for continued following on faith. You can achieve the disappearance by closing your hand and moving it up to your shoulder or across your waist. Repeat this version until the dog demonstrates the same recognition that the lure disappearing altogether is a good thing.

Once this is accomplished, start extending duration. From one second, go to two seconds, then three, four and five. As usual, drop the standards and go for shorter bursts if the dog falls apart and starts performing badly. In a few sessions, you should be able to heel the dog without a lure for ten or fifteen seconds per reinforcer, with the dog riveted in position.

Making Sits Automatic

The most efficient way to install automatic sits is to heel the dog with frequent halts. The initial sequence is as follows: 1) stop walking and 2) hand-signal the dog to sit, near a wall or barrier if he's a butt-out swinger. Your eventual goal is for the cessation of walking to become the sit cue. This is why it comes first. Avoid the common error of prompting or signaling the sit *before* you halt or *as* you halt. If you do this, the known hand gesture will block the event you are trying to establish as a cue: your coming to a halt.

The correct order of events - halt then hand-signal - may cause the dog to continue past the point at which you stopped. Don't panic and fall into the trap of preemptively cueing a sit before halting. It is tempting to do so, because it seems to solve the problem. Actually, it is merely postponing the problem to the inevitable day when you want the dog to sit for cessation of walking alone. Cessation of walking must, therefore, come first in the sequence if it is to ever be established. So, the solution is to get your prompt in with some urgency as soon as you have stopped walking, to reduce the overshooting. If you're doing a series of sits, selectively reinforce those sits which are in better position.

When the dog is no longer overshooting on halts and his sits are relatively well positioned, start fading the hand signal. Start off with a series of halts and signals as usual, reinforcing the nicest sits. Then, after halting, try a smaller hand signal for the sit and see if you get one. If you do, reinforce. If you don't get a sit, give your broader signal but don't reinforce the sit thus produced. Then repeat the exercise. If the dog is consistently failing to sit for your faded signal, try a less faded signal, something between what works and what doesn't. Try your verbal if he's got a good one. Then say it more and more softly. You are searching for a new standard. The goal is to fade the hand signal or verbal to nothing. A lot of dogs pick up automatic sits very readily, partly because sit is such a strong behavior to start with. If the dog doesn't catch on quickly, fade systematically. If the dog is a crooked sitter, use your barrier prompt all the time you're working on getting the sit automatic. Only when it is very fluently automatic will you start weaning off your straight-sit prompt wall. When you do, don't panic if the automatic sit gets a little wobbly. It'll come back. This is why dog training is so much like juggling.

High School Level Heeling

The goal now is to extend lure-free heeling up to a minute per reinforcement. To maintain quality control over this duration, you will initially use your voice liberally. Build duration in increments of a few seconds. If the dog is riveted, add a few more. As duration grows in this exercise, remain very aware of exactly what you're clicking. Trainers quickly fall into the trap of thinking they are reinforcing the heeling as a whole when they click and treat but, in reality, the click is selecting a particular *moment* of heeling. This is particularly troublesome when one pushes the dog past the point of destruction: the dog's performance starts to deteriorate and the trainer clicks and treats to regain the dog's interest. This common error results in reinforcement going to exactly what you

234

don't want: poorer heeling. Get in the habit of clicking the nice instants and noting what durations between reinforcers he can tolerate with razor sharp position. If position starts to deteriorate, it is a reflection of lackluster voice prompting, selective reinforcement of inferior moments and/or a too-low rate of reinforcement. Reinforce before deterioration sets in. If the dog consistently deteriorates right after reinforcement, that is an indication that you are reinforcing in a too-predictable way and, likely, not frequently enough. As duration grows, you should occasionally click and treat two or three times almost back to back, to counteract the post-reinforcement blahs. When he's up to a minute, lure free and sharp, you may start heeling the dog in less quiet locations. When you first do this, drop the duration requirement considerably, still using your voice to encourage. Build duration back gradually.

College Level Heeling: No Prompt

When the dog heels nicely for at least a minute for verbal encouragement only and no food target, the next task is to fade the voice. This is an optional step if you do not intend to compete in licensed obedience trials. In these events, the dog is expected to heel for durations of around a minute at a time with no feedback from the handler. The way there is to: gradually fade the verbal coaching, selectively reinforcing after increasingly long stretches of good heeling without this prompt. Then take it on the road to proof location changes and various flavors of ambient distraction.

If your goal is to compete, use obedience fun matches as a main training location. Not surprisingly, they afford the best simulation of the location where you will most want nice responses: obedience trials. This doesn't mean you necessarily have to enter the first few times, simply hang out and train. The main goal is for the dog to learn this location predicts the usual reinforcer contingencies.

A frequent error is prematurely entering obedience trials where the rules forbid feedback from handler to dog. Good performance goes

235

completely unreinforced. Imperfections in performance are not worked on. There is no difference between great and terrible heeling – it's all unreinforced. Performance drifts inevitably under this contingency. It is as though the dog asks himself, "What's different? Why no R+?" and the resounding answer is "this context," which includes give-away elements like the presence of other dogs, nervous people milling around, and people with corsages who are carrying clipboards barking out commands like "forward!" etc. Dogs discriminate environmental differences with great ease and the context of a dog show will quickly come to equate "no contingencies in effect" if the dog is not initially reinforced in this.

Competitors label dogs like this "ring-wise." Many assume some malicious intent on the part of the dog, rather than accepting the predictable and mundane learning phenomenon of operant discrimination. The contingencies *are* different in an obedience trial and the dog, perfectly obedient to the laws of learning, will perform accordingly. That is, unless he is never allowed to perceive the lack of contingency. This means 1) lots of training, (training, not performing) in this context and 2) entering trials only when the dog's performance is extremely tight and on a thin enough reinforcement schedule that minimal damage will be done to the behaviors by the feedback-free experience. Obedience trials can be very damaging. The worst thing is that, once the dog has learned that obedience rings are where reinforcement never happens, all subsequent work will be affected, even if performance is made slick elsewhere. This goes for any performance situation where the feedback density changes, not just obedience trials. Dogs discriminate context variations and their associated contingencies brilliantly. You can make this work for you or against you.

Tug Toy Motivators

Tug toys can spice up heeling quite splendidly in dogs that are high drive. Introduce tug toy motivators if you haven't already. Before proceeding, review the rules of tug and teach them if you haven't.

236

When you use tug to reinforce nice turns in heeling, a great recall or lighting fast drop, produce a hidden tug toy from your pocket or up your shirt and engage in a brief round of tug of war. Keep it brief. This means a few seconds only: the idea is to keep him ultra-motivated. Longer tug sessions are reserved for two occasions: when the dog really hits the jackpot with some wondrous response or when you're ending the training session, a fun time for an extra-large reinforcer.

The reasons for adding tug toy motivation to the arsenal are:

1) varying reinforcers is always a good idea (rotation preserves some novelty, plus the "money effect" of conditioning a secondary reinforcer – your clicker - to multiple primaries)

2) many dogs work more enthusiastically for tug than for bait – for speed and intensity behaviors, it's a great choice

3) the interactive game provides good bonding in the form of cooperative killing

4) it's a great energy burner for the dog

5) it provides an opportunity to improve control of your dog, especially his jaws, when he is in an excited state

The mechanics of dispensing a tug toy reinforcer during heeling take practice. Try stashing it in your shirt, in your (dog side) armpit and in your other hand. Select a moment of excellence, click and produce the toy. It's crafty to give the toy to the dog in position to that his (eventual) toy grab anticipation will work to solidify rather than undermine positioning. Play a few seconds of intense tug, then cycle back into heeling.

Competing Motivation

A dog who has a strong and well-generalized response to a particular cue and who is normally very motivated by food and tug games may fall apart under certain conditions. Stress can make behavior fall apart. A much more common interference is competing motivation. The dog hears and understands the cue but something else in the environment potently reinforces an alternative behavior. Your bait and tug toy are losing out to dog play or the trail of a rabbit in the woods. What do you do? The first line of defense is to make the behaviors you want strong: recalls, downs, stays etc. and to rehearse them in areas with gradually increased distraction. In the case of recalls, go the added distance of proofing for competing motivation, as described earlier. If you'd like to bump other behaviors up to the level of withstanding strong competing motivation, the same principle – that of making the thing he wants to do contingent on first doing the behavior you're asking for – is a good tool to understand. This is Premack's Principle.

The first thing is to understand that there is always a hierarchy of reinforcers and that it's useful to label them as activities rather than things. What I mean is that rather than saying "rabbit trails are more reinforcing than food so he didn't do his down-stay in the field," say "hunting rabbits is currently a preferred activity to down-stay." Now, in those cases where you are willing and able to grant the activity that he wants most to do, he can do that activity *provided he does the other activity – the obedience one you want – first.* (This is known to children as "eat your broccoli to get your ice cream.") His access to rabbit trails, dog playmates, etc. is contingent on his snappy response to obedience cues. Dogs fail to comply around competing motivations because the best way to get the things at the top of the reinforcer hierarchy has always been to simply access them directly. The behaviors you want would get in the way, delay or pre-empt altogether the preferred activity. This is where you must prove the dog wrong. Not only does the down-stay not interfere with the dog's access to the rabbit trails, it becomes the *only way* the dog may obtain access to rabbit trails.

You must, therefore, resolve to set things up so that he is unable to engage in these super-high-value reinforcing activities unless he has earned them. If you say sit and the dog ignores you, carries on sniffing or running towards another dog, explode into action. Get yourself quickly to the scene of the crime ("cut him off at the pass") and prevent or cut short the activity. Vow to next time set it up so you can prevent him more elegantly (i.e. have a leash on). Failure to do this means the dog directly accesses the reinforcer at the top of the hierarchy for engaging in the direct access strategy. This is not good. You must go to Training DefCon One and build a program to teach the dog that the world doesn't operate this way. Performing requested behaviors on cue makes you say things like "go see the dog" or "find rabbits." Trying to access these things directly gets nothing or, worse, makes walks end. Simply be prepared to put your money where your mouth is. If you're out on a walk and ask for a sit before going to greet a person or dog down the block, and the dog simply wiggles and pulls, say "too bad" and walk away in the other direction. You don't *have* to let him do anything, including greet people or dogs.

If you rehearse this enough, the dog gets the picture. No anger, no frustration, just a simple rule: comply and you get the good stuff dogs like. Don't comply and you don't get them. Dog's choice. If you give the dog this choice, he will comply, no matter what else is out there because you are exploiting rather than competing with the reinforcer hierarchy. You are using the laws of learning to which he is always, without exception, perfectly obedient.

Suggested Dissertations

If you want a greater challenge, here are some suggested "post-graduate" projects, the nuts and bolts of which you may work out for yourself based on the same principles you've used up to now.

- ✓ Random position changes at thirty feet for verbal-only cue in a distracting environment

- ✓ First-cue discrimination of ten to twenty verbal cues

- ✓ Ten-minute sit or down-stay with handler out of sight (spying) and heavy distraction

- ✓ Heeling with no food or verbal prompts through heavy distraction environments

Final Note

If you have not already done so, please spay or neuter your dog. Millions are euthanized at shelters every year and we are all party to this national disgrace if we let our dogs breed.

Recommended Reading

Abrantes, Roger: *Dog Language* (Wakan Tanka, 2001)

Dawkins, Richard: *The Selfish Gene* (Oxford University Press, 1976)

Dawkins, Richard: *Climbing Mount Improbable* (Norton, 1997)

Dunbar, Dr. Ian: *How to Teach a New Dog Old Tricks* (James & Kenneth, 1991)

Fox, Dr. Michael: *Understanding Your Dog* (St. Martin's Press, 1972)

Hetts, Dr. Suzanne: *Pet Behavior Protocols* (AAHA, 1999)

Kahneman, *Thinking Fast and Slow* (Farrar, Straus and Giroux, 2011)

Mech, L. David: *Alpha status, dominance, and division of labor in wolf packs* (Canadian Journal of Zoology, 1999)

Pinker, Steven: *The Blank Slate* (Penguin, 2002)

Pinker, Steven: *The Better Angels of Our Nature: Why Violence Has Declined* (Viking, 2011)

Pryor, Karen: *Don't Shoot the Dog!* (Bantam Books, 1999)

Reid, Dr. Pamela: *Excel-Erated Learning!* (James & Kenneth, 1996)

Ridley, Matt: *Nature Via Nurture* (Harper Collins, 2003)

Ridley, Matt: *The Origins of Virtue* (Penguin, 1998)

Sdao, Kathy: *Plenty in Life is Free* (Dogwise, 2012)

Serpell, James (Ed): *The Domestic Dog* (Cambridge University Press, 1995)

Singer, Peter: *Animal Liberation* (Avon Books, 1975)

Wright, Robert: *The Moral Animal* (Vintage, 1995)

Zulch, Helen and Mills, Daniel: *Life Skills for Puppies* (Hubble & Hattie, 2012)

Acknowledgements

The great Bob Bailey has been the single greatest influence on my thinking about dog training over the years, and I also feel enormously privileged to have known Marian Breland Bailey. Thank you, Bob. I've had the delicious pleasure of ah-ha moments from the work and wisdom of numerous friends and colleagues in applied behavior, including the incomparable Karen Pryor, Nicholas Dodman, Susan Friedman, Suzanne Hetts, Delva Howell, Paul Klein, Amy Marder, Cathy McNaughton, Jennifer Messer, James O'Heare, Kathy Pickel, Kathy Sdao, and uber-angel-to-dogs Sandi Thompson. I will always be grateful to Ian Dunbar for his many contributions to dog training, especially his untiring advocacy of early-and-often socialization and anti-aggression training.

The folks at Dogwise are simply wonderful. Charlene, Larry and Nate Woodward, Kristy Allen and Jon Luke have been uniformly professional and a pleasure in all dealings.

I owe a debt of gratitude to this book's supporters over the years, and to those who disliked it but took the time to deliver thoughtful criticism.

Finally, my students over the years have quite literally kept me in the game, many becoming close friends. Their intelligence, compassion, curiosity, humor, commitment to science, and unwavering focus on the human-animal bond are inspiration beyond measure. They are the future of dog training.

About the Author

Jean Donaldson is the founder of The Academy for Dog Trainers (www.academyfordogtrainers.com). Her books include *Mine!, Fight!, Dogs Are From Neptune, Oh Behave! Dogs From Pavlov to Premack to Pinker*, and *Train Like a Pro*. She holds degrees in Comparative Psychology and Music, and competed successfully in numerous dog sports before transitioning full time to pet dog training in 1990.

The Academy has over five hundred graduates training and counseling in most US states and 25 countries world-wide. Jean lives in the San Francisco Bay area with her dog, Buffy, adopted in 2002. When she is not working, she is an ardent baseball fan and student of evolutionary biology.

Index

D

E